THE DESPOT'S GUIDE TO
WEALTH MANAGEMENT

THE DESPOT'S GUIDE TO WEALTH MANAGEMENT

On the International Campaign against Grand Corruption

J. C. SHARMAN

CORNELL UNIVERSITY PRESS
ITHACA AND LONDON

First published 2017 by Cornell University Press
Printed in the United States of America

Library of Congress Cataloging-in-Publication Data

Names: Sharman, J. C. (Jason Campbell), 1973– author.
Title: The despot's guide to wealth management : on the international
    campaign against grand corruption / J.C. Sharman.
Description: Ithaca : Cornell University Press, 2017. |
    Includes bibliographical references and index.
Identifiers: LCCN 2016045920 (print) | LCCN 2016049372 (ebook) |
    ISBN 9781501705519 (cloth : alk. paper) | ISBN 9781501708435 (ret) |
    ISBN 9781501708442 (pdf)
Subjects: LCSH: Corruption—Prevention—International cooperation. |
    Political corruption—Prevention—International cooperation. |
    Money laundering—Prevention—International cooperation.
Classification: LCC JF1525.C66 .S47 2017 (print) |
    LCC JF1525.C66 (ebook) | DDC 364.1/323—dc23
LC record available at https://lccn.loc.gov/2016045920

Contents

To my family and Bilyana

PREFACE

This book examines the rise of a global norm and associated rules prohibiting one country from hosting money stolen by senior officials from another country. State leaders, generally from poorer countries, have routinely looted millions or even billions of dollars from their national treasuries. Where does the money go? All too often, it is spent or stashed in rich countries. Until very recently, rich countries have had no moral or legal obligation to do anything about these inward flows of dirty money. Now states have a moral and legal duty to screen, seize, and return such illicit wealth to the victim state.

The main aim of this book is to answer a few simply stated but difficult questions. First, why did this normative and policy change occur? Why did a situation that had long been seen as common and unremarkable come to be viewed as immoral and a policy problem in need of a solution, especially given the powerful vested interests favoring the status quo? Second, how well is this campaign against hosting the proceeds of "grand corruption" working? To what extent are shortcomings in effectiveness a product of a lack of will, because governments are not really trying to fix the problem, or a lack of capacity, given that the problem is hard to solve? Finally, the book concludes with some suggestions on how we could do a better job of holding corrupt leaders to account.

To sketch out the answers in brief, there is a surprising degree of consensus that change was a result of the coincidence of the end of the Cold War and the need to explain failures in Western development policies in poor countries. Media and policy accounts began to perceive widespread, persistent poverty as the flip side and result of the vast wealth accumulated by corrupt elites. In the 1990s, kleptocratic but reliably anti-Communist client governments in the Third World were subject to new scrutiny and pressure from Western patrons in the name of "good governance." The change in global standards occurred rapidly, but in a decentralized, uncoordinated way, rather than being the deliberate result of calculated strategy by either self-seeking states or vanguard "norm entrepreneurs." In countries with the largest banking and financial systems, favorable external conditions for action were catalyzed by scandals involving foreign despots laundering their ill-gotten gains.

Although there are some recent successes in countering kleptocracy, so far only a small minority of corrupt leaders have been held to account through the confiscation of their stolen wealth. Though shortcomings are in part a product of realpolitik, and even more so of banks' commercial incentives and influence over politicians and regulators, there are genuine policy challenges that have been more important in explaining the effectiveness gap. The inherent difficulty of international legal action in a world of sovereign states, the expense and complexity of bringing such actions, and the legitimate protections accorded to private property and those accused of crimes mean that asset recovery is a long shot. Prevention and deterrence seem to be more promising options, with asset recovery a last resort.

The broader conclusions are that even in an area where there is much room for cynicism about the dominance of money and national self-interest in politics, this is not the whole story. If it were, there would simply be no campaign against kleptocracy. The status quo suited banks and rich and poor governments alike. The interplay of noble sentiments, power politics, and financial greed makes this issue typical of messy political life, a messiness that demands a detailed exploration of events.

Assessing the incidence of secret criminal activity is difficult. Evidence to back up the claims above is drawn from four studies of rich countries that host significant sums of money stolen by senior officials from poor countries: the United States, the United Kingdom, Switzerland, and

Australia. With varying speed and effectiveness, each of the first three states has taken some action to trace, seize, and return these illicit funds to their countries of origin. On the other hand, Australia typifies a larger group of countries that has not matched fine words with action, instead turning a blind eye to the laundering of foreign corruption proceeds. In concentrating on "host" states, my aim is thus different from fascinating recent studies of grand corruption that focus on "victim" countries from where the money is stolen. I draw on extensive interviews in the period 2006–2015 with those in government, law enforcement, regulatory bodies, international organizations, nongovernmental organizations (NGOs), and private sector law firms and banks. The book also draws on participation and observation in bodies such as the Stolen Asset Recovery Initiative (a joint enterprise of the World Bank and the United Nations Office on Drugs and Crime, covered in chapter 1), the G20 Anti-Corruption Working Group, the World Bank, the Financial Action Task Force on money laundering, and the Asia-Pacific Group on Money Laundering. To gather evidence for the Australian case study, I engaged a private investigator to analyze corporate and property records to track the inward flow of corruption funds to specific properties, companies, and banks.

In addition, brilliant and fearless investigative journalists, sometimes working with even more courageous whistle-blowers, have provided intimate detail on particular schemes (the importance of journalists, NGOs, and whistle-blowers in pushing the anti-kleptocracy agenda generally, but also in driving forward cases against particular leaders, is an important lesson of the book). Information from a variety of official sources, from government agencies to intergovernmental organizations to courts, has also been invaluable. Finally, though the academic literature on grand corruption is relatively small, there is a much larger body of work on corruption, money laundering, and other related financial crimes that has strongly informed and shaped the argument of this book.

Although I had written on financial crime before, I was at first reluctant to study corruption because I thought that the hypocrisy might be a little too much. Officials from governments and international organizations devoted to fighting money laundering and tax evasion are generally sincere and are seldom guilty of the same crimes they denounce. When it comes to corruption, this is less clear. One of the reasons corruption is so insidious is that a fair number of the people preaching against it are themselves corrupt. Policy makers generally can't say this, whereas academics can (one reason it's good to be an academic).

What I had failed to appreciate, however, and what in many ways more than compensated for this rather depressing realization, was the opportunity to read about and in some cases meet people who are fighting corruption at great personal risk (unlike those who just study corruption; another reason it's good to be an academic). It has been a humbling but also uplifting experience to learn something about these people and in a very small way to recognize their work and problems in this book.

I wrote the first sentence of this book on August 2, 2014. That I finished it is thanks to many different kinds of help I received. I would like to acknowledge that parts of chapter 5 derive from an article, "Illicit Global Wealth Chains after the Financial Crisis: Micro-states and an Unusual Suspect," to be published with the *Review of International Political Economy*.

In a book about a lack of financial transparency, the first priority is to make clear that I could not have done this research without a lot of other people's money. The most important of these sources is the Australian Research Council; I am extremely grateful for the four-year teaching buyout I received (grant FT120100485), as well as supplementary funding from ARC grant DP120100937. I am also indebted to the Norwegian Research Council (STEAL Project 212210/H30). The STEAL Project was ably led by Duncan Wigan and Len Seabrooke, who put together fascinating and stimulating workshops that fed into this book.

This money enabled me to spend two long periods overseas to conduct primary research. Thanks to Alex Cooley, I had the fall semester of 2014 at the Department of Political Science at Barnard College, Columbia University. The department, the university, and New York City provided as stimulating an environment as it is possible for me to imagine, so I am incredibly thankful to Alex for taking time away from the burdens of his role as head of department to set up this opportunity and to be a consummate host as well. Further thanks in New York go to Anne Wolff-Lawson, Séverine Autesserre, Peter Romaniuk, and Tonya Putnam, and beyond the ivory tower to David Spencer. Mark Blyth put on an excellent seminar and provided characteristically sophisticated hospitality during a brief visit to Brown University, as did Odette Lienau and Sarah Kreps at Cornell.

The second spell away from home was at the Centre for International Studies at the London School of Economics, once again an invaluable opportunity. Here I owe a debt to Jeff Chwieroth for making the initial connection; to the director, Kirsten Ainley, for generously hosting me; and to Sophie Wise and my CIS office mates for their help and company, especially fellow Queenslander Andrew Phillips. While I was in London, Iver Neumann, Julia Gray, George Lawson, Anastasia Nesvetailova, and Ronen Palan served to make it a wonderfully rich intellectual atmosphere. I tested some of the arguments in the book at seminars at the University of Exeter and the University of Warwick, and thanks here are due to John Heathershaw, André Broome, Juanita Elias, and James Brassett for organizing these events.

Much of the book, and especially the conclusion, depended on people in policy, industry, and the NGO sector being very generous with their time in helping me understand the technical details of the cases, the backstage politics that provided crucial context, and their thoughts on what is working and not working in anti-corruption policy. Among the more than one hundred fifty people I spoke with, I acknowledge in particular Elise Bean, Geoff Cook, Tim Daniel, Richard Gordon, Larissa Gray, Richard Hay, Mark Matthews, Rick Messick, Maggie Murphy, Stefanie Ostfeld, Robert Palmer, Jean Pesme, Peter Ritchie, Emile van der Does de Willebois, Angelo Venardos, Simon Whitfield, and Bruce Zagaris (many of them will disagree with much of what I have said here). The person I have not yet met who contributed most to the book is Gretta Fenner Zinkernagel, who was incredibly helpful in opening doors for me in Switzerland. A few organizations also stand out for their assistance, especially Global Witness and the International Financial Centres Forum, as well as Transparency International, the Society of Trust and Estate Practitioners, and the International Centre for Asset Recovery.

Griffith University has once again proved to be the perfect congenial and collegial place to write a book. Among all my colleagues, Pat Weller, Haig Patapan, Wes Widmaier, and A. J. Brown stand out for the support they have provided me on this project. Among academics elsewhere, Kate Weaver, Mike Levi, Peter Reuter, Terry Halliday, and Eleni Tsingou were patient in hearing out or reading and commenting on more or less inarticulate earlier statements of my theses. At the sharp end of proceedings, John Chevis, Gill Donnelly, and Sam Koim all have my great appreciation and boundless respect—key parts of the book could not have been written without them.

Roger Haydon has again taught me why he and Cornell University Press are the best in the business, and two anonymous reviewers took a lot of their time to offer very thoughtful and constructive feedback on the draft manuscript.

Finally, my biggest thanks go to Bilyana, even though she is now lagging rather badly in the book dedication stakes.

INTRODUCTION

Power and Money

The link between money and power is seldom more apparent than when state leaders loot their own countries. The spectacular excesses of corrupt dictators ruling over impoverished subjects has become a recurrent theme, from the Swiss bank accounts of Ferdinand Marcos and his wife's gargantuan shoe collection, to the Nigerian dictator Sani Abacha, who looted cash from his own central bank by the truckload, to the palatial London and Paris dwellings of the rulers overthrown in the Arab Spring of 2011. Obnoxious enough in its own right, this conspicuous corrupt consumption is especially offensive when contrasted with the grinding poverty of those ruled by such kleptocrats. Yet the story of grand corruption is by no means just one of degenerate, insatiable despots and suffering masses in faraway poor countries. This kind of industrial-scale corruption depends on the services of the world's largest banks and expert financial professionals, and the ill-gotten gains are hosted in the very same countries that are loudest in preaching the gospel of "good governance." For the trail of money taken from these exotic locales usually leads back to Western financial centers like New York and London.

Threatening to disrupt this nexus of money and power, however, new global rules to combat grand corruption are challenging the status quo. Shortly after the turn of the twenty-first century, the world's most powerful governments made far-reaching political and legal commitments to track down stolen wealth that had entered their financial systems and to return these funds to the countries from which they were taken. This book explains what these new rules are, how they came about, how well they work, and how they could work better.

The campaign against grand corruption, or kleptocracy ("rule by thieves"), including the finance centers that host the resulting plundered wealth, is perhaps one of the starkest contests between power and principle in global governance. On these grounds, it is easy to be pessimistic or cynical in assuming that the global campaign against corruption is nothing more than a particularly grotesque example of hypocrisy at work. Yet such a view fails to explain change. There was a time quite recently when international corruption was just not talked about in diplomatic circles, especially corruption involving senior government officials. At the smallest possible scale, what at first seemed to be a wasted interview in fact served to bring this point home.

At a meeting in the Asian Development Bank Institute in Tokyo in 2012, I was indelicate enough to ask whether those at the institute researched corruption.[1] On finding out that they didn't, I compounded my indiscretion by asking why not. After all, extolling the fight against corruption was practically obligatory for other multilateral development banks and international organizations, even if couched in the more euphemistic terms of "good governance." Somewhat embarrassed by my obtuseness, the official explained that member-states found corruption to be a very delicate matter and preferred to confine the institute's work to other areas. Regarding this as strange at the time, I was struck only much later that the institute's attitude of letting sleeping dogs lie and avoiding awkward subjects was entirely what we should expect. It was in fact the behavior of all the other multilateral bodies—their readiness to talk about, and sometimes even act in response to, corruption—that demanded explanation.

Considering that it directly implicates such powerful parties, there are good reasons for corruption not to be on the international policy agenda. The anti-corruption agenda has moved well beyond rhetoric to a variety of international and domestic laws and standards. Furthermore, these laws have been backed up by law enforcement and investigative agencies, along with rules and regulations that impose greater financial transparency on politicians and other officials. At the very least, even if the officials themselves do not believe what they are saying about the importance of transparency and accountability, they run the risk that others might. Even insincere commitments can have consequences down the line. One of the case studies in this book shows a prime minister subject to an arrest warrant issued by the very same anti-corruption agency he created. Occasionally, powerful individuals are caught out and held accountable for their corruption crimes. Many others who are not may nevertheless be put to significantly more expense, risk, and inconvenience in enjoying and safeguarding their ill-gotten gains as a result of the new rules. The extent of the anti-corruption movement and institutions that have developed over the last couple of decades casts doubt on the idea that the whole edifice was always intended to be purely window dressing.

Rather than consider the whole gamut of corrupt activities, this book focuses on one particular aspect: instances of corruption committed by senior public officials involving large sums of money that are held in a foreign country. The class of such instances is known as kleptocracy or grand corruption, terms that I use interchangeably. To get a sense of the specifics, consider one example.

Teodoro Obiang came to power in the small West African nation of Equatorial Guinea in a 1979 coup that resulted in the death of his psychopathically brutal uncle, who had ruled since independence from Spain in 1968. Life and politics in Equatorial Guinea is richly described by the former World Bank staffer and prominent scholar of corruption Robert Klitgaard in his aptly titled book *Tropical Gangsters*.[2] At the time Klitgaard was writing, in the late 1980s, the country's economy, dependent on cocoa, was close to collapse. In the 1990s, however, the country struck it rich with oil. Then a strange thing happened: huge revenues began flowing as Equatorial Guinea's government started signing deals with Western oil firms, but the benefits failed to reach the large majority of the population. The African Development Bank has noted, "Equatorial Guinea has the characteristics of a low income country while having one of the highest per capita GDPs in Africa. About 75% of the population live below the poverty threshold and get no benefit from the oil economy,"[3] living on less than two dollars per day with no access to running water.[4] Why has a huge increase in Gross Domestic Product per capita failed to improve development outcomes? More bluntly, where has all the money gone? One clue is provided by the habits of the heir apparent.

Teodorin Obiang is vice-president of Equatorial Guinea and son of the president. His official annual salary is less than $80,000, yet from 2004 to 2011 he went on a $314 million spending spree. Purchases included an $80 million mansion in Paris (after renovations valued at double this figure), another in California for $30 million, and a third in São Paulo for $15 million; a $38.5 million Gulfstream jet, two yachts (with a down payment on another 280-foot vessel), five Rolls-Royces, a Maserati, two Ferraris, four Bugattis, and two Bentleys; $44 million spent on fine art, $14 million on antiques, $20 million at Yves Saint Laurent's estate auction, four wristwatches worth more than a million dollars each, $5 million on wine, and, finally, $1.8 million worth of Michael Jackson memorabilia, the centerpiece of which was a $275,000 crystal-studded white glove from the "Bad" tour.[5] Not to be left out of the frenzied spending, in 2012 the United Nations Educational Scientific and Cultural Organization (UNESCO) accepted funds from the Obiang family to establish a prize in their honor for advancing the life sciences.[6]

Is this kind of abuse a new topic? "Kleptocracy" was added to Webster's dictionary only in 1996.[7] To be sure, domestic corruption has been illegal for centuries.[8] To this extent, moral and legal prohibitions against corruption are nothing new. Yet what is novel is the internationalization of this anti-corruption norm and laws. From the end of the 1990s it became illegal in many OECD countries to bribe foreign government officials, a practice that was previously not only widespread but often actually tax-deductible as a legitimate business expense. The norm and resulting system of rules at the heart of this book, however, are different: simply stated, they prohibit countries from hosting money stolen by senior officials of another country. As of only a few years ago, there is an international moral and legal responsibility for states to prevent the proceeds of foreign corruption offenses from entering their financial systems and, to the extent that such illicit wealth does filter through, to trace, freeze, and return it to the source or "victim" country.

Here it is important to note the relationship between the norm and the regime, which overlap but are not the same thing. A norm is a generally shared conception of appropriate behavior for a particular individual in

a particular community. Some norms, like table manners, remain informal, while others become formalized in laws and institutions.[9] The anti-
kleptocracy norm is the shared belief that it is wrong to host wealth stolen
by foreign government officials. The corresponding regime is the system
of national and international hard and soft laws, policies, regulations, and
institutions that formalize and aim to enforce this normative prohibition.[10]

After explaining the rise of the norm, this book aims to find out how
well the resulting regime works. It investigates the extent to which shortcomings reflect a lack of genuine effort, in that anti-corruption measures
were never sincerely designed to work, or the fact that taking on the rich
and politically powerful is just very difficult. One obvious but inadequate
answer is "perhaps a bit of both." While probably true, this answer is
hugely unsatisfying. We want to know the relative balance between a lack
of commitment and the inherent difficulties of the mission, and when,
why, and under what conditions one or the other is more important. Answering these questions is complicated, and the attempt to wrestle with
them informs the structure of this book. The immediate tasks at hand,
however, are first to establish why grand corruption is an inherently international activity and then to explain why it is surprising that this issue ever
made it on to the global policy agenda.

Why Is Kleptocracy an International Issue?

I argue that grand corruption is an inherently international phenomenon
involving at least two countries: the victim country, whose leaders steal
money and whose citizens suffer as a result, and the host country, where
the looted wealth ends up. Though it is important to study both, I pay
more attention to the host countries than the victim, as distinct from fascinating recent works like *Thieves of State* and *The Looting Machine*.[11] In
many of the cases examined here, however, matters are more complicated,
as kleptocrats may spread their looted wealth through half a dozen different countries or more. From a kleptocrat's point of view, shifting looted
wealth abroad is an eminently sensible decision, for several reasons.

Corrupt officials know that whenever criminal activities cross borders,
this immediately complicates any investigation. Law enforcement authority
is parceled out into bounded, sovereign states. For all the progress that has

been made in international cooperation in criminal matters, mutual legal assistance remains a slow, laborious, and unreliable process. Just the prospect of the time, effort, and money involved in trying to secure international legal cooperation often stops investigations before they really start. A foreign refuge provides corrupt officials with a haven in case they lose power at home, and luxury real estate abroad is a useful sanctuary and store of value. Major financial institutions, most obviously banks but also lawyers, accountants, and other professionals, are concentrated in a few cities in the developed world. These locations also provide corrupt officials with opportunities for conspicuous consumption that are not available home, whether it is palatial real estate in London, luxury attire in Paris, or extravagant parties in New York. Kleptocrats have a strange relationship with the rule of law: contemptuous and corrosive of it at home, they are nevertheless keen on locating their wealth in states with strong property rights and effective laws. Thus the logic of a campaign against kleptocracy in relatively weak, poor countries very quickly comes back to powerful, rich countries.

Aside from the tendency of stolen wealth to be moved abroad, the international cast of the campaign stems from the fact that if the incumbent rulers are corrupt, probably the only way that they can be held accountable is through action by those outside the country. Corrupt rulers are likely to have bribed or intimidated judges and prosecutors, law enforcement, and the other local institutions of accountability. Of course the domestic justice system may catch up with such rulers after they have been overthrown, perhaps under the rubric of transitional justice.[12] Even international actors are often likely to wait until individuals are out of power before taking action. Typical examples are those rulers overthrown in the Arab Spring of 2011, feted by both Western governments and financial institutions until almost the last moment before they lost power. Yet sometimes even those still securely in power may now be targeted for their corruption.

Against the Odds: The Surprising Campaign against Kleptocracy

Although many more corrupt leaders get away with their crimes than face justice, the rise of the expectation from shortly after the turn of the century that host countries have a duty to take action to block or seize their illicit funds is a new and in many ways remarkable development. It runs contrary to the doctrine of sovereign immunity, according to which individual state leaders cannot be prosecuted by third countries for acts committed in office. While this immunity has been successfully challenged in some cases of human rights abuses, perhaps most famously with the decision to arrest Augusto Pinochet in response to a Spanish warrant during a visit to Britain in 1998, recent moves also bring this immunity into question for corruption offenses. Considering the incidence of serious corruption among the world's leaders, if this expectation were ever to be generally enforced, the consequences for international diplomacy would be enormous. Thus US diplomats resisted a law to bar senior officials suspected of corruption from being admitted to the United States because "senior State Department people especially from Africa kept saying that if something like this is used they wouldn't have anyone to talk to."[13] Yet as discussed in chapter 1, African governments have been some of the keenest supporters of vital parts of the anti-kleptocracy regime. A wide range of governments from the developing world, and more recently those of China and Russia as well, have pressed for rules allowing them to reclaim stolen assets transferred abroad.

Instead of looking at poorer countries that may have been forced to act against corruption by outside political pressure (e.g., as a condition of World Bank loans), the book focuses on four rich countries where such pressure has played little or no role. The United States, Britain, Switzerland, and Australia have freely made demanding commitments to detect and return looted wealth from abroad, and it is difficult to see these promises reflecting outside coercion. It is equally hard to find a conventional national interest rationale for pushing anti-kleptocracy campaigns. Rather than lecture poor foreign governments about the error of their ways, rich countries have invited scrutiny from international organizations and peer countries of their own performance in the sensitive areas of money laundering and corruption. In security terms, the status quo arrangement of rich-country governments averting their eyes from dictators laundering their illicit funds worked perfectly well. With the end of the Cold War there was much less need to fund such client governments, but there was also no national security logic in actively seeking to promote transparency and accountability, especially considering the extent of patron states' complicity in past shady affairs.

Adding to the puzzle is a lack of a domestic electoral logic behind the anti-kleptocracy campaign. Rather than look to investigate the misdeeds of national politicians, the aim is to hold senior officials from foreign countries accountable. While American voters, for example, are likely to care about corruption by American politicians, they are much less exercised about Ukrainian politicians laundering the proceeds of their corruption in US banks or real estate. Though this sort of activity is clearly a problem for Ukraine, it is much less apparent why US national interests would demand an investigation. It is even more puzzling when the Ukrainian government itself may show at best sporadic interest in pursuing such matters. The same goes for Nigerian leaders laundering their funds in the United Kingdom, Pakistanis in Switzerland, or Chinese in Australia.

As rhetorical commitments have been translated into treaties, laws, and regulation, this work has been done by and with the support of senior government officials. Yet the main thrust of many of these rules is to place exactly this class of people under suspicion. According to the system they have instituted, even those with a spotless record face extra scrutiny and inconvenience in their financial affairs. And of course many such officials have a great deal to hide in their financial lives. As such, on a personal level, for senior officials to support an anti-corruption campaign specifically directed at senior officials as they have seems a little like the proverbial turkeys voting for Christmas.

Finally, beyond states and politicians, the new rules cut across the interests of perhaps the most politically influential industry within such countries: the finance sector. As described in chapter 1, much of the actual enforcement of the new rules has been delegated to private financial institutions, especially banks. They must screen new and existing customers, compile risk profiles, and report suspicious financial activities to authorities. Not only must these firms act as unpaid policemen, they can and have been sanctioned for failing to carry out these unwanted duties (though there are many more instances of lapses remaining unpunished). The finance industry has sometimes tried to argue that it has its own intrinsic business and moral reasons for screening out the proceeds of corruption, and other criminal activity, due to commercial and reputational concerns.[14] This claim is not convincing. Criminal funds and clients generate the same stream of fees and revenue for banks as legitimate ones. To the extent that banks are dealing with wealthy kleptocrats in their private client sections, the rewards are especially high. There is little or no evidence to support the idea that banks suffer significant damage to their reputation when they are found to have done business with such unsavory customers. Nearly all the world's major international banks have been caught out on these grounds, with very little damage to show for it. The same applies to other related law and financial firms. The new rules against kleptocracy thus run contrary to financial firms' interests in that they endanger these firms' single most important goal: profit.

In sum, the campaign against grand corruption by states, intergovernmental organizations, and NGOs is centered on an extremely delicate issue, is in tension with fundamental laws and norms of sovereign immunity, focuses on the powerful countries that are most resistant to outside political pressure, provides little or no electoral payoff for politicians in these countries, threatens the personal interests of all senior officials, and runs counter to the interests of perhaps the most powerful business lobby in developed states. The deck would seem to be heavily stacked against this issue ever making it on to the policy agenda, and yet it has.

Explaining New Norms and Changing Policy Agendas

The question of how kleptocracy came to be defined as an international policy problem ties in with a much broader set of questions asking why certain practices or institutions that are at one time almost universally accepted as being part of the natural order of things later come to be seen as a problem to be solved, or perhaps even anathema to civilized sensibilities.[15] A prominent example might be slavery, a social institution that was accepted as an integral part of a huge range of societies from antiquity down to the nineteenth century;[16] another case might be the decline of interstate war.[17] Currently, although other forms of unfree labor exist, slavery as a system in which some people own others as property is outlawed in every single country in the world. Considering the inertia created by socialization in line with prevailing social institutions, how can we explain the kind of fundamental change whereby a practice that was regarded as entirely accepted, and that was backed up by powerful economic vested interests as well, came to be seen as completely illegitimate and repugnant? The contemporary shift, in Western countries at least, toward acceptance of homosexuality indicates that normative shifts may happen relatively rapidly, in a matter of years rather than generations.

Scholars have often focused on small, dedicated groups of pioneering activists in explaining large-scale international moral and legal transformations. These activists are said to both prick the conscience of policy makers and provide a blueprint for reform that goads these officials into action.[18] These "norm entrepreneurs" are said to initiate the process of a normative change in such a way that the momentum of this shift becomes self-sustaining. The more states and other actors that come to see something like slavery, gender discrimination, or the use of anti-personnel land mines as illegitimate, the greater the social pressure on others to conform with this view. Eventually the activists do themselves out of a job, or at least an issue; their formerly radical, perhaps even utopian, idea becomes mainstream and taken for granted.[19] As well as being an explicit account of how norms and regimes arise, this account implicitly predicts a high level of effectiveness in norms causing compliant behavior; most actors do not even consider violating the taken-for-granted norm, while the few who do are ostracized and sanctioned.

In studying the rise of an international responsibility to combat grand corruption through following the trail of dirty money, we find that campaigning nongovernmental organizations certainly have played an important role. While Transparency International has achieved a public profile that is the envy of many such groups, Global Witness has been even more important on the specific topic of kleptocracy and asset recovery. Yet as significant as the crusading activism of these groups has been, rather than change being the result of revolutionary vanguards, or campaigners possessed of Steve Jobs–like entrepreneurial genius, the argument presented here emphasizes a more decentralized, undirected, and coincidental process of change.

Another even more prevalent approach focuses on explaining states' behavior as the product of rational mean-ends calculations to achieve national interests, usually defined in material terms. The actors are different from the norm entrepreneurs noted above: states, rather than NGOs, are central. The goals are different too, being self-interested rather than altruistic. Yet there is the same tendency to explain the social world and political outcomes as the result of deliberate action by strategic actors.

The idea of states acting in a way that they think will enhance their national interests certainly sounds plausible, if not a truism. As discussed in the chapter to follow, many of the most important moves in instituting the anti-kleptocracy regime were taken by states, such as the United States and Switzerland, or clubs of states, such as the World Bank and the United Nations. To what extent is this states-as-rational-actors account an answer to the puzzle? Though the concept of "the national interest" is almost infinitely elastic, often being used to justify (or "explain") diametrically opposed courses of action, from host states' point of view, tracking down and returning stolen money from elsewhere is an unlikely fit. The central problem right from the start, in both a policy and intellectual sense, has been that if a victim state loses money to a host state, why is this a problem for the host state?

Hosting foreign dirty money has no particular costs and some benefits for the banks involved. Conversely, going to the effort and expense of tracing foreign illicit wealth and then handing it over to another government is a strange sort of selfishness. As discussed, since the victim states are usually poorer and less powerful than the havens for the looted wealth, it cannot be international coercion or arm-twisting that explains the change (the example of China as source and Australia as host discussed in chapter 5 may be the exception that proves the rule). The normal idea of reciprocity, whereby states may take short-term costs to receive larger benefits over the longer term, is also unlikely. That Switzerland and the United Kingdom are repatriating money to the Philippines and Nigeria so these two developed countries can receive the same cooperation with respect to corrupt Swiss and British politicians hiding money in Philippine and Nigerian banks sounds very implausible. The evidence suggests that explaining the anti-kleptocracy regime as a product of strategic rational action by states seeking material benefits is not convincing, and neither is the idea of strategic NGOs deliberately aiming at normative change. If both these kinds of strategic action fall short, what is the alternative?

From the perspectives sketched out above, political change may be driven by the strategic action of states in pursuit of the national interest or by the strategic action of vanguard activists or entrepreneurs in pursuit of norm change. In either case, the logic is broadly the same. To explain the success of the vanguard movement, however, we must explain why the masses are receptive to their appeals. To explain the successful business entrepreneur, it is necessary to explain the market and consumers' tastes. So too in explaining norm change we must explain why audiences are willing to buy the framing that norm entrepreneurs are selling. Just as political revolutions may be the product of subterranean, slowly unfolding processes of economic and social change, so too revolutions in norms may reflect undirected, unintended, and uncoordinated processes that are neither steered nor anticipated, nor perhaps even understood by those caught up in them. Rather than being a product of farsighted entrepreneurs or self-seeking states, the emergence of the anti-kleptocracy norm owes more to just this sort of deep, structural change, specifically the end of a need to support corrupt anti-Communist client governments after the fall of the Soviet Union and a diagnosis among development experts and policy makers that corruption causes poverty. Like the idea of a spark that lights a prairie fire,[20] individual scandals revealing the presence of foreign dirty money activated these background conditions by creating media and political pressure on governments in host countries to break from the status quo and take action. Yet it is the background conditions, and not the spark itself, that are most important in explaining the cause and content of the resulting action.[21]

Social scientists often have the unfortunate habit of turning relatively minor differences of language or emphasis into fierce debates and intellectual zero-sum contests. In refocusing attention from crusading groups to the evolving context, in portraying change as more a result of human action than human intention, the difference is a matter of degree. The example of the first of the Arab Spring revolutions, in Tunisia, provides an illustration of the broader point at issue and returns us to the subject of kleptocracy.

On December 17, 2010, in the Tunisian town of Sidi Bouzid, Mohamed Bouazizi, a street vendor selling vegetables, was insulted and fined by a policewoman for trading without a permit, though in fact no permit was required. Lacking the funds to pay a bribe, he sought redress at a local government office, where he was turned away. Shortly afterward he returned to the street in front of the office with a can of gasoline, doused himself, and set himself alight. Sustaining burns to 90 percent of his body, Bouazizi lingered on for eighteen days. His story prompted growing protests in sympathy with his anger at the authorities and later a visit from President Zine al-Abidine Ben Ali to his hospital bed. Seeking to explain the situation, his sister commented to reporters, "In Sidi Bouzid, those with no connections and no money for bribes are humiliated and insulted and not allowed to live."[22]

The contrast with the ruling family is jarring and instructive. On visiting Ben Ali's twenty-three-year-old daughter and twenty-eight-year-old son-in-law in 2009, the US ambassador described an opulent scene in his hosts' mansion (at the time they had another, even bigger residence under construction nearby). They had numerous servants, a caged tiger, and ice cream flown in especially for the meal. In between yelling at their servants, the young couple reminisced about their recent holiday in Saint-Tropez and opined about a variety of topics: the prospects for Middle East peace, how McDonald's makes Americans fat, and the virtues of organic food.[23] In another cable the ambassador presciently drew out the political implications of this obvious diversion of public assets: "Corruption in the inner circle is growing. Even average Tunisians are now keenly aware of it, and the chorus of complaints is rising. . . . Meanwhile, anger is growing at Tunisia's high unemployment and regional inequities. As a consequence, the risks to the regime's long-term stability are increasing."[24]

One way of explaining the Tunisian revolution is to look at the events from Bouazizi's self-immolation until Ben Ali and his despised wife fled into exile in Saudi Arabia scarcely a month later. The focus would be on the protest leaders and union heads that led the opposition, and the key defections of regime supporters and army officers that brought down the regime. Another approach is to zoom out and consider longer-term trends like those noted in the ambassador's second secret cable. These might include the rising number of unemployed university graduates, widening income disparities, or more intangible factors like the decaying legitimacy of the regime as its malfeasance became more and more obvious. The response that a full explanation should include both immediate and longer-term causes is a reasonable one, but it does not change the fact that in practice explanations tend to weight one or the other more heavily. When it comes to revolutions in norms like that against corruption, most commentators tend to concentrate on actors' shorter-term strategic decisions, whereas this book instead favors structural trends.

Assessing Effectiveness, Addressing Bias

The questions as to whether leaders really put any stock in their rhetoric about tackling "the cancer of corruption" and whether the rules on following the trail of dirty money have actually done any good in reducing the incidence of grand corruption are related but distinct. Answering these questions is tricky. The first depends on being able to judge policy makers' true intentions, the second on finding some yardstick to measure the amount of corruption and related laundering before and after the relevant international standards were put in place. But to simply throw up our hands when asked about effectiveness is not a defensible response. If there is an imperative to fight corruption, then there is also an imperative to find out if these efforts are doing any good.

Whether or how well international rules work would seem to be a fundamental concern for students of international relations, yet intractable problems have hamstrung research in this area, even when (unlike in the case of corruption) the degree of compliance is easier to see and measure. Behavior consistent with international standards may not be a result of these rules causing states to act in a more law-abiding fashion but instead the fact that law-abiding states are more likely to sign up to these rules in the first place.[25] Imagine a situation in which a group of countries agree to an international rule to make their currencies freely convertible and then subsequently introduce this reform. The temptation is to reason that the international agreement caused the subsequent policy change.[26] In fact, however, the international agreement may have been a mere ratification of a decision that this group of countries had already taken for unconnected domestic reasons.[27] When in 2009 the G20 leaders committed to increase government spending to mitigate the effects of the global recession, this seemed much more like an endorsement of what states would have done in isolation anyway than a substantive international commitment that changed behavior in and of itself.

When it comes to kleptocracy, the problem is not one of wondering whether high levels of compliance reflect a situation in which the presumed effect is really the cause or one where only law-abiding states sign up to international treaties. Over 175 countries have signed up to the UN Convention Against Corruption, and many of them have corrupt governments. Despite manifest problems of evidence, no one really thinks that most of the money stolen by corrupt officials and secreted across borders is intercepted and returned, or even detected. The total of looted state wealth repatriated as of 2014 is about $4.5 billion,[28] but the guesses of the total money stolen usually amount to at least the hundreds of billions. A United Nations study of the effectiveness of efforts to stop all kinds of criminal financial flows (not just corruption) estimated that the detection rate was around one cent per dollar, with perhaps as little as one-fifth of one cent of every dollar of illicit funds confiscated by law enforcement.[29] One could reasonably argue whether the true figure is one cent, a tenth of a cent, or maybe even five cents, but the judgment of another UN report from 1998 that money laundering in general is an area "characterized by criminal successes and law enforcement failures" is widely agreed to still ring true today, including by law enforcement agencies themselves.[30] The campaign against kleptocracy may have an even less flattering strike rate. Most money laundering prosecutions tend to be of relatively low-level criminals, usually connected with the drug trade.[31] Grand corruption is only a recent priority. Furthermore, thanks to the very scale of the wealth stolen, kleptocrats are often able to pay for the very best legal representation to deter, delay, or defeat efforts to seize their illegal assets.

Yet the consensus around the low level of effectiveness in absolute terms does not render further investigation pointless. A very small proportion of drivers who speed may be fined, but this does not mean that speed limits make no difference to people's driving or to the number of road deaths. Even if few kleptocrats are actually stripped of their assets, new rules designed to prevent the laundering of corruption proceeds could deter some from moving their money abroad, complicate the calculations of those who do, and introduce an idea of risk and vulnerability among these corrupt officials where previously there was complete impunity. Complex laundering schemes to disguise the illicit origins of dirty money may actually be a backhanded indication that the system has had some effect.

An important source of bias in almost any study of corruption is that from the criminals' point of view the success stories will never be known outside those directly involved. Those held to account for such crimes, especially grand corruption, are the unlucky and atypical few. If the instances of kleptocracy we know about are unrepresentative, how can we get anything like an accurate picture of the overall phenomenon? Though this bias is definitely a problem, and thus we should be modest about the certainty of any conclusions, it may not be as crippling as it first seems.

Somewhat surprisingly, much kleptocracy is a fairly public affair. Because impunity for so long has been the rule and accountability the exception, up until quite recently leaders have not really had to take many precautions to hide their crimes. Indeed, in a strict legal sense, taking public assets for private benefit abroad often may not have constituted a crime at all in the country that ended up hosting the stolen assets. Even if there were laws on the books against hosting the proceeds of foreign corruption, for the political reasons described above, kleptocrats knew that their chances of being investigated, let alone prosecuted or convicted, were close to zero.

Kleptocracy can be like daylight robbery, much more conspicuous and visible than petty corruption. After all, the sudden effort to trace the illicit wealth of leaders from Ferdinand Marcos after his downfall in 1986 to President Yanukovych of Ukraine from 2014 was not due to a sudden revelation that they had acquired vast sums of money illegally. Although the details of where these stolen assets are hidden are still coming to light after extensive investigations, the corrupt nature of these regimes was clear well before the revolutions, even among many of these rulers' own citizens.

For example, the French authorities should not need Sherlock Holmes–style powers of deduction to see that there is something suspicious about the assets in France held by the ruling Bongo family of Gabon.[32] On an annual presidential salary of $300,000, the family purchased thirty-nine luxury properties in France, one in Paris valued at €18.9 million, and hold seventy bank accounts.[33] Pascaline Bongo, the daughter of the former president Omar and sister of the incumbent Ali, spent $86 million in 2008–2010 on air travel for herself and friends. Meanwhile, at home, the head of the Gabonese budget watchdog complained in 2014 that "half of the [state's] budget simply vanished," and a third of the population lives below the poverty line.[34] When the French government hinted at an investigation, Gabon changed its official language from French to English in retaliation.

A further example is Denis Sassou-Nguesso, who has ruled Congo-Brazzaville on and off since 1979. The fact that 70 percent of his citizens live on under a dollar a day has not cramped the president's style. Thus the €60 million the Sassou-Nguesso family spent on luxury goods in France has gone on purchases ranging from twenty-four properties to ninety-one designer suits in a single twelve-month period.[35] Inheriting his father's taste in clothes, son Denis Christel spent €474,000 on shirts alone.[36] In 2006 the presidential party spent $400,000 during two weekend stays in the Waldorf Astoria in New York (they took up forty-four rooms) on a mission to the UN to explain why Congo needed to have its debts forgiven to alleviate poverty. Then–World Bank head Paul Wolfowitz was so incensed by press reports of this splurge that he unilaterally sought to veto the debt relief. He was defeated by a French-led revolt in the World Bank Board, which maintained it was important "to stay engaged with stake-holders" (a phrase that one former World Bank staffer translated to me as meaning "continue giving money to crooks").[37] Such examples of gross excess could be multiplied, but the picture of rulers and their families blatantly living beyond their official means is clear.

Why concentrate the search for illicit funds on the United States, Switzerland, Britain, and Australia? The best guess is that the bigger the financial center, the more dirty money flows through it, including the proceeds of foreign corruption.[38] As the hosts of the world's two leading financial centers, New York and London, and vital players in shaping the international anti-kleptocracy regime, the United States and Britain are obvious choices. Though having much less presence in international politics generally, Switzerland plays host to more wealth from rich individuals and families than any other country. Between them, these three countries dominate the international financial system and hold more foreign wealth than the rest of the world combined. As such, they are the key actors if the campaign against grand corruption is to succeed. All three states provide well-documented examples of kleptocrats laundering their money unhindered, but also more recent successful and unsuccessful efforts to attack their stolen wealth. In fact, the United States, Britain, and Switzerland are the only three OECD countries to have repatriated stolen wealth between 2011 and 2014.[39]

Australia has neither particular political nor financial significance but is nevertheless a vital case. Precisely because the other three countries are the exceptions in returning looted wealth, it is important to also look at a more typical situation of government inaction in response to transnational grand corruption, of the dogs that don't bark. Because in the past and probably even now government inaction in the face of corrupt monies from abroad is more common than action, Australia may be the most representative case of the four countries examined. Looking at Australia affords a uniquely close view of laundering the proceeds of corruption with impunity and a government in denial. Considering the lack of relevant public evidence, how can we know that there is in fact foreign loot in Australia? To answer this question I had to adopt an unorthodox research strategy. I hired a private detective and then worked with foreign anti-corruption officials to directly follow the path of dirty money into the country. These investigations turned up tens of millions of dollars of real estate owned by foreign corrupt officials. Much of this material is now in chapter 5, as well as being provided to the Australian government and law enforcement (which have generally ignored it) and to foreign agencies (which are using this information in various criminal cases).

The Shape of the Argument: Big Questions and Provisional Answers

How has this generalized international duty to chase kleptocrats' loot arisen in light of the unpropitious circumstances described earlier? Even more important, how well is the campaign against grand corruption working (if at all)? Are governments really trying to make these rules effective? Do disappointments about the results so far reflect cheap talk and cynically crafted window dressing, or are sincere efforts falling short because of the difficulty of the task at hand?

In line with contemporary accounts and subsequent scholarship, I argue change was a result of a conjunction of factors, particularly the geopolitical earthquake represented by the end of the Cold War but also a reevaluation of the failure of Western development policies. While the Soviet Union was still a going concern, the attitude of the United States and other Western powers toward corrupt anti-Communist dictators in the Third World echoed that of Franklin Roosevelt toward Nicaraguan dictator Anastasio Somoza: "He may be a son-of-a-bitch, but he's our son-of-a-bitch." Beginning in the 1990s, the national security rationale for propping up such unsavory client rulers was much less compelling. The geopolitical change coincided and overlapped with changing beliefs in the development policy community, which came to see corruption as one of the main causes of poverty. These two trends mutually reinforced each other. As a result of these intersecting factors, normative and policy change occurred rapidly, but in a decentralized, uncoordinated way, rather than being the deliberate result of calculated strategy by self-seeking governments or crusading "norm entrepreneurs."

The timing of change in particular countries has often been driven by a common pattern of events. Journalists and/or NGOs in host countries uncover looted wealth and through the resulting publicity create pressure for subsequent formal investigations. The role of activist victim governments, doggedly and publicly pressing for recompense, has also been vital for breaking the torpor of host states. Nevertheless, the story here does not fit the template of a "whodunit." The individual scandals and exposés that brought to light the secret wealth of corrupt dictators were certainly important in explaining the timing of change in individual countries. But the general trend, the rise of the anti-kleptocracy system, cannot be explained in terms of these particular episodes.

Despite some successes in countering grand corruption, most kleptocrats get away with their crimes and are still able to freely enjoy their ill-gotten gains at home and abroad. Though shortcomings are in part a product of the structural power of the finance industry, real policy challenges mean that even those governments that are sincerely trying to implement the rules (and many aren't) face high hurdles. A dauntingly large number of things have to go right in both victim and host countries for asset recovery to work as it is meant to. The upshot is that the preventive aspects of the anti-kleptocracy regime become even more important, because once dirty money has entered a foreign financial system, it is often prohibitively difficult and expensive to recover it.

The chapter immediately following analyzes the rise of the new norm and regime, while most of the rest of the book is primarily focused on the question of effectiveness. Chapter 1 sets the context for the subsequent chapters on the United States, Switzerland, Britain, and Australia. In order to ground the discussion of grand corruption, it begins with an example of what has been described as "the kleptocracy to end all kleptocracies": President Mobutu, who systematically pillaged the Congo during the three decades of his rule. The most important task of the chapter is to explain the rise of the anti-kleptocracy norm and the resulting global regime. The 1990s saw a growing global consensus that corruption was not merely a domestic matter but something that states should come together to fight in a coordinated fashion, associated with more general worries about states' loss of control in the face of financial globalization.[40] This shift is explained by the confluence of the end of the Cold War and the need to account for development policy failures. Anti-corruption NGOs like Transparency International were more an effect of this shift than a cause. This norm has been instantiated in an interlocking series of global and regional treaties and conventions, increasingly replicated in national legislation and regulation, as well as the commercial and compliance procedures of banks and other private financial institutions. The last part of the chapter presents a summary of the main elements of this regime to show how the system is supposed to work.

Each of the four case study chapters has some common elements, yet they also highlight important differences. In many instances the fact that the same scandal spilled over borders to cover more than one of these countries helps to illustrate similarities and differences between them. I seek to show how the various scandals and successes fed into interactive changes, both in a formal legal sense and informally in terms of policy priorities. The more contemporary instances illustrate the strengthening of the regime, as reflected in some partial successes. These chapters finish with a discussion of the major obstacles remaining in chasing kleptocrats' loot, an assessment of the overall effectiveness of standards, and some ideas as to how shortcomings might be overcome.

The Conclusion compares the patterns of strengths and weaknesses among the four case studies and offers some policy recommendations. Given the inherent difficulty of international legal action, the problems faced by victim countries, which almost by definition have limited resources, and the fact that even "bad guys" are allowed due process and human rights in rule-of-law democracies,[41] it seems that asset recovery as a purely criminal law strategy will seldom work. The idea that asset recovery will ever generate a meaningful amount of money for development purposes is an illusion, once we take into account investigative and legal costs, the costs of monitoring repatriated wealth, and the danger that these funds will once again be stolen.

A more hopeful strategy is to move away from the criminal justice system and interstate law, and instead use a mix of strategies pursued by states but just as importantly nonstate actors also, from NGOs, to vulture funds, to private individuals. States can sanction firms that play host to stolen wealth, especially banks but also lawyers, and make much better use of the tax system to pursue corrupt wealth. A blacklist of the worst kleptocracies should be drawn up, with officials from listed states being denied physical and financial access to countries hosting major financial centers. Such a list could be created either by an intergovernmental organization or by the United States unilaterally, or even perhaps by NGOs. With the rise of a private compliance and ratings industry hungry for data to feed into their financial risk software and models, such a list would to a significant extent be self-enforcing. Although jointly a radical package of measures, each solution has already been at least partially adopted in some settings. This package of reforms would be relatively cheap and significantly more effective than the status quo.

1

The Rise of the Anti-Kleptocracy Regime

Political leaders by definition have power over the use of public money. Perhaps unsurprisingly, many take this opportunity to transfer this money from state accounts to their own, behavior that according to one common definition, the abuse of public power for private gain, constitutes corruption. Aside from direct theft, senior officials may enrich themselves at the expense of the public interest by receiving or extorting bribes, trading in influence, or appointing their friends and families to sinecure posts. Corruption is a difficult problem to address at the best of times, but most of all when the state apparatus used to enforce laws is controlled by people dedicated to breaking them. In the absence of a world government, how can those at the apex of political power in sovereign states ever be punished for their corruption?

In responding, this chapter has three main aims. The first is to flesh out the brief discussion of kleptocracy in the Introduction by providing a portrait of one of the most publicized and influential early examples of kleptocracy, that of Mobutu Sese Seko in the Congo (renamed Zaire

1971–1997). This sketches out the corruption of Mobutu and his clique while they were in power from 1965 to 1997 and the unsuccessful efforts to recover the loot held abroad after their fall.

The second and most important aim is to show how the global anti-kleptocracy norm and the resulting regime came into being. Though there are many reasons, two in particular stand out. The first is the incremental process of building a policy consensus concerning why measures designed to foster growth in poor countries had failed. Beginning in the 1990s, policy makers and others became convinced that corruption prevented development, and hence that fighting corruption was necessary to reduce poverty. Even more importantly, at around the same time the sudden end of the Cold War undermined the security rationale for the United States and other Western powers to support kleptocratic client governments in the Third World.

For different reasons, a wide variety of intergovernmental organizations, NGOs, and governments from Africa, Asia, and Latin America stressed that corruption implicated rich countries as well as poor, because funds looted from poor countries tended to end up in rich ones. The United States independently had previously sought to co-opt other governments to join its attempts to tackle cross-border corruption. Looking at havens for the proceeds of corruption, rather than just corrupt governments as such, put the issue of returning stolen assets on the agenda. Most of the policy tools for tracing and confiscating illicit funds were already at hand, thanks to unrelated efforts as part of the "war on drugs" and broader efforts to combat money laundering. The story of intertwined normative and policy change at the global level in this chapter provides context for the subsequent analysis of how well these rules work at a national level in the later chapters on the United States, Switzerland, Britain, and Australia.

The final part of the chapter briefly summarizes the main features of the resulting system of rules. It focuses on how the central elements of the global anti-kleptocracy regime have been institutionalized in law and practice by considering two important examples. The first is the United Nations Convention Against Corruption, the primary formal statement of the underlying anti-kleptocracy norm. The second is the most specifically relevant international organization, the joint UN–World Bank Stolen Asset Recovery Initiative (StAR), designed to mobilize both technical assistance and moral pressure to combat kleptocracy.

The Scope of the Argument

Although most of the financial flows associated with grand corruption tend to go from poor countries to rich ones, it is important to highlight exceptions. Clearly, senior officials in developed states are also prone to corruption.[1] Former French president Jacques Chirac was convicted of embezzlement in 2011, and his successor Nicholas Sarkozy has been investigated for corruption offenses.[2] Former German chancellor Helmut Kohl was placed under criminal investigation in connection with kickbacks from a Saudi arms deal that were laundered as undeclared campaign donations to the Christian Democratic Union, though this matter was settled without a conviction.[3] Most of the Italian political class was found to have been corrupt in a series of investigations in the early 1990s.[4] At one stage more than half of the members of the legislature were under indictment. In an ironic reversal in light of later events during the Arab Spring, former prime minister Craxi received refuge from Ben Ali in Tunisia so as to avoid a twenty-seven-year jail term. Craxi's "defense," both before and after his flight, was that although he was taking bribes, so was everyone else. More recently, Silvio Berlusconi avoided jail on corruption charges thanks to a series of legal amendments to the criminal code introduced by his own government.[5]

Across the Atlantic, the term "money laundering" was first used in connection with the criminal conspiracy of the Nixon administration in the Watergate scandal.[6] Some US states have had endemic problems with corrupt senior officials. For example, the Senate seat vacated by Barack Obama was filled at the discretion of Illinois governor Rod Blagojevich, who was wiretapped musing, "I've got this thing, and it's fucking golden. I'm just not giving it up for fucking nothing." In December 2011 he was sentenced to fourteen years in prison for corruption offenses. Former Canadian prime minister Brian Mulroney accepted paper bags stuffed with $1,000 notes from an Airbus lobbyist in 1993 and 1994. Despite denying the payments under sworn testimony and failing to declare these cash payments of C$ 225,000 on his income tax return, Mulroney successfully sued the Canadian government when it alleged corruption.[7] Japan and South Korea have also had major corruption scandals at the highest level of government.[8] The list could be extended much further, but the point is that leaders in many rich countries also have been engaged in serious corruption offenses.

Why, then, the disproportionate focus on corrupt leaders from Africa, Asia, eastern Europe, and Latin America in this book? One answer is that recent corruption among senior officials in North America and western Europe does not seem to have had the same effect on the economy in general and hence the welfare of their citizens. Reasoning from the analogue of post-Communist Russia, one former CIA official explained to Congress what the United States would look like if it were a kleptocracy:

> It would be necessary to have massive corruption by the majority of the members of Congress as well as by the Departments of Justice and Treasury, the agents of the FBI, CIA, DIA, IRS, Marshal Service, Border Patrol, state and local police officers, the Federal Reserve Bank, Supreme Court justices, US District Court judges, support of various Organized Crime families, the leadership of the Fortune 500 companies, at least half the banks in the US, and the New York Stock Exchange. This cabal would then have to seize the gold in Fort Knox and the federal assets deposited in the entire banking system. It would have to take control of the key industries . . . and claim these items to be their private property. . . . This unholy alliance would then have to spend 50% of its billions in profits to bribe officials that remained in government and be primary supporters of all the political candidates. . . . The President would not only be aware of such activities but would support them.[9]

While all political systems probably suffer from some form of corruption, it is untrue and unhelpful to say that all such systems are equally corrupt.

A last caveat is that although the focus here is on looted wealth that is moved across borders into major financial centers, a lot of this wealth is spent at home. Aside from the palaces and opulent domestic living, kleptocrats may dissipate much or even most of the money they steal in maintaining the support of subordinates, perhaps especially in the army and police. Their political edifice is usually built on a network of patronage and payments that demands a constant supply of money and favors, often involving a subcontracting out of bribe-taking opportunities.[10]

What Does Kleptocracy Look Like?
Mobutu in Congo/Zaire

The case of Mobutu Sese Seko in Zaire (now the singularly misnamed Democratic Republic of the Congo) is an iconic instance that powerfully shaped popular and policy perceptions of kleptocracy and was important in putting this issue on the international policy agenda. In particular, this case is notable in fixing the notion of a link between the rapacious predation of the ruler and his family in stripping out the national patrimony, the baroque opulence of their lifestyle, and then the extreme poverty of those they ruled and the dysfunctionality of the state. The emerging policy narrative interpreted the former as the cause of the latter. As discussed later in this chapter, kleptocracy came to be seen as an extreme form of the bad governance that was held to be responsible for a wide range of development failures. This case also highlights a change in the international landscape that was crucial for bringing kleptocracy on to the agenda: the end of the Cold War. As with the foibles of other reliably anti-Communist US client dictators like Ferdinand Marcos in the Philippines and the Duvaliers in Haiti, before the end of the East-West confrontation the grand corruption of Mobutu and his inner circle had been ignored in favor of overriding geopolitical concerns.

Mobutu came to power in 1965 promising to live on a soldier's salary, but during his thirty-two-year rule he instead set up a system referred to as "a kleptocracy to end all kleptocracies."[11] Born Joseph-Désiré Mobutu, in an indication of his vaunting ambition and self-regard, Mobutu adopted the full name "The warrior who knows no defeat because of his endurance and inflexible will and is all powerful, leaving fire in his wake as he goes from conquest to conquest" (Mobutu Sese Seko Kuku Ngbendu Wa Za Banga). Congo, renamed Zaire from 1971 to 1997, became synonymous with both grand corruption and poverty.

Mobutu and his family and associates benefited from a wide range of corrupt schemes.[12] The most direct routes of enrichment were special presidential budget items in the national accounts. At one stage, Mobutu's personal allocation comprised 17 percent of the total budget, more than the totals spent on health, education, and welfare combined.[13] There were additional direct transfers from the central bank into Mobutu's personal foreign accounts. Western governments paid bribes to Mobutu without even pretending they were part of a development package (these were put at $150 million in the 1960s).[14] The state-owned diamond mine was reportedly instructed to divert 30 percent of its proceeds to private accounts, while there were other ad hoc sales of large quantities of copper and cobalt in which all the proceeds were corruptly diverted. Mobutu and his inner circle routinely demanded and received bribes and kickbacks from domestic and foreign investors. A campaign of nationalization in the early 1970s saw prime assets and key monopolies end up as the private possessions of the ruling clique. Borrowings from foreign private lenders, governments, and the Bretton Woods institutions were prone to expropriation, and development and military aid was similarly vulnerable.[15]

The politics of the national debt was particularly incendiary in the way it implicated Western banks and governments in the despoiling of the country and the illicit enrichment of its elite. Until the mid-1970s the Mobutu regime borrowed extensively from private Western lenders, the money often frittered away on graft-plagued white elephant projects. Realizing the slim chances of ever getting their money back, these banks stopped lending. Yet Zaire's foreign debt ballooned through the 1980s as the World Bank and the International Monetary Fund stepped into the breach. Despite the serious and sometimes public misgivings of senior staff from both institutions, US and French political pressure ensured that new loans were granted under repeated pretenses of reform and restructuring.[16] Mobutu's willingness to let Zaire be used as a base for various anti-Communist guerrillas and covert actions was seen to far outweigh his venality and ensured that loans and direct aid payments kept on flowing. By 1986, debt servicing took 43 percent of the national budget.[17] After billions of dollars of development lending, annual GDP per capita stood at $130 in 1994.[18]

The Search for Mobutu's Loot

In the wake of his fall in 1997, the new government set up an Office of Ill-Gotten Gains to recover the assets stolen by Mobutu and his coterie. The search began in the newly renamed Congo but quickly extended abroad. The result was almost complete disappointment. Even though these efforts predated many of the new anti-kleptocracy measures discussed later in this chapter, the roadblocks encountered still stand today as a reminder

of the difficulties facing a government from the developing world looking to recover illicit wealth transferred abroad. The problems encountered
in the search for Mobutu's foreign wealth have plagued many other similar efforts.

The French government was completely uncooperative from the start,
despite Mobutu's high-profile properties there. From before the fall of
Mobutu right up to the present day, France has been a reliably unfussy host
for the proceeds of grand corruption from Africa.[19] The Swiss and Bel-
gians, however, were initially willing to help. Journalist Michela Wrong
recounts that freezes were placed on the assets of the former Zairean president as well as those of eighty of his senior officials. Interviewing a representative from the Swiss police, Wrong recounts a problem that would
sound familiar to those searching for many other kleptocrats' wealth: "We
need more information and it has never come from Kinshasa. . . . They
must at least show us there is some link between these assets and supposed
crimes, a suspicion, if not actual proof, for the dossier to go further."[20] The
information never came, and the freezes lapsed. A search of Swiss accounts
that was expected to come up with $8 billion instead netted only $4 million.[21] Why had the process failed, when Mobutu's corruption was so blatantly obvious, when at least some of the assets like properties were not
hard to find, and when at least for a time some important host country
governments were keen to help?

The point about a lack of necessary information from the victim country to establish a link between particular crimes and particular assets
would be repeated again and again in subsequent cases. As discussed in
relation to the Mubarak money in chapter 4, matters sometimes descended
into an acrimonious exchange of charge and countercharge: the victim
country complains of a lack of cooperation from the host country, and
the host complains about a lack of specific information from the victim
government. When Wrong inspected the asset freeze request sent by the
Congolese government to counterparts overseas, she was amazed by how
little information it contained. When the public prosecutor was questioned
about this perfunctory document, which had only five lines on Mobutu, he
insouciantly replied that "we're leaving it to our friends abroad to fill out
the details."[22]

There are several reasons why the new government did not provide the
information needed to track down the looted wealth. There was certainly

no shortage of other pressing issues to worry about. The machinery of government, such as it was, had fallen apart during the closing stages of Mobutu's shambolic rule, and so too had the economy. Most urgently, a falling-out with former allies Rwanda and Uganda had led to an invasion from the east and a new war.[23] As a result, there was a political imperative to reconcile with many members of the old elite so they would help shore up the new government.[24] This decision to let bygones be bygones later extended to taking Mobutu's son, a prime beneficiary of his father's looting, into the cabinet.[25] Furthermore, the very officials charged with recovering corrupt assets were themselves accused of misusing their powers of seizure to acquire prime real estate in Kinshasa, leading to dismissals and further disruption. The lesson of subsequent asset recovery efforts is that even a determined and reasonably organized government seeking the return of stolen assets has to persevere for many years to recover even a fraction of the wealth in question. The Congolese government was neither determined nor organized.

Even allowing for the meager information they were given, why was such a small sum found in Swiss banks, a fraction of 1 percent of the expected total? One suggestion might be that Mobutu and his family made sure to conduct both the initial theft and later laundering at arm's length by using proxies or associates rather than carry out this risky business in their own names. Especially after the end of the Cold War, once Zaire's Western backers began distancing themselves from the regime, the ruling clique had several years' advanced warning that their ill-gotten wealth abroad might be vulnerable. Mobutu often gave verbal orders to underlings, who then signed the necessary documentation.[26] As a result, a simple search of bank accounts under the Mobutu name may not have revealed the stolen wealth. The habit of using front men is certainly common to other kleptocrats and has posed a considerable obstacle to other asset recovery efforts. Yet this strategy is risky. The front men themselves may decide to abscond with wealth that is in some sense legally theirs.

A closely related gambit is using companies or trusts to obscure the money trail. Rather than the bank account being held in the name of a real person, such as a friend or family member, it is held in the name of a legal person, for example, a shell company. Given that companies and trusts can be easily and cheaply created, dissolved, and renamed at will, they can provide an invaluable concealment function. There may be layers or chains of companies and trusts between the real owner, the corrupt official, and the assets.[27] For example, one company might own a second that holds the bank account or property. Or one company may function as a trustee of a trust that in turn owns a second company that holds an account or property. The Congo's original kleptocrat, the Belgian king Leopold, used Congo Free State shell companies to hide profits from his rubber monopoly, in addition to holding property in the name of his doctor and architects.[28] Perhaps Mobutu also used corporate intermediaries to keep his name off bank records.

Another, more fundamental reason why there was no huge recovery of Mobutu assets may have been that there simply was no fortune, or at least not on anything like the scale that was commonly alleged. There is a tendency in talking about crime for completely unsubstantiated huge numbers to be quoted back and forth until they attain the status of fact.[29] In 1997 the new government of the Congo put the sum of Mobutu's stolen wealth at $14 billion, with the implication that this stock of wealth still existed and thus was potentially recoverable. No basis for this figure was offered, but it happened to exactly coincide with the nation's foreign debt at the time. This paralleled an estimate in 1982 when the former prime minister estimated that Mobutu had $4 billion in foreign bank accounts; at the time, Zaire's foreign debt was also $4 billion.[30] This gave rise to the notion, reported in the media both at the time and shortly after his fall from power, that Mobutu could have personally paid off the national debt with the proceeds of his corruption.[31]

The notion of equivalence, that the national debt of this desperately poor country was the direct consequence of its ruler's corruption, strongly shaped the subsequent thinking about kleptocracy (as a later Philippine election slogan put it, "If there's no corruption, there's no poverty"). Thanks to Mobutu's disastrous, rapacious style of "government," living standards actually declined during his rule. Yet as one IMF official was quoted as saying in 1989: "The typical number, that the wealth of Mobutu equals the debt of the country, this is taken out of the sky. There's no question that he's taken plenty of money out of the country, but I don't think anybody knows how much, except possibly him, and even he might not know."[32] Furthermore, the idea that this looted money might represent a fixed sum of invested wealth patiently accumulating interest seems very wide of the mark, given the amount of money that was squandered (e.g., cellars full of the most expensive French wine spoiling in the tropical heat, luxury cars abandoned for lack of maintenance, leasing of the Concorde for Madame Mobutu's shopping trips to Paris) and the cost of keeping the system of patronage going. A World Bank official noted, "The country was kept together by the loyalty of the regional governors, who were essentially warlords. Mobutu was milking whatever cows he had and sending the money to these guys. It was a very, very expensive business."[33] Nor did these payments stop at the border, with allegations that prominent Belgian politicians were on the payroll, that a brother of French president Valéry Giscard d'Estaing had been awarded hugely valuable building contracts, and that campaign donations from Mobutu had also bought influence in Washington.[34]

After the freeze on Mobutu's accounts eventually lapsed in 2009, the Swiss government issued a scathing rebuke of the Congolese government for its lack of interest in recovering the funds.[35] The statement noted that of ten countries contacted by the Congo government, all the others had let the freeze lapse after a few years, thanks to a lack of any follow-up from the government in Kinshasa. It listed a chronology of efforts by the Swiss to encourage the Congolese government to pursue the funds, including a visit to Kinshasa by the Swiss president and an offer to pay a private lawyer to conduct the case. Over a twelve-year period the Swiss government had unilaterally extended the freeze, even though there was no criminal case or mutual legal assistance request in process. The official statement concluded: "This episode has put an end to all hopes of being able to restore at least a part of Mobutu's assets to the Congolese people. A highly symbolic opportunity for various states to show their commitment to combating corruption and impunity has thus been squandered." While the Swiss frustration was genuine, it did not address the point of how funds from this "notoriously corrupt regime" (as the statement puts it) had been allowed to be laundered in Switzerland with impunity for decades.

The Rise of the Anti-Corruption Agenda

How did kleptocracy and the hosting of stolen assets in foreign countries come on to the international policy agenda? Because kleptocracy is a subset of the broader topic of corruption, I first take a step back to consider how the taboo surrounding corruption in policy and diplomatic circles was broken. Once corruption was on the agenda, it was a short step to focusing on kleptocracy and the hosting of stolen assets. The remainder of the chapter thus explains the interlinked process of normative and policy change, as the shifting climate of opinion was increasingly reflected in new laws and new institutions. The novel shared belief that fighting grand corruption constituted a general international responsibility, and the corresponding regime constituted by the various overlapping global, regional, and national rules, was the result of a confluence of underlying trends. It was not caused by the deliberate action of farsighted strategic actors. A disparate group of rich and poor states, intergovernmental and nongovernmental organizations converged on the position that corruption was an international problem that required a coordinated international response, and furthermore that addressing grand corruption more specifically necessitated tracking and repatriating looted wealth from host countries.

Breaking the Corruption Taboo: The End of the Cold War

If the Mobutu case is an exemplar of the problem of grand corruption and catalyst for change in the global policy agenda, what were the other, more general forces at work? First, the end of the Cold War removed the perceived need to overlook the grand corruption of various anti-Communist client states (the Soviet Union had been equally indifferent to corruption among its clients). Not only did the geopolitical utility of such government decline, but of course there was no longer a danger of these states switching sides after the collapse of the Soviet Union. Writing on African client states more broadly, William Reno has in part ascribed the rise of "failed states" in the early post–Cold War period to this shift.[36] Previously such states were held together thanks to a network of patron-client relations and rent seeking funded in significant part by flows from the United States, other Western allies, and the Bretton Woods institutions. As these flows tailed off and the pressure to dismantle such networks increased in line with the new template of "good governance" reforms, the state apparatus fell apart.

Domestically, the related "third wave of democratization" meant that newly free media and civil society organizations could investigate and publicize corruption scandals. These often became important election issues, creating strong pressure for past and present corrupt politicians to be held accountable for their crimes. For example, some of the main drivers of the continuing search for money stolen during the presidency of Ferdinand Marcos were bodies like the Philippine Center for Investigative Journalism.[37] In formerly Communist Europe, the transition away from state socialism provided opportunities for new forms of corruption, especially that associated with privatization programs, but also gave journalists and other investigators much more room to publicize the self-enrichment of the old regime.[38]

A coincidence of high-profile national corruption scandals tainted leaders in the mid to late 1990s in countries as diverse as Indonesia, Pakistan, South Korea, Brazil, Venezuela, Ecuador, Mexico, Colombia, Spain, and the Czech Republic.[39] Even in established democracies like Italy, the end of the East-West confrontation shook up the political system in a way that made long-standing corruption much more visible. The Italian Communist Party split, and with its anti-Communist role now much less relevant, the Christian Democrats and their allies became much more susceptible to investigation.[40] One observer holds that in the early 1990s no fewer than six heads of state and over fifty ministers lost power as a result of corruption investigations, not to mention the dozens of officials who committed suicide after their misdeeds were exposed.[41] Given the plethora of such scandals, the *Financial Times* dubbed 1994 "the Year of Corruption."[42]

Corruption and Development

After the end of the Cold War a further cause of change was development policy failures that demanded explanation; corruption became the prime suspect. The IMF and the World Bank had spent much of the 1980s promoting economic liberalization, deregulation, and more generally a move to increase the role of markets while decreasing the role of the state among its developing country borrowers.[43] Reforms were bundled together in Structural Adjustment Programs. These programs became synonymous with government cuts to health, education, and welfare and with hardship among the general population. The resulting stigma meant that both the specific policy measures but also the two Bretton Woods institutions as a whole became the targets of a highly critical NGO campaign. To make matters worse, the evidence that IMF and World Bank prescriptions for development actually worked was at best mixed.[44] The 1980s had been a "lost decade" for Latin America, and most African countries had actually become poorer since independence. Something had gone badly wrong, but what?

A growing consensus suggested that shortcomings among recipient governments were to blame. It is difficult to separate the mix of expediency and genuine intellectual conviction behind this shift. It was more palatable for the World Bank and the IMF to blame borrower governments than to admit that they themselves, and by implication the Western governments behind them, had been in the wrong for years or even decades. Certainly there was some plausibility to this account about the importance of government policy and institutions.[45] Somewhat later the botched privatization in eastern Europe and especially in the former Soviet Union that saw huge swaths of the economy transferred to a few well-connected insiders and oligarchs again put the spotlight on corruption.[46] These emerging currents of thought were cross-fertilized and bolstered by contemporaneous theoretical and empirical trends in academic thought.

The growing popularity of New Institutional Economics as pioneered by Nobel Prize–winning scholars such as Douglass North and Oliver Williamson emphasized the importance of governments in providing institutions that fostered growth. North in particular attributed continuing poverty in the developing world to institutional failures, especially institutions that favored rent seeking and corruption over productive economic activity.[47] This view, championed by Joseph Stiglitz as World Bank chief economist from 1996, challenged the more neoclassical orientation of professional economists in development organizations that had previously ignored or downplayed the role of the state.[48]

The relatively scarce literature on corruption before this point had suggested that corruption might actually increase growth, for example by allowing bribe givers to cut through red tape and get on with business.[49] Pioneering work by Susan Rose-Ackerman and Anne Krueger,[50] however, followed up by others in the early 1990s, drew the opposite conclusion, increasingly equating corruption with rent seeking and underdevelopment.[51] One of the seminal empirical assertions of this relationship was in a 1995 article that found that high perceived commercial corruption scores were associated with reduced investment and growth.[52] The production of academic work on corruption rose substantially in the 1990s, much of it probing the link with development.[53] Both at the time and since, the causal relationship between corruption and poverty has been questioned, and countries like Bangladesh, Indonesia, and especially China have managed sustained economic growth despite widespread corruption.[54] But as far as policy makers were concerned, by the late 1990s there was a consensus not only that poorer countries tended to have higher levels of corruption but also that corruption retarded growth.[55] Indeed, by 2004 the World Bank held that corruption was "the single greatest obstacle to economic and social development."[56] In his foreword to the United Nations Convention Against Corruption, Secretary-General Kofi Annan similarly talked about "the devastating effect that corruption has on development."[57]

A key signal of changing priorities was the 1989 World Bank report "Sub-Saharan Africa: From Crisis to Sustainable Growth." In terms that would later become the conventional wisdom, then-president Barber Conable reasoned in the foreword, "A root cause of weak economic performance in the past has been the failure of public institutions. Private sector initiatives and market mechanisms are important, but they must go hand in hand with good governance—a public service that is efficient, a judicial system that is reliable, and an administration that is accountable to the public."[58] The report explicitly said that many African governments were "wracked by corruption,"[59] including "at the highest levels."[60] An earlier draft of the report had been even more pointed, explicitly blaming Africa's kleptocratic elites for much of the continent's misfortunes. A later review of the causes of the World Bank's ineffectiveness, the 1992 Wapenhans Report, argued that the corruption was a problem generally, not just in Africa.[61]

Such assessments of the Bank's performance were complemented by new leadership when in 1995 James Wolfensohn (by training a lawyer rather than an economist) took up the presidency and quickly made corruption a priority with his oft-repeated metaphor of the "cancer of corruption." Wolfensohn held that corruption was the number-one obstacle to development.[62] In 1996 a Corruption Action Plan Working Group was established. The resulting report stated that "a window of opportunity had opened up" in combating corruption because "staff, donors, and many borrowers" had come to support such efforts,[63] and that "corruption is no longer a taboo subject in the Bank."[64] The report clearly raises the central feature of laundering the proceeds of kleptocracy: "Grand corruption is often associated with international business transactions and usually involves politicians as well as bureaucrats. The bribery transaction may take place entirely outside the country."[65]

Converging Currents in the Rise of the Anti-Corruption Agenda

The World Bank was by no means the only, or even the first, intergovernmental organization to take up the anti-corruption cause. Early World Bank publications on this topic refer to OECD efforts to counter foreign bribery as blazing a trail for the Bank and other international organizations looking to break the corruption taboo. This work was focused on the problem of firms from OECD countries bribing foreign government officials, rather than kleptocracy. Nevertheless, efforts to counter foreign bribery are important for the story here because they show the transition from corruption as a purely domestic issue to one at the center of the international policy agenda. The origins of this initiative begin with the United States.

After passing the Foreign Corrupt Practices Act criminalizing the bribery of foreign officials in 1977, the United States sought to advance an anti-corruption agreement through the United Nations, without success.[66] One of the staffers who had assisted in drafting the bill, Jack Blum, was invited by the United Nations to write an outline of what an international anti-corruption instrument might look like. As he recounts it, the initial twenty-page draft was drastically rewritten by UN officials for the various constituencies in the organization. They explained that for the Communist bloc, capitalism was corruption; for the African group, racism was corruption; for the Arab states, Zionism was corruption, and so on; and that all these concerns had to be acknowledged in the document. The resulting ninety-page document was unworkable and unreadable, and it was junked.[67] In 1989, however, at the urging of the United States, the OECD set up an ad hoc working group to look at international corruption.[68] The broader ambitions of this ad hoc group were flagged in April 1993, when it was noted that aside from the OECD membership the goal was to include countries like Hong Kong, South Korea, Malaysia, Thailand, Singapore, and Taiwan.[69] In 1994 a nonbinding resolution was passed by the OECD Ministerial Council (and the working group made permanent), and in December 1997 the OECD anti-bribery convention was opened for signatures.[70] It is worth remembering that at this time not only was bribing foreign officials legal in many Western European states, it was also a legitimate, tax-deductible business expense.

The period 1994–1997 saw a rush of international anti-corruption agreements. Following on from initial discussions in 1993 and led by the United States, Chile, Ecuador, and Venezuela,[71] in December 1994 a Summit of the Americas initiated work on what became the Inter-American Convention Against Corruption, with agreement reached in March 1996. At the time of the summit Ecuador had committed to be the first country to adopt Transparency International's new standards (discussed below), while Brazil and Venezuela were seeking the extradition of former presidents accused of corruption.[72] The European Union approved an anticorruption convention in 1997.[73] The IMF formally signed up to the cause in the same year, following important publications by economists at the Fund on the negative effect of corruption on development a few years before.[74] The United Nations General Assembly passed a resolution on the control of corruption in 1996.[75] At a ministerial conference in mid-1994 the Council of Europe mandated work on a convention against corruption, launching the resulting legal instrument in 1999,[76] and founded the Group of States Against Corruption (GRECO) peer-review monitoring group. In December 1994 a meeting of African heads of state in Pretoria called for a regional anti-corruption agreement, though the African Union anticorruption convention was concluded only in 2003. International business also pushed this topic, prompted in particular by US firms. The World Economic Forum meeting that gave rise to the Davos Summits made corruption a centerpiece of its January 1994 meeting.[77] The International Chamber of Commerce released a set of recommendations in response to extortion and bribery in international transactions in 1996.[78] The Federation of Consulting Engineers and the International and American Bar Associations published recommendations along similar lines in 1995 and 1996 respectively.[79]

At around the same time, the first NGOs explicitly devoted to fighting corruption began to coalesce, the best known being Transparency International, which was founded in Germany in May 1993. Former World Bank regional director for East Africa Peter Eigen was the first chairman, and three other early members of the Board of Directors had also been senior World Bank officials, indicating the close links between the two bodies.[80] Eigen and others had become frustrated with the World Bank's cautious attitude in condemning corruption and hoped to achieve more in a new body unconstrained by member-state politics. In particular,

Eigen traces the initial impetus of his move from the World Bank to found Transparency International to the 1989 report on Africa referenced above.[81] Much of the preparatory work for the launch had been done in 1992, when many of the principals had come together to draw up a draft charter and set the goals of the new organization.[82]

Although understandably keen to play up their own role, even those from Transparency International acknowledge the importance of coincidence, good timing, and deep trends completely outside their control in explaining the rise of an anti-corruption norm. For example, speaking of a 1990 meeting in Swaziland, Eigen noted: "The timing was propitious: international corruption had reached crisis-level proportions, and many countries that were undergoing political transition were in desperate need of stronger integrity systems. . . . At the end of the Cold War, the time was right."[83] "When TI was launched in 1993, none of its founders could have anticipated how quickly it would be accepted as an idea whose time had come."[84] Writing almost twenty years later, Eigen judges, "Looking back we have to recognize that many factors came together, including an opportune time at the end of the Cold War, courageous personalities and institutions, and a growing demand of the people for better governance."[85] Another key founder agrees that "against a background of a post–Cold War era and rising public concerns about corruption our timing was right."[86]

This view was also expressed in interviews with Transparency International members, who echoed word for word this phrasing that anti-corruption was "an idea whose time had come," thanks to the end of the Cold War and frustration in the development community with repeated policy failure.[87] One TI official in Berlin made a similar reference to the importance of the "zeitgeist."[88] Transparency International built on extant anti-corruption sentiment among a wide range of constituencies, from elites in intergovernmental and national policy networks to local, grassroots anti-corruption movements. As early as 1995 there were already fifty national chapters, with more than a hundred by 2000. The invention of the organization's most successful public relations tool, the Corruption Perceptions Index, was "more or less a coincidence."[89] Since 1995 the index has scored and ranked countries annually from most to least corrupt on the basis of aggregated surveys. This high-profile measure was created by a young intern (Johann Graf Lambsdorff) and first published without permission by a German journalist.[90]

Global Witness was also founded in 1993, in Britain. Although not having the public profile of Transparency International, it now has an even more prominent role in the campaign against kleptocracy and money laundering. Global Witness's original purpose was to examine the link between the plundering of natural resources, conflict, and corruption. Early research concentrated on the illegal logging trade in Cambodia,[91] work that was later expanded to include conflict diamonds and a wide range of other activities.[92] This NGO was important in shaping the direction of the corruption policy agenda from the late 1990s on, especially with regard to kleptocracy and asset recovery. Together with the umbrella group Publish What You Pay, Global Witness was instrumental in the Extractive Industries Transparency Initiative, launched in 2002 to combat international corruption in the energy and minerals sectors.[93]

In the second decade of this century a swarm of other NGOs became active in the area of combating illicit international financial flows, particularly the related areas of cross-border corruption, money laundering, and tax evasion. Thus while Transparency International and Global Witness play a leading role in the Financial Transparency Coalition, this umbrella group contains a total of 150 member organizations, usually smaller NGOs and foundations along with some trade unions.[94] Some members' primary concerns lie in cognate areas (e.g., tax or aid), but each body endorses the positions of its fellows. The representatives of such groups often have impressive policy expertise, and they sometimes enjoy important access to such organizations as the World Bank, OECD, and Financial Action Task Force, as well as key national governments like those in the United States and United Kingdom.[95] In turn, these groups derive their funding from a mix of OECD governments (Britain and especially Norway being prominent thanks to their outsized aid budgets and leaders' personal interest in the anti-corruption cause) and philanthropic bodies like George Soros's Open Society Foundations.

Playing a different role is the Basel Institute on Governance, and within it the International Centre for Asset Recovery. Funded from 2006 in large part by the Swiss development agency as part of Bern's more public diplomacy campaign in this area (see chapter 3), and supplemented by aid agencies from the United Kingdom and Liechtenstein, the center is staffed by lawyers and former prosecutors and law enforcement officials.[96] It provides training, technical assistance, and policy advice to government agencies from the developing world seeking to recover stolen funds abroad.

Explaining Norm Change and the New Regime

The story put forward above about why corruption came to the fore of policy debate when it did after long being taboo at the international level is widely supported by other accounts.[97] As noted, this view also matches activists' opinions at the time and since. Thus, in 1995, Naím spoke of a structural change (giving Transparency International only a fleeting mention): "Changes in the political, economic and social standards of the world have opened a window in the fight against corruption."[98] Hotchkiss agreed that "a serendipitous combination of geopolitical events has created a very favorable climate for anti-corruption campaigns. These campaigns, however, would not be possible without new ways of thinking about the problems of corruption and its political impact."[99] Abbott and Snidal wrote: "The confluence of development and democracy concerns led to a rapid transformation of attitudes among key actors."[100] More recent academic verdicts have the same view: "The end of the Cold War, the liberalization of the global economy and the advance of globalization, the spread of liberal democratic principles, and the emergence of game-changing corruption scandals among business and political elites in Western Europe brought about a shift in global norms concerning corruption."[101]

The contrast with accounts centered on the trail-blazing norm entrepreneur is striking. In this version, a small group of principled "true believer" activists in NGOs work hard for a fairly lengthy initial period to convince a much larger audience, especially powerful states, that a certain practice that has been regarded as normal is in fact immoral.[102] The cause might be the exclusion of women from the suffrage,[103] the environmental damage caused by damming rivers,[104] human rights violations,[105] or the use of anti-personnel land mines.[106] Gradually the cause gets traction, and at a certain "tipping point" enough actors subscribe to the new perspective that the onus is on those laggards maintaining the old view to justify themselves in the court of public opinion. Increasingly the new sentiment is institutionalized in domestic and international law, and it becomes taken for granted as the natural order of things. Thanks to their dedicated, vanguard activism, the true believers overcome the odds to achieve their normative and policy goals. Norm change (and the resulting institutional change) is portrayed as directly resulting from the intentions of strategic actors.

With the fixing of an international anti-corruption norm, however, the timing and sequence, and the nature of the actors, are very different.

Rather than a long, slow build to a tipping point or cascade, there is the "corruption eruption," a very rapid and near-simultaneous normative and international legal change across a wide variety of different contexts. This shift did not come out of the blue. But rather than the prime suspect norm entrepreneur (Transparency International) leading the way, the birth and growth of this group and others largely coincided with the explosion of international policy activity on this front in 1994–1997. The timing alone gives a strong indication that this explosion could not have been a result of Transparency International's previous activism. Instead, Transparency International seems to have been an effect of this outburst rather than a cause. The World Bank and the OECD had made their first, tentative steps to put corruption on the agenda in 1989. The United States had moved even earlier, passing its own unilateral measure in 1977 and then unsuccessfully trying to bring developed and developing countries into a multilateral agreement through much of the 1980s.

Where the norm entrepreneur literature would expect the activists to be the first mover dragging powerful states and intergovernmental organizations along in their wake, in the case of corruption this sequence was reversed. Officials of the Clinton administration brought together business interests and activists beginning in 1993,[107] with the German and Dutch governments also being key initial supporters. Since that time, many of the most active NGOs in the area have been substantially funded from government sources, including Transparency International, Global Witness, and the International Centre for Asset Recovery. In terms of timing and support, governments have led NGOs at least as often as the other way around. Rather than transnational activists effecting deliberate normative and policy change, both participants and academic observers, at the time and in retrospect, explain the rise of the anti-corruption norm by unanticipated transformations in the broad political context, which meant that, in the recurring phrase, the international anti-corruption norm was "an idea whose time had come."

Why Kleptocracy and Asset Recovery?

This book is not about corruption in general, but rather the specific subtype of kleptocracy, or grand corruption, and the associated financial flows. When and why did these come to the fore? For the media, kleptocracy had always been central to coverage of corruption. The Lockheed bribery affair in the 1970s that had helped lead to the initial US foreign anti-bribery legislation claimed a Japanese prime minister, an Italian president, and a Dutch prince, while the Watergate affair had of course finished Nixon's presidency. The wave of corruption scandals in Europe and Latin America in the mid-1990s was disproportionately focused on heads of government and ministers. Elsewhere high-profile cases like Mobutu and Ferdinand Marcos had formed the stereotype of the kleptocratic Third World dictator. The academic literature on corruption took it as a given that corruption was often concentrated at the apex of political power.[108] Transparency International's first report in January 1994 was titled "Grand Corruption in Third World Development."

Yet the World Bank, along with regional development banks and national development agencies, was very much wedded to notions of "partnership" with developing country governments and other "stakeholders," which would supposedly have "ownership" over the resulting "client-centric" and "demand-driven" policies. Western-dominated international organizations were wary of putting developing country governments offside by suggesting corruption was all their fault. Although the notion that all states suffered from corruption to a greater or lesser extent was a common theme, measures like the Corruption Perceptions Index sent an unequivocal message that poor countries were the most corrupt, a conclusion that was already apparent in the notion that corruption causes underdevelopment. To avoid confrontation, officials and activists styled international anti-corruption policy in terms of helping national governments deal with their corruption problems. It was much less clear how such an approach would work if the government itself *was* the major corruption problem, however. Similarly, Transparency International avoided confrontation with either specific governments or companies in seeking a Fabian, cooperative approach. Through its decentralized, franchise model of autonomous national chapters, Transparency International consistently sought to downplay the idea that it was a Western organization seeking to expose and discipline degenerate governments in the Third World.

Taking on the incumbent leaders of sovereign states, and thus in some sense these states themselves, poses the exquisite political difficulties that give the campaign against kleptocracy its special character. A much less awkward problem, however, is when a new government takes power and seeks to hold the previous leadership accountable, either through direct prosecutions or through efforts to recover stolen wealth. In such cases sovereign amity can be maintained, and the rhetoric and resources of mutual legal assistance, technical assistance, and capacity building can be deployed. For developed and developing country governments alike, as well as NGOs and international organizations, this framing of action against former kleptocrats was highly convenient in providing a formula all could agree on.

In the negotiations over the United Nations Convention Against Corruption (UNCAC) from 2000, poor countries helped to further extend the picture of corruption, and especially grand corruption, as a transnational issue that intimately involved rich countries as well. To be sure, this was not the first time the culpability of the rich world in international corruption had been raised.[109] It was, after all, Western firms that were first targeted by the OECD's anti-bribery agreement. Yet the unmistakable tone of the development and corruption literature was that corruption was disproportionately a problem for, and of, governments in poor countries.

The accumulation of kleptocracy scandals, however, made it clear that as well as the flows of bribes from the West to the rest of the world, there was another, perhaps more important flow of illicit funds in the opposite direction, from grand corruption in poorer countries to the major financial centers in rich countries. The succession of exposés and the agitation of NGOs helped push the issue of the hosting of the proceeds of corruption up the agenda. Capturing the tone of these sentiments, in March 2001 the African national chapters of Transparency International jointly issued the Nyanga Declaration, which stated in part: "It is not only illegal but blatantly immoral that so much wealth stolen from some of the world's poorest countries is allowed to circulate freely in the economies of some of the world's wealthiest nations in Europe, the Americas, the Middle East and diverse offshore havens . . . it is inherently inconsistent to call for the cancellation of Africa's debts while much of the money originally lent remains illegally invested or banked in privately held accounts abroad."[110]

Transparency International's *Global Corruption Report* in 2004 contained a small but widely publicized section on kleptocracy, including a table of the top ten kleptocrats and estimates of the amounts they stole while in office (see Table 1.1).

Despite the disclaimer that the figures in the report were "extremely approximate" and that "very little is known about amounts allegedly embezzled by many leaders,"[111] the report is still a standard reference point for discussions of grand corruption today. Inflated estimates of the assets looted may be part of the explanations for the disappointing totals recovered.

Poorer countries made a determined push for strong asset recovery provisions in the negotiations over the UNCAC.[112] The complaints from the Philippines government about the lack of cooperation in the search for the Marcos loot from countries like the United States, Switzerland, and Liechtenstein, and the questions about why banks in these countries accepted what was so obviously criminal money in the first place, were echoed by other governments in a similar position. As a result, in the negotiations over the UNCAC, "victim" states made a

TABLE 1.1. Exemplary Villains

Head of Government	State and Term in Office	Estimated Loot	GDP per capita 2001
Mohamed Suharto	Indonesia 1967–98	$15–35 billion	$695
Ferdinand Marcos	Philippines 1972–86	$5–10 billion	$912
Mobutu Sese Seko	Congo/Zaire 1965–97	$5 billion	$99
Sani Abacha	Nigeria 1993–98	$2–5 billion	$319
Slobodan Milosevic	Yugoslavia/Serbia 1989–2000	$1 billion	n/a
Jean-Claude Duvalier	Haiti 1971–86	$300–800 million	$460
Alberto Fujimori	Peru 1990–2000	$600 million	$2051
Pavlo Lazarenko	Ukraine 1996–97	$114–200 million	$766
Arnoldo Alemán	Nicaragua 1997–2002	$100 million	$490
Joseph Estrada	Philippines 1998–2001	$78–80 million	$912

Transparency International, *Global Corruption Report* (Berlin, 2004), 13.

strong and successful push for asset recovery to be a priority. African leaders were vital. In particular, Nigeria pushed the cause of asset recovery in light of its difficulties in seeking the return of assets stolen by former dictator Sani Abacha. In a speech before the UN General Assembly in 1999, Nigeria's President Olusegun Obasanjo called for a new international convention for the repatriation of wealth looted from Africa and held abroad, asserting, "It is morally reprehensible, unjust, unfair and against all established human values to engage in actions that actually encourage corruption in poor nations to fatten your own country. . . . The thief and the receiver of stolen items are guilty of the same offense."[113] He estimated the total wealth looted from Africa and held in foreign countries at $400 billion, of which $100 billion was taken from his own country (though, once again, there was no evidence provided for these figures), compared to a then-current Nigerian foreign debt of $28 billion.[114]

Instead of being a subject that divided rich and poor countries, there was a pronounced common ground between the two. The United States shared this priority of fighting kleptocracy. In a meeting of fifty-eight states in December 2001 to consider proposals for the Convention, the US submission was exclusively devoted to asset recovery.[115] For all its delays and frustrations, the Marcos case (discussed in chapter 3) could not have been brought to a successful conclusion without the support of the Swiss government. Although the UK response to its banks' laundering of money for the Nigerian dictator Sani Abacha was underwhelming (as discussed in chapter 4), the Blair government maintained a close interest in foreign development, and the Department for International Development was a major supporter of efforts to combat kleptocracy. Thus a disparate range of state and nonstate actors came to similar conclusions about the need to follow the money from grand corruption at about the same time, rather than one group leading the rest.

In December 2000 the UN General Assembly announced the need for an international anti-corruption agreement and requested that the secretary-general put together an expert group to prepare terms of reference for the negotiations.[116] A follow-up resolution later in that same month called for a particular focus on the international transfer and repatriation of the proceeds of corruption.[117] A 2002 report from the experts' group laid out the same logic: "The exporting of funds derived from corruption has a number of severe consequences for the country of origin. It undermines foreign aid, drains currency reserves, reduces the tax base, harms competition, undermines free trade and increases poverty levels. Corruption and laundering can therefore operate in tandem to limit every advance (social, economic or political) of countries, especially developing countries and countries with economies in transition."[118]

Most of these groups advanced very similar arguments as to why asset recovery was needed. The money was important for governments to address the damage done by corruption, to strengthen the integrity of government, and more generally to provide public services. Sums of hundreds of millions of dollars could go a long way in poor countries. Reaching out to claw back stolen wealth sent a message of accountability to the populations that had suffered. This approach might also deter some of those with the opportunity to engage in grand corruption from doing so.

The years following saw the G20 focus on kleptocracy and asset recovery in large part thanks to an accident of timing. By the time the Arab Spring and associated revelations on kleptocracy hit the headlines in early 2011, the most urgent demands of the financial crisis had waned and members were looking for new goals. The G20 created an Anti-Corruption Working Group as a way to leave its mark on the policy agenda.[119] The G7 Deauville Partnership to help Arab states trace and repatriate stolen wealth responded to the same circumstances at the same time.

The more recent interest of Russia and China in recovering the overseas assets of senior officials accused of corruption adds a new twist to the story. It shows why even governments with no principled commitment to the rule of law at home or abroad might nevertheless strongly favor the new regime. As discussed in chapter 5, a secret Chinese government report estimated that over 16,000 officials fled the country in the period 1993–2008 for the United States, Canada, Australia, and elsewhere, taking with them over $120 billion of state funds.[120] Beginning in 2014 the Communist leadership initiated an unprecedented worldwide effort to bring these officials back. Even before the Russian invasion of Ukraine, the Putin regime's "de-offshorization" initiative aimed to force all state officials to bring their assets home to Russia.[121] In both cases there are strong suspicions that these parallel campaigns are motivated at least as much by power political considerations as any commitment to the cause of anti-corruption as such.

Despite the political impetus created by the Arab Spring revelations, the multiplication of NGOs, and the intervention of the G20 and G7, the substance of the anti-kleptocracy regime was in place shortly after the turn of the century. The final section of the chapter briefly describes two of the main planks of the global anti-kleptocracy regime: the UN Convention Against Corruption, which came into force in 2005, and the Stolen Asset Recovery Initiative, launched in 2007.

Institutionalizing the Global Anti-Kleptocracy Norm

The global normative shift against corruption in general and kleptocracy in particular was quickly institutionalized in formal rules and policies. The set of rules that jointly constitute the anti-kleptocracy regime are a mix of international and domestic hard and soft laws. These rules shade into and overlap with others relating to money laundering, transnational crime, terrorism, tax, and more general financial supervision. Rather than attempt a detailed legal primer, this section instead provides a brief sketch of the main features of this system to give an idea of how it is meant to work. This summary provides a baseline or point of comparison for the detailed studies of how the system seems to work in practice, as laid out in the chapters to follow.

The most complete formal statement of the international anti-kleptocracy norm is in the United Nations Convention Against Corruption. The Stolen Asset Recovery Initiative is a collaborative venture of the UN and World Bank aimed at providing assistance to governments seeking the return of looted wealth. It is the only intergovernmental organization with the specific mission of countering kleptocracy. Thus the legal provisions of the UNCAC and the mission and practices of StAR both represent the products of underlying norm change and are two of the main components of the new global regime.

Opened for signature in December 2003, the UNCAC came into force on December 14, 2005. Thanks to building on prior national and multilateral hard and soft law rules, the UNCAC is almost as significant for its strong normative statement of principle as it is for any legal innovations.[122] The most important of these principles is the necessity of funds being repatriated to the victim country. Foreshadowing this and other key principles was the earlier UN Convention on Transnational Organized Crime (the Palermo Convention), which came into force only a little more than a month before the UNCAC was opened for signature.

After first laying out the need for a meritocratic and transparent state bureaucracy, the articles of the UNCAC suggest a range of measures to prevent corruption. One example is the use of asset declarations and registries for public officials (Article 8). These are declarations of all wealth and liabilities when people take up public office, usually updated each year, which form a baseline against which to detect a suspicious enrichment out of keeping with officials' salaries that may indicate corruption. The UNCAC defines corruption to include bribery, embezzlement, nepotism, and trading in influence (Articles 15–22). The Convention contains clauses on freezing and confiscating the proceeds of foreign corruption offenses (Article 31). In keeping with the inherently cross-border nature of the problem, it includes detailed provisions on the exchange of information, evidence, and suspects between states (Chapter IV), aiming to facilitate mutual legal assistance.

Many of the specific measures to help in the detection and interdiction of corrupt monies restate existing soft law principles designed earlier by the Financial Action Task Force (FATF) to counter money laundering (e.g., Articles 14, 23, 52, and 58). Thus provisions necessitate that banks adhere to the "Know Your Customer" rule by finding the true identity of their account holders, including the identity of the real people in control of accounts held in the name of companies, as well as the source of their funds. The aim here is to screen out criminal proceeds and prevent dirty money from entering the financial system. Additional components of anti–money laundering policy in the Convention include the requirement that private financial institutions report suspicious transactions and that a national Financial Intelligence Unit be created to receive, analyze, and distribute such reports. State signatories are committed to ensure that their banks exercise particular caution in dealing with foreign senior public officials, their family members, and other close associates, on the grounds that these individuals are disproportionately likely to be engaged in serious corruption.

The whole of Chapter V of the Convention is devoted to asset recovery. Article 51 states that restitution of stolen assets is a "fundamental principle" (a principle also referred to in Articles 1 and 3). Given that so many of the provisions of the UNCAC were already foreshadowed in the UN Convention on Transnational Organized Crime, foregrounding asset recovery was seen as providing some distinct contribution for a treaty that was otherwise viewed as derivative and unnecessary.[123] The head of the United Nations Office on Drugs and Crime (UNODC), Antonio Maria Costa, pointed to this provision as the main achievement of the treaty,[124] as did UN Secretary-General Kofi Annan.[125]

Victim governments can effect asset recovery using different strategies. One is to obtain a criminal conviction in a domestic court for a corruption offense in the victim state or for a derivative money laundering offense in the host state. On the basis of this conviction, either the victim state could place a confiscation order with the host state or the host state could obtain the money laundering conviction and repatriate the funds to the victim. Ideally, both states could work simultaneously from each end. Yet getting a conviction might be impossible if the official in question is a fugitive or dead. Furthermore, it has been extremely difficult to first prove a case beyond a reasonable doubt against a person and then link a particular asset to a particular crime (for example, just which one of Mobutu's crimes gave rise to that $4 million in Swiss accounts?).

An alternative route is to use a civil case brought by the victim government in the courts of the host state. Aside from avoiding the problem of missing defendants, the major advantage of this strategy is a reduced burden of proof, whereby the case can be decided on the balance of probabilities rather than the prosecution having to prove matters beyond a reasonable doubt. The related strategy of non-conviction-based forfeiture is also directed at assets rather than at persons as such.[126]

Although invaluable in codifying the anti-kleptocracy norm into law, by itself the UNCAC does little to practically help victim countries get their money back. Responding to this need, in September 2007 the World Bank and United Nations Office on Drugs and Crime jointly formed the Stolen Asset Recovery Initiative (StAR). This body is the most prominent international institution instantiating the norm against grand corruption and the corresponding duty to repatriate the proceeds of corruption. As explained in the founding document in 2007, the rationale for this new initiative was that anti-corruption efforts were said to have concentrated too much on the source countries for grand corruption, largely poorer countries, and not enough on those hosting the resulting wealth, rich countries and offshore financial centers. This report rehearsed all the familiar themes covered earlier about corruption undermining development and democracy, as well as most of the conventional guesstimates about the scale of the problem (e.g., Transparency International's top ten kleptocrats list).

StAR was not to have an investigative or operational role, nor was it entrusted with new standard-setting powers. Instead, the goal was to help overcome what were said to be the two greatest obstacles to asset recovery: the technical legal difficulties developing countries faced and the lack of political will among host countries. Technical problems could range from the availability and admissibility of foreign evidence, to the immunities enjoyed by public officials, to the fact that the same behavior might fall under different offenses in different countries, to the management of assets after freezing and confiscation.[127]

The second priority, of strengthening political will, relates to one of the fundamental questions motivating the book: to what extent are implementation problems a product of a lack of inclination to comply, particularly among those countries hosting looted wealth, as opposed to a lack of capacity? StAR aimed to solve the first problem by providing expert advice to victim countries and to work with governments and NGOs to keep up the pressure on havens for the proceeds of corruption. The immediate impetus for StAR came from the difficulties faced by the Nigerian government in recovering Abacha's looted wealth from Switzerland.[128] World Bank president Paul Wolfowitz had antagonized the Bank's board with his unilateral measures against corrupt governments, but after his ousting there was a desire for the Bank to reiterate its anti-corruption credentials. Given the passage of the UNCAC, policy makers inside and beyond the Bank considered that anything like StAR would have to be a partnership with the UN. StAR was initially funded from ad hoc grants by Norway and Sweden, later bolstered by Britain and Canada, but most of its staff were paid on secondment from the UNODC and World Bank.[129]

During its first years of existence, in the period 2007–2011, much of StAR's work was focused on research on topics like identifying suspicious bank accounts, improving mutual legal assistance procedures, and discerning the real owners of shell companies.[130] After the Arab Spring, however, it was tasked by the G20 with a more applied mandate of supporting particular governments' restitution efforts. As of 2014, it was assisting twenty-nine different governments.[131] Although StAR was directed to focus on "quick

wins," this proved easier said than done. In a verdict that was only confirmed over the following years, an early review document admitted that
"the assumptions regarding the progress of asset recovery programs have
been too optimistic."[132] By using its connections to rich-world governments
and other international organizations, StAR pressed for specific reforms
relating to the regulation of corporate transparency, enhanced scrutiny of
Politically Exposed Persons (i.e., senior public officials), and the use of non-
conviction-based forfeiture, and more generally for governments to ratify
UNCAC. It also campaigned hard for the FATF to pay more attention to
corruption offenses, a priority later imposed by the G20.[133]

Much of this chapter has looked at how and why a subject that was formerly taboo came to the forefront of the global policy agenda. Although
everyone agrees that international policy on corruption has been transformed beyond recognition since 1990, there is a nagging sense of doubt
that the basic problem is largely untouched. The estimates of the total
funds stolen are still huge, while the amounts recovered are proportion-
ately tiny. Harking back to the fiasco of the search for Mobutu's looted
wealth, what difference has the shift in the climate of opinion, the plethora
of international conventions like the UNCAC and its regional equivalents,
and the emergence of actors like Transparency International and StAR
made to the fight against grand corruption? Is there any less grand corruption around? Norms and laws may be loosely coupled with practice and
behavior, or even completely divorced. Most of the rest of the book tries to
answer these sorts of questions.

The actors most involved in fighting kleptocracy are sometimes susceptible to getting drawn into the minutiae of various legal provisions and
specific policy reforms without asking the bigger and more important
questions relating to general effectiveness. Questions about effectiveness
(or the lack of) are closely entwined with questions about the extent to
which governments have really "got religion" in fighting grand corruption. Even assuming that the leaders of the powerful, rich states that tend
to host the proceeds of foreign corruption genuinely care about doing the
right thing in this respect, they have many other competing and conflicting
priorities. How do governments trade off economic, diplomatic, or national
security concerns against the moral and legal requirements of following the
money trail of corrupt leaders?

The next chapters look at how similar challenges and controversies have played out in four different national arenas. In each instance the general goals are to investigate how well the anti-kleptocracy system works, how hard governments are actually trying to make it work, and what are the most important vulnerabilities. Rather than four isolated national case studies, each chapter is a story of the interplay between local and international dynamics in different national settings. Grand corruption and the associated efforts to recover the proceeds tend to sprawl across borders and decades. While this presents difficulties in bounding the coverage of any one case, it often has the advantage of showing how efforts to recover the wealth of a particular kleptocrat vary across national jurisdictions and as new international instruments are brought into play.

2

The United States

A Superpower Stirs

In many instances since 1945, the United States has provided the moral leadership, the side payments, and the necessary arm-twisting to effect change in world politics. More recently, the United States has sometimes played the role of the spoiler, whether it is on climate change or the International Criminal Court. In many ways the campaign against cross-border corruption was made in the United States. When it comes to the norm against kleptocracy, Washington has proved to be a leader, though competing foreign policy priorities and the power of domestic lobbies have tempered effectiveness.

The United States has had a mixed record on screening and returning stolen wealth. Just like the other three countries, the United States has a politically powerful financial sector, and the profit motive creates strong pressures for banks to accept large foreign deposits without asking too many difficult questions. Lawyers, real estate agents, and other professionals face the same incentives. Unlike that of most other countries, however, the US government has a massive network of security ties and alliances, with security interests in every region of the world. This can often mean that, besides commercial incentives and corporate lobbying, there is a national security constituency that may well favor turning a blind eye to wealth of dubious provenance invested in the United States by senior foreign officials. With these often reinforcing pecuniary and foreign policy motives, it is all the more surprising that the United States has shifted from a position of inaction, or in some cases the active encouragement of kleptocracy as a strategy to buy the support of Cold War allies, to one that often favors strong action at home and significant diplomatic effort abroad in promoting the fight against grand corruption.

When, why, and to what extent are the US government and American banks really interested in clamping down on such illicit financial flows? To what extent are continuing flows of the proceeds of corruption into the United States a product of lack of genuine will to stop such funds or lack of capacity?

I begin by briefly tracing the origins of the anti-kleptocracy cause in the United States, starting with the unpropitious Cold War environment and the Foreign Corrupt Practices Act of 1977, then moving to the growing drive to internationalize anti-corruption measures from the early 1990s. I examine the status quo ante of dictators being able to launder their funds in the US financial system with impunity immediately before and after the turn of the century. At this time, there was no law prohibiting American banks and other institutions receiving the proceeds of foreign corruption. In October 2001 the USA Patriot Act closed this legal loophole, yet practice lagged, and laws at first failed to have much of an impact. More recent cases evidence at least partial effectiveness, however, with instances of successful prevention and some looted wealth confiscated and returned. There is evidence of genuine positive change in both the government and the private sector, but also continuing serious problems with effectiveness. These flaws are a product of powerful political lobbies in the legal, real estate, and company formation sectors that have blocked efforts to address important vulnerabilities. More broadly, the basic difficulties of cross-border legal action, and human rights and property protection, stack the deck against those hoping to attack kleptocrats and their illicit wealth, a more general discussion developed in the conclusion of the book.

Prologue: The Cold War and the Foreign Corrupt Practices Act

The US government was well aware of the scale of looting conducted by many allied governments during the Cold War. Not only did the United States fail to do anything to stop this corruption, it actively hindered efforts to promote accountability, for example by pressing the Bretton Wood institutions to continue lending to many such countries. This complicity in the wholesale looting of Zaire, Haiti, the Philippines, and other countries was seen as a price worth paying in the geopolitical struggle against Soviet Communism. Although the end of the Cold War certainly has not made such national security arguments obsolete (as evidenced by the toleration of corrupt leaders from Pakistan, Angola, Afghanistan, Iraq, Kazakhstan, and many other states), the fall of the Soviet Union marked a significant break point.

Yet the first key steps followed from the Watergate scandal. This affair put the abuse of government power and the role of money in politics at center stage. Over the opposition of both the business community and the executive,[1] the Foreign Corrupt Practices Act (FCPA) was passed through the Senate Banking Committee in 1977. The act prohibited American firms from paying bribes to foreign government officials, and it served as a marker that the corruption of foreign government officials, not just Americans, was legally and morally unacceptable to the US government. For at least the first decade, little effort was made to enforce the act. As long as the FCPA was in being, however, it created an incentive for the US government and business community to spread these standards to other countries. The constant complaint was that as long as US companies alone were prohibited from paying kickbacks to foreign officials, they were at a competitive disadvantage.

As part of the "war on drugs" in the 1980s, there was a broad coalition between Congress and the executive that the main parts of US domestic anti–money laundering legislation should also be adopted at the international level. At a G7 summit in 1989 the Bush administration succeeded in this aim with the support of the French and British governments by creating a new Financial Action Task Force. This new body was responsible for designing, diffusing, and enforcing international anti–money laundering standards. Over the next decade or so this organization had spectacular success in persuading or coercing most of the world's states to legislate a standard package of anti–money laundering policies.[2] These came to form much of the basis of the UN Convention on Transnational Organized Crime, the UN Convention Against Corruption, and the G7/8 and G20 measures against corruption, as well as national responses to deterring, detecting, and confiscating the proceeds of corruption.

The end of the Cold War simultaneously removed much of the rationale for propping up corrupt anti-Communist governments, stimulated new scrutiny of foreign aid and development policies, and elevated organized crime and criminal financial flows as national security priorities.[3] The Clinton administration vigorously pushed the anti-corruption agenda within the Organization for Economic Cooperation and Development, the Organization of American States, and the World Bank. The FCPA began to be much more vigorously enforced. In 1999, in Washington, D.C., Vice-President Al Gore organized the first Global Forum on Fighting Corruption, a body that has subsequently met biennially. The Global Forum brought together a wide range of those with an interest in anti-corruption, from government officials, to NGOs, to academics. Some credit this gathering with helping to displace the view that corruption was an inevitable fact of life and to recast it as a policy problem that could and should be addressed.[4] Yet for all this progress, at the end of the 1990s a series of revelations concerning kleptocrats laundering their funds in the United States raised the central question of this book: what difference did all these rules make?

An Era of Impunity: Corruption Proceeds in the United States in the 1990s

One of the most persistent and effective champions of the anti-kleptocracy cause has been the Senate Permanent Subcommittee on Investigations, under the stewardship of Sen. Carl Levin from the late 1990s until his retirement in 2014. Reports from the subcommittee both provide a trove of information on various murky affairs and have been a significant stimulus for policy change, directly in legislation but perhaps more significantly indirectly, as the glare of publicity stimulated both private actors and regulators to act where they had previously been passive. The first of these reports, released in November 1999, looked at the role of private banking in laundering criminal funds, focusing on Citibank.[5]

The investigation began by uncovering how funds stolen by Raúl Salinas, brother of Mexico's then-president, were laundered in the US banking system. It subsequently expanded to include Asif Ali Zardari, at the time husband of Pakistani prime minister Benazir Bhutto, and after her assassination president in his own right; three sons of Nigerian dictator Sani Abacha; two daughters of Indonesian president Suharto; a former president of Venezuela; and President Omar Bongo of Gabon. In every case these individuals had faced little difficulty in laundering corruption funds in the United States. Levin put the issue of hosting looted assets succinctly: "America cannot have it both ways. We cannot condemn corruption abroad, be it officials taking bribes or looting their treasuries, and then tolerate American banks making profits off that corruption."[6] Levin's interest in the matter had first been piqued through media coverage. He and his staff were keen to find out what they could accomplish in the committee, in particular using their powers to subpoena bank records and other legal documents, as well as bringing witnesses before the committee.[7]

The Salinas case saw Citibank engaged in elaborate precautions to protect his finances from scrutiny, which, beginning in 1992, included setting up accounts under code names, accepting the use of aliases, routing wire transfers through the bank's own accounts to break the link with Salinas, and setting up offshore shell companies and trusts to hold accounts. The level of secrecy provided fooled many of Citibank's own internal controls. For all the effort put into veiling Salinas's financial affairs, however, the bank put none into customer due diligence. Once Salinas was arrested in February 1995, three years after he had opened his accounts and deposited $87 million, Citibank reviewed the file on the source of Salinas's wealth only to find out that no information had been entered.[8] This lapse came despite outside and internal rules mandating extra scrutiny for clients who were senior public officials or relatives thereof, and despite press speculation about his corruption.

It was a similar story with reference to the other individuals investigated. Benazir Bhutto's husband, Ali Asif Zardari, used Citibank accounts in Dubai and Switzerland to receive bribes (see the following chapter). Once again the money escaped scrutiny, even after Zardari had been charged with corruption offenses. President Omar Bongo of Gabon

moved tens of millions of dollars through Citibank New York in the 1980s
and 1990s. The internal bank documents of the source of wealth reasoned
as follows: "Head of State for over 25 Years. . . . Source of Wealth/busi-
ness Background: self-made as result of position. Country is oil producer."[9]
(The Citibank file on Abacha sons similarly observed, "Wealth comes
from father who accumulated wealth as head of state of major oil producing country."[10]) After scrutiny from US regulators asking about the Bongo
accounts in 1996 and 1997, internal correspondence speculated that "the
French government/French oil companies (Elf) made 'donations' to him
(very much like we give to PACs in the US!)"[11] Media coverage at the
same time reasoned along the same lines (though without the euphemism
"donation" for "bribe"). A criminal probe was launched, and the Swiss authorities froze several related accounts, yet senior Citibank officials urged
employees to disregard these developments.[12] Citibank eventually decided
to begin closing the accounts in 1999. Although Bongo's corrupt conduct
touched the United States through his finances, it is important to note that
the French government, and especially its national champion oil company
Elf Aquitaine, have been much more deeply implicated.[13] Until his death
in 2009 Bongo kept his luxury real estate in France and his close personal
friendship with Jacques Chirac (himself convicted of corruption offenses
after finishing his term as president).

This report and its sequels are replete with lurid details of kleptocrats'
foibles and corporate conniving, often picked up and amplified in the
media. Were these instances highlighted because they are the worst of the
worst, and therefore unrepresentative of general practice? Time after time,
senior bank executives hauled in front of the committee have alluded to
fact that they are in charge of very large organizations, often with tens of
thousands of employees spread over dozens of separate country offices, and
that by implication any such large organization is going to have a few bad
apples and policy glitches.

Yet rather than just being sensational anecdotes, the reports show general failures. Thus with specific reference to Citibank, the single largest US
multinational bank at the time, the chair of the committee, Sen. Susan Collins noted that there was a "systematic pattern of deficiencies that allowed
Citibank to be vulnerable to money-laundering." John Reed, Citibank
CEO, replied, "I think you are correct."[14] Illustrating the gap between
rules on the books and those applied in practice, Citibank had had internal

policies for thirty years specifying that the private bank should establish that clients' funds were not derived from crime.[15]

The Senate report identified the basic conflict of interest that has repeatedly led many banks to accepting criminal funds.[16] Private bank clients are usually signed up to a particular relationship manager who then coordinates the provision of all financial services from the bank and its associates to the client. Relationship managers are rewarded via commissions and performance bonuses for preserving and enhancing existing relationships and for bringing in new clients. Yet they also may function as the initial gatekeeper responsible for screening the legality of the wealth being invested. Given this conflict of interest, incentives suggest not asking clients or would-be clients too many hard questions about the sources of their wealth. Furthermore, relationship managers may actually coach their clients on how to avoid scrutiny from the bank's own internal compliance section.[17]

What light do the cases investigated in the report shed on the basic questions at issue? On the available evidence, banks had internal policies designed to screen out the wealth of corrupt senior officials, but these were not enforced. In practice, these policies took a back seat to the revenue associated with such clients, running at something like $1–2 million in annual fees per individual.[18] Handling foreign corruption proceeds was at this stage legal, the US government was not even trying to keep kleptocrats' loot out of the country, and at this time there was no international responsibility to do so. During George W. Bush's presidency, however, political change at the domestic and international level instituted for the first time a duty to chase looted foreign wealth.

Changing Rules, At Home and Abroad

By the end of Bill Clinton's time in office, the US government was firmly committed to internationalizing the fight against corruption. George W. Bush's administration gave continued backing for the negotiation of the UN Convention Against Corruption, and in particular placed a strong emphasis on countering kleptocracy and recovering assets. The US delegation to the talks arrived with a full draft of the asset recovery chapter but then modified it in line with draft text put forward by the Peruvian government,[19] which at the time was engaged in hunting for funds looted by former president Alberto Fujimori and his spymaster Vladimiro Montesinos.[20] The United States and Peru jointly put forward a hybrid text on asset recovery, which became Chapter 5 of the Convention.

The most important domestic legal reform relating to US efforts against kleptocracy was contained in the USA Patriot Act, passed a month after and in direct response to the terrorist attacks of September 11, 2001. The act made it a crime for US institutions to accept the proceeds of foreign corruption offenses. Banks now had to reckon with criminal penalties if they held accounts for kleptocrats. However, the new rules were weakened in 2002 when as a result of lobbying, Treasury agreed to temporarily exempt a range of professionals, including real estate agents, who had been bound by the act. This "temporary" exemption is now well into its second decade and shows no sign of expiring.

The act gave teeth to earlier guidance from Treasury and other federal regulators to US banks on preventing foreign senior officials from laundering proceeds of corruption.[21] This document advised banks, "The institution should take reasonable steps to determine the official salary and compensation of the Covered Persons [i.e., foreign public officials] as well as the individual's known legitimate sources of wealth apart from his or her official position." It suggested that banks that failed to follow such procedures risked prosecution or reputational damage. Neither of these claims was accurate. At the time, accepting the proceeds of foreign corruption was not a predicate offense for money laundering. The idea of reputational risk for those institutions banking kleptocrats is a stubborn myth, then and now something of an article of faith for regulators, despite the near-complete lack of evidence to support this assertion.[22]

Good Laws, Bad Enforcement: Riggs Bank

The powerful provisions of the Patriot Act might seem to have transformed banks' attitudes toward handling the foreign proceeds of corruption. Conduct that had been legal, if disapproved of, now constituted the crime of money laundering. Yet several failures sharply demonstrated the difference between laws on the books and laws that are actually enforced. The scandals associated with Riggs Bank, outlined briefly below, fed into dedicated anti-kleptocracy measures adopted by the US executive shortly afterward.

Riggs Bank was a pillar of the Washington financial and political establishment. Another report released in 2004 by the Senate Permanent Subcommittee on Investigations revealed that Riggs was serially incompetent in screening out dirty money, and in some instances was actively complicit in helping clients hide the proceeds of corruption.[23] Furthermore, the regulatory agency supposedly enforcing the stringent new post-2001 regulations, the Office of the Comptroller of the Currency (OCC), was shown to have been timid and ineffectual (a shortcoming that changed little until at least 2012[24]). The report focused on three sets of Riggs clients in particular: Saudi diplomats allegedly linked to the 9/11 hijackers; the ex-dictator of Chile, Augusto Pinochet; and the ruling Obiang family of Equatorial Guinea. The first showcased Riggs's errors of omission, while in the second the bank actively assisted Pinochet in hiding money after he had been indicted for human rights and financial crimes. But it is the third that is most relevant here, relating to the Obiang family.

The ruling family, especially the president, Teodoro Obiang Nguema Mbasogo (commonly referred to as Teodoro Obiang), and his son and the current vice-president, Teodoro Nguema Obiang Mangue (better known as Teodorin Obiang), have become something of the epitome of the twenty-first century-kleptocrat, a level of infamy compounded by this government's abysmal human rights record.[25] As discussed below, for more than a decade after the Riggs scandal, Obiang Jr. in particular has suffered various legal entanglements in several countries in relation to his looted wealth.

Both the Senate investigation and the belated regulatory enforcement action took place in large part thanks to the investigative reporting of Ken Silverstein and coverage in November 2002 alleging a link between Riggs and the 9/11 hijackers.[26] This sequence is a recurring pattern in investigating kleptocracy: journalists, NGOs, and/or whistle-blowers discover key initial facts, and the resulting publicity creates pressure for subsequent formal investigations.

Beginning in 1995, Riggs opened around fifty accounts for various members of the Obiang family, close associates, or companies controlled by them, holding up to $700 million. The Equatoguineans were jointly Riggs's single biggest source of custom and, presumably, fees. The bank

engaged in a wide range of unusual or downright illegal behavior in allowing the Obiangs to move proceeds of foreign corruption into the United
States. It also facilitated suspicious transfers of money from US oil firms
to the family. One account was capitalized with several deposits of over $1
million in cash, including two deposits of $3 million in cash in suitcases,
weighing sixty pounds.[27] Riggs personnel saw no reason to report these
deposits as suspicious.

The Senate report stresses that it is not picking isolated examples of bad
practice, but rather highlighting particular episodes that exemplify general
and systemic failures. An internal investigation by Riggs in 2004 found
that of 15,000 embassy and international private banking accounts, only
15 percent had the proper Know Your Customer documentation, a clear
violation of both law and bank policy.[28] The US government Financial
Crimes Enforcement Network determined that the bank's Suspicious Activity Report processes "were either non-existent or not implemented."[29]
The year before (March 2003), a frustrated OCC inspector complained
about her own agency's inaction over the years, asking in an e-mail "if
not Riggs who and if not now, when?"[30] While the OCC identified many
of the deficiencies in the bank's policies, it repeatedly declined to take
any action. One key OCC official who urged leniency, Ashley Lee, took
a job with Riggs less than two months after leaving government service
in 2002.[31] In general, the conduct of the officials who were supposedly supervising anti–money laundering standards was indicative of a classic case
of regulatory capture. According to the authors of the report, the OCC's
tolerance of lax bank practices in this domain continued long afterward,
until 2013 at least.[32] A separate government review concluded that a variety of other federal regulatory agencies had been equally unresponsive
with respect to other banks that had had similarly egregious anti–money
laundering failures.[33]

After paying $41 million in penalties to various federal regulators, Riggs
was taken over by PNC Bank in 2005. The offending Obiang accounts
were closed in 2004, but as discussed later in the chapter, an important se-
quel played out between the US government and Obiang Jr. in 2008–2014.

What, if anything, can be said in the bank's defense? During the testimony of Riggs CEO Lawrence Herbert, Sen. Levin quoted a sycophantic
letter from Riggs Board members to President Obiang praising his "pru-
dent leadership and administration," before asking the CEO, "How do

you write stuff to a man as abominable as this guy, and known to be abom-inable? How do you write—how do you, basically, live with yourself?"[34]

Levin had earlier pointed out that Obiang was a "dictator" who com-monly featured on the "worst of the worst lists" for human rights.[35] Herbert's answers were as self-serving and unconvincing as those of the oil executives who followed, who asserted that their dealings with the Obiang government were not only legal but met "the highest ethical standards" as well.[36]

Yet presumably both the bank and oil companies could have asked why, if Equatorial Guinea's government was so far beyond the pale, the US government had chosen to reopen diplomatic relations and energeti-cally woo Obiang after 2001, and why Secretary of State Colin Powell and Energy Secretary Spencer Abraham had accorded Obiang a private meeting in Washington in 2004.[37] Washington had closed its embassy in Malabo (the Equatoguinean capital) in 1995 partly in response to death threats by the Equatoguinean foreign minister against the US ambassador and partly in protest against the government's flagrant human rights and corruption crimes. With the discovery of oil, however, the United States began to reconsider, as part of a strategy of sourcing more oil from West Africa to reduce dependence on the Middle East (Equatorial Guinea is Africa's third-largest producer after Nigeria and Angola).

Riggs drew the obvious conclusion in internal correspondence. After noting the country's "well documented" problems with human rights and corruption, the memo continued: "However, any hesitancy on the part of the US or European countries toward Equatorial Guinea will be tempo-rary, due to the rising importance of the oil sector."[38] Since the US govern-ment was so friendly with Obiang (Condoleezza Rice referred to him as a "good friend" of the United States in 2006), why shouldn't banks and oil companies court his business?

George W. Bush Administration
Anti-Kleptocracy Initiatives

The Clinton, Bush, and Obama administrations all supported initiatives to combat grand corruption (although each continued to turn a blind eye to the corruption of favored clients). Interviewees explain this bipartisan support on the grounds that fighting foreign corruption provided an opportunity for moral leadership, that "everyone likes to be wearing the white hats," and that investigating foreign corruption is often more politically palatable than investigating corruption in one's own system.[39] This moral support translated into a series of executive measures targeting foreign kleptocrats. One of the first was to set up a dedicated team in Miami drawn from the Treasury, Justice, and State Departments in August 2003 with the specific mission of tracking proceeds of foreign corruption laundered in the United States and targeting the assets and individuals involved.[40] This new team, the Miami Foreign Corruption Investigation Group, soon got results.

The first target was Arnoldo Alemán, until 2001 president of Nicaragua. Alemán was sentenced to twenty years in jail in his home country for embezzlement in 2003, landing in ninth spot on Transparency International's 2004 top ten kleptocrats list. US officials seized $2.7 million in bank deposits and property, on the grounds that these assets were part of a US money laundering scheme deriving from a foreign corruption offense, conduct that had only recently been criminalized in the Patriot Act. These funds were returned to Nicaragua to be used for education programs.[41] This decision demonstrated the principle that stolen assets should be returned to the victim government, but also the idea that returning governments could put conditions on how the money is used. A further civil forfeiture case in 2005 targeted an additional $700,000. In both the criminal and the civil actions, US authorities were closely advised by their Nicaraguan counterparts, and both actions were greatly aided by the fact that Alemán had already been convicted at home. In 2009, however, Alemán's embezzlement conviction was controversially overturned in a Nicaraguan court, leading to speculation of a deal with his erstwhile political opponent Daniel Ortega.

Actively seeking out foreign corruption proceeds in the United States, like those recovered from Alemán, represented a new approach. One official explained this shift by reasoning, "We have indications that it's not uncommon for corrupt leaders in foreign countries to put their money in United States banks and institutions."[42] The same article suggested that the lead agency involved, Immigration and Customs Enforcement, was looking for a new job after having lost purview of countering the financing of terrorism to the FBI.

An earlier example of some success in foreign asset recovery is the case of Peruvian spymaster Vladimiro Montesinos. Montesinos had been the right-hand man of Alberto Fujimori, who had won election as Peru's president before later suspending democracy. Among his other intelligence and security duties, Montesinos had orchestrated a campaign of domestic bribery to shore up political support and buy off opponents, while also embezzling tens of millions in state funds.[43] The Fujimori government collapsed in late 2000, and Montesinos went on the run. The new government took a series of positive steps that, with foreign assistance, led to significant sums being recovered from the United States as well as Switzerland (covered in chapter 3).

In November 2000, Citibank New York lodged two Suspicious Activity Reports concerning a close associate of Montesinos, Victor Venero-Garrido, who was trying to close two accounts in Miami worth a combined $10 million. With unusual speed, the report was passed on to an interoffice anti-drugs unit operating under the gung-ho moniker of the South Florida Money Laundering Strike Force, which passed it to the FBI.[44] A search of Venero-Garrido's apartment produced extensive financial records. Peruvian authorities had meanwhile been able to strike deals with other highly placed officials to return embezzled money and hand over financial records in return for a pardon. The US and Peruvian authorities compared notes to build up a fuller picture of the case. Just over $20 million was found in US banks. The Justice Department took legal action against the funds directly, using non-conviction-based forfeiture provisions (the Patriot Act did not yet exist, so a money laundering conviction of the individuals involved would have been much more difficult). The case had only to be proved on the balance of probabilities, not the higher criminal standard of beyond a reasonable doubt, though it turned out that no one contested the claim. At this stage, although there was a Peruvian arrest warrant out for Montesinos, there was no criminal case and hence no conviction. The US Attorney General agreed to turn the money over to the Peruvian government in January 2004, conditional on its being spent on anti-corruption programs.[45]

The relatively speedy success of these efforts (at least compared with other asset recovery cases) seems to have owed a great deal to the widespread international media coverage of the hunt for Montesinos and his money, and the political priority Washington placed on supporting the new government of Peru. These factors seem to explain why Citibank first lodged the two crucial Suspicious Activity Reports, why of all the thousands of such reports made each year these were picked up so quickly, and why the FBI and US government made such a sustained effort to recover the money. US Justice Department officials were adamant that the money could not have been recovered if not for their ability to bring civil confiscation orders, given the lack of a conviction or even a criminal trial in Peru.[46]

A third relevant case is that of Pavlo Lazarenko, Ukrainian prime minister from 1996 to 1997. He was detained while trying to enter the United States illegally in February 1999. At the time, Lazarenko was fleeing an investigation for corruption and murder at home after being stripped of parliamentary immunity, and he had earlier been charged with money laundering in Switzerland. He had been accused of corruptly obtaining up to $200 million, putting him just ahead of Alemán in eighth place on Transparency International's 2004 top ten kleptocrats list (Lazarenko's declared annual income was $3,000). In large part this wealth was said to represent kickbacks from gas deals with Russia and Turkmenistan.[47]

In May 2004, Lazarenko was convicted in a California court of money laundering, conspiracy to commit money laundering, and wire fraud, leading to a sentence of eight years one month in prison, a $9 million fine, and a $21 million forfeiture order. The US Attorney's Office stated that "the sentence should send a strong message to corrupt foreign public officials— they will be held accountable if they misuse their office and try to make safe harbor in the United States."[48] US prosecutors had achieved the difficult task of establishing the "specific unlawful activities" abroad and then traced the flow of $15 million of these illicit funds into specific assets in the United States, aided by the guilty plea and testimony of co-conspirator Peter Kiritchenko.[49] Financially and politically, the United States had little to gain from the case. One FBI agent remembered that Ukrainian officials were confused as to why the United States was even pursuing the matter, given the lack of a US stake in the outcome.[50] Despite this success, the fact that as of late 2014 (two years after his release from jail) Lazarenko was still able to defend millions of dollars of what was almost certainly dirty money in US legal action shows the limits of accountability.[51] His extensive use of US shell companies to retain property estimated to be worth $72 million demonstrates a more general weakness discussed further below.[52]

The cases against Alemán, Montesinos, and Lazarenko represented some success in holding foreign kleptocrats accountable by targeting their stolen assets in the United States. In all three cases it is hard to determine a selfish national interest rationale for why the US government would take action and then return most of the money. On the other hand, moves to target this wealth were made only once Alemán, Montesinos, and Lazarenko had fallen from power, even though the most superficial scrutiny of their wealth should have aroused banks' and regulators' suspicion well beforehand. A charitable interpretation of this sequence is that banks had not appreciated the scale of the corruption until the media coverage after these three lost office, and that law enforcement could do little until it got assistance from victim countries. The more realpolitik version is that both banks and the authorities in the United States were well aware of the corrupt conduct but for reasons of commercial and diplomatic expediency chose to turn a blind eye until the political winds changed.

Building on these cases, the Bush administration continued to strengthen US policy domestically and multilaterally. In January 2004 the president issued a "proclamation to deny entry into the United States of corrupt foreign officials, their dependents, and those who corrupt them" (Presidential Proclamation 7750), a measure enshrined in legislation in 2008.[53] A later series of measures comprised the National Strategy to Internationalize Efforts Against Kleptocracy. These focused on aggressive US investigation and prosecution of kleptocracy, repatriating stolen wealth, providing intelligence and technical assistance to other countries so they could do the same, and strengthening the framework of multilateral rules against corruption. Explaining the rationale behind this policy in August 2006, President Bush spoke of kleptocracy in the following terms:

> For too long, the culture of corruption has undercut development and good governance and bred criminality and mistrust around the world. High-level corruption by senior government officials, or kleptocracy, is a grave and corrosive abuse of power and represents the most invidious type of public corruption. . . . It impedes our efforts to promote freedom and democracy, end poverty, and combat international crime and terrorism. Kleptocracy is an obstacle to democratic progress, undermines faith in government institutions, and steals prosperity from the people.[54]

A second part of this response was a joint effort with other G8 members. The US government put an emphasis on anti-kleptocracy multilaterally through the G8 summit it hosted in 2004. This built on the G8 "Fighting Corruption and Improving Transparency Action Plan" agreed at the previous year's summit in Evian, France.[55] As well as calling on members to complete the negotiation of the UNCAC, this statement committed members to increased scrutiny of senior foreign public officials operating within their financial systems and to denial of entry to corrupt foreign officials. Many of these and other G8 measures were later transposed into the G20 Anti-Corruption Working Group starting in 2011.

Banks Step Up: Preventive Successes

In 2010 the Senate Permanent Subcommittee on Investigations released another report examining the laundering of foreign corruption proceeds in the United States, comprising case histories of officials from Angola, Nigeria, Gabon, and Equatorial Guinea. Though the report was mostly negative, there was also a more positive side. Detailed evidence demonstrated that many attempts at placing dirty money in the US financial system were defeated, while others succeeded only after deliberate efforts to evade banks' screening procedures. The report concludes that "although U.S. financial institutions have become more vigilant over time and less willing to harbor suspect funds, PEPs [Politically Exposed Persons, i.e., senior foreign officials] are still often able to bring millions of dollars into the United States without having to answer questions about the source of their funds."[56]

The significance of the two examples discussed below, first Angola and then Obiang, is that American banks acted to block corrupt wealth from entering the United States, even when Washington was at the time on cordial terms with the regimes concerned. Because banks are the key point of compliance with the anti-kleptocracy regime, the detailed coverage of banks' internal decision making presented in the 2010 report is invaluable. Banks claim that they routinely turn down would-be clients whom they suspect of corruption, and block suspicious transfers, but that this good behavior never comes to light.[57] It is hard to get independent evidence to confirm this, however. The section immediately following this one turns the spotlight to two of the most important anti-kleptocracy actions brought during the Obama administration, the first again concerning Teodorin Obiang, the second targeting a former ruler of Guatemala.

The most positive example of private sector preventive action concerns an unsuccessful effort to defraud Angola's Central Bank (BNA) of $50 million. The scheme was hatched by the bank's director, Anguinaldo Jaime (later deputy prime minister), together with a collaborator in the United States, Menehou Satou Amouzou. It is sometimes difficult to determine whether the story is one of conspirators working toward a common aim or conspirators scamming other conspirators. In 2002 Amouzou formed a US shell company, MSA Inc., ostensibly offering consulting and investment advice (consultancy is a recurring cover story for corrupt payments[58]). In June 2002 Jaime authorized $50 million to be wired from the central bank's account in Citibank London to MSA Inc.'s Bank of America account in San Diego. The latter account had been opened the month before, with Jaime a co-signatory. Amouzou had promised outlandish returns on the money, which would supposedly be channeled back into Angola for development purposes. At first things went well: the money arrived on the same day it was sent from London, and for a week no suspicions were aroused. Yet a Bank of America representative testifying before the committee recalled that when she asked Amouzou in person about the source of the funds, he "got very upset and said the funds were good, clean funds and why was I so suspicious."[59]

Not especially reassured by this answer, Bank of America and Citibank made further inquiries that only deepened their concerns. An e-mail from Bank of America security on June 20 picked up the anomaly of Jaime both authorizing the initial transfer and being a signatory on the receiving account. The e-mail continued, "Please ensure that the money stays frozen, deeply frozen! . . . Citi are obviously extremely worried about what has been uncovered and my contact [at Citi] has promised to keep me well informed but he's 'pleaded' with us not to release that money!!!!"[60] Finding that their money was frozen, both Amouzou and his attorney began to put pressure on the bank to release the funds, while shortly afterward Jaime wrote in his capacity of head of the central bank asking that the wire transfer be reversed for a "clarification." At the same time, Bank of America was approached by the State Department, which urged it to release the money,[61] a solution that suited both banks involved. The money was returned to BNA's Citibank account in London.

Yet this was by no means the end of the story. Bank of America closed the MSA Inc. account due to worries about money laundering. More significantly, in 2003 Citibank closed all accounts linked to the Angolan government, including its notoriously corrupt state oil firm Solangol,[62] and withdrew its presence in that country, incurring a significant loss of revenue in the process. This decision was explicitly based on the mysterious $50 million transfer.[63] Jaime's successor as central bank director informed Citibank that this episode was one of a number of problems he was dealing with; the relevant internal bank memo rather drily observed, "This does not add to our comfort on the inner workings of the BNA."[64] Bank of America and Citi's performance is especially impressive given that at the time handling foreign corruption proceeds had been a crime for less than a year, but even more so because then and now the US government has found it politic to ignore the kleptocratic nature of Angola's government. There was no political pressure on Citibank to cut ties with Angola; if anything, the State Department intervention might be read as an attempt to smooth things over.

Not the types to be discouraged, Amouzou and Jaime quickly embarked on another attempt to move the $50 million, this time involving US Treasury Bills, various HSBC subsidiaries, and Wells Fargo. More middlemen and another shell company (again offering "consulting") were brought into the equation as part of a deal promising returns that would be attractive to any investor: 300 percent . . . per month.[65] Once again, though, after early success, problems arose. Despite some queries, HSBC carried out the purchase of $50 million in bonds and transferred them to Wells Fargo. An officer at the latter bank, however, was suspicious and asked a private due diligence firm to investigate. The investigation concluded that the transaction was probably part of a scam, and so the funds were returned to HSBC and the account closed. Another attempt to transfer the funds failed when HSBC mistakenly entered the wrong account number.[66]

The final effort was to ask HSBC to provide a "safekeeping receipt" for the $50 million. If endorsed by HSBC, a safekeeping receipt would function as a bearer security, that is, essentially like cash, in the sense that anyone who had the original document could claim the $50 million. In a hurry to get out of the office to start a vacation, an HSBC employee endorsed the document against bank policy, but only faxed a copy rather than sending the original.[67] Desperate to get their hands on the original document, Jaime and his co-conspirators put increasing pressure on HSBC, a stance that backfired. An HSBC compliance officer wrote concerning the requests for the safekeeping receipt: "These bearer instruments have been used in scams and have a negative connotation associated with them. A request to have us issue something like this to support what sounds like a secured credit facility is very unusual. Furthermore, your indicating that the transaction details are confidential and that there is tremendous pressure to have the receipt issued today makes the entire transaction look suspect to us. . . . Based on what I see here it appears to me that this is part of some elaborate scam to defraud the Central Bank of its securities."[68] At this stage the money was returned to the original BNA account in London.

Unlike Citibank, however, HSBC did not make any moves to distance itself from the Angolan government. In his testimony before the committee, the HSBC compliance director explained this decision by noting that USAID maintained a close relationship with BNA, while also referring to Secretary of State Hillary Clinton's remark concerning her desire "to deepen and strengthen the relationship between the United States and Angola" during her visit to Angola in August 2009[69] (when asked about corruption during a visit to Angola, Clinton replied, "Corruption is a problem everywhere. . . . It's only fair to add that Angola has begun taking steps to increase transparency"[70]). If the US government was (and is) so relaxed about Angolan grand corruption, why should HSBC or any other bank suffer pangs of conscience?

Obiang versus the Banks

The hostility that erupted between Equatorial Guinea and the United States over the family's outrageous corruption is notable because it is such a radical departure from what had been the conventional script. Bluntly put, this script might be that kleptocrats and their money can be pursued only once they lose power, not when they are in office, and especially not when they are rulers of oil-producing nations and hence of geopolitical importance.

Beyond being the son of "El Liberator," Obiang Jr. was made minister for forestry and agriculture in 1994 and has been second vice-president since 2012. Despite his modest official salary of around $80,000,[71] Obiang insisted that a "revolutionary tax" be paid by logging firms into a shell company corporate account he controlled (Somagui Forestal). Teodorin spent all this money and more on a vast array of luxury cars (numerous Bugattis, Rolls-Royces, Maseratis, Ferraris, etc.), property (including a $30 million property in Malibu, California, next door to Britney Spears), a Gulfstream private jet ($38.5 million), and $1.8 million of Michael Jackson memorabilia. All told, his spending spree in the period 2004–2011 was estimated by the US Justice Department at $314,868,310.62.[72]

In late 2006 the NGO Global Witness discovered the true ownership of Obiang's Malibu mansion, "looking through" a shell company set up to obscure this link, and then obtained two crucial secret law enforcement documents. The first, dated September 4, 2007, is from US Immigration and Customs Enforcement asking for legal assistance from its French counterpart in an investigation of the Obiangs' corruption and money laundering. It includes the comment that "prosecutors suspect that most, if not all, of Teodoro Nguema Obiang's [i.e., Teodorin's] assets are derived from extortion, bribery or the misappropriation of government funds."[73] The second document was an undated PowerPoint presentation from the interagency anti-corruption unit in Miami. The information contained held that Obiang had managed to route at least $70 million into the United States (later information suggested a total in excess of $100 million[74]). US law enforcement apparently had Teodorin in its sights, outlining a strategy to "identify, trace, freeze, and recover assets within the United States illicitly acquired through kleptocracy."[75]

Over the next few years, however, nothing happened. Global Witness, lawmakers, and journalists increasingly asked why the Obiangs were not on the list of those senior public officials to be denied entry on the grounds of corruption (apparently around three dozen in 2009)[76]. The omens did not seem good when a beaming President Obama posed with Obiang Sr. for a photo opportunity with their respective first ladies in New York in October 2009. In querying the lack of action until late 2009, the Global Witness report asks the questions at the heart of this book: "Could the lack of legal action against TNO [i.e., Obiang Jr.] stem from political pressure to ignore the crimes of a possible future president of an oil-friendly ally? Or are there insurmountable legal obstacles to prosecuting TNO, who has diplomatic status from his government?"[77] For the former US ambassador to Equatorial Guinea, the answer was easy: "Of course it's because of oil."[78] But even highly sympathetic lawyers quoted in the Global Witness report noted that, putting political and diplomatic considerations to one side, legal action would be difficult.[79] Given that no cooperation would be forthcoming from Equatorial Guinea, a criminal prosecution for money laundering would almost certainly fail to prove the case beyond a reasonable doubt. Getting the assets in question forfeited in line with the lower balance of probability criterion was still said to be difficult.

Despite the criticism of the government's inactivity, Teodorin was not having things all his own way in laundering the proceeds of his corruption in the United States. The Justice Department took action against Obiang's assets on April 28, 2011 (with the case specified as "United States v. One White Crystal-Covered 'Bad Tour' Glove and Other Michael Jackson Memorabilia," followed by the house and a Ferrari), but for years anti–money laundering screening by US banks had forced Obiang into ever more elaborate ruses to gain access to the financial system. In this unworthy enterprise he was ably assisted by California lawyers Michael J. Berger and George Nagler.

Initially, from 2001, Obiang would wire money from Equatorial Guinea to accounts held in the name of one of his shell companies or to his secretary's personal accounts at Union Bank of California (UBOC) and Bank of America. In late 2004 and early 2005, however, Union Bank categorized Equatorial Guinea as a "high risk" country in its anti–money laundering software, basing this on the various rankings issued by the Financial Action Task Force, Transparency International, and other organizations. It closed all the Obiang-linked accounts. Bank of America also drew the connection with Equatorial Guinea and closed the accounts. Subsequently, however, Obiang would move money from accounts in Equatorial Guinea in the name of companies he controlled to Berger's law firm trust accounts. Berger then moved the money via checks from the trust account to US accounts held by Californian shell companies that were set up by Berger and had Berger as the signatory but acted on Obiang's instructions.[80] On other occasions, Berger paid Obiang's bills directly out of the trust account.[81] Berger was paid $60,000 a year for these services, and Nagler almost $200,000 over two years. Even with these precautions in place, however, Union Bank cottoned on. Internal correspondence from June 2007 reasoned: "The use of multiple corporate vehicles by Michael Berger, the lawyer of Politically Exposed Person (PEP) Teodoro Nguema Obiang, in order to disguise the identity of his client as well as to place, layer, and integrate Obiang's funds derived via international wire transactions from Equatorial Guinea, a high risk jurisdiction . . . had the appearance of money laundering activity conducted by a UBOC client on behalf of Obiang."[82] The bank closed the accounts. This time Bank of America was less vigilant. It closed the shell company accounts in 2005 but did not pick up that Berger was using his law firm account as a conduit for Obiang until Senate investigators approached the bank in mid-2008. Berger opened a final account at Citibank in 2007, but this was closed by Citibank less than a year later.

Nagler opened similar accounts on behalf of Obiang with California National Bank, but despite Obiang's name being kept off the documents, the bank made the link and, after finding coverage of the Riggs scandal, closed all accounts within the month.[83] A further bank where Nagler introduced Obiang in person as the account holder, Pacific Mercantile Bank, at first accepted his business but then thought the better of it several months later. Finally, City National Bank not only closed Obiang shell company accounts but froze $700,000, forcing Obiang to go to court to recover the money. On investigation in 2004, the bank found Obiang had opened the account with someone else's Social Security number, had given the wrong birth date, had not disclosed his PEP status, and had not explained the source of the funds, meaning that City National Bank never should have opened the account in the first place.[84] Nagler also used his firm's trust account to conceal Obiang's finances.[85]

How significant is this risk-screening behavior by banks? On the one hand, it could be said that thanks to the publicity surrounding Riggs Bank, Obiang was in a risk class all of his own. On the other, Obiang's name was not associated with most accounts or the corporate entities that held them, thanks to Berger's and Nagler's careful work, and yet in most cases the banks could make the link, closed the accounts, and reported their suspicions to the authorities.

To give some context, it was in 2006 that Condoleezza Rice referred to Obiang Sr. as a "good friend" of the United States. In a secret cable available on WikiLeaks from 2009, the US ambassador in Malabo noted that Equatorial Guinea supplied 20 percent of US national energy imports and hence "it is time to abandon a moral narrative that has left us with a retrospective bias and an ambivalent approach to one of the most-promising success stories in the region." It went on to say that Equatorial Guinea's government is "no worse than many of our energy allies, and better than some," that President Obiang was "one of the good guys," but that US policy had been too swayed by "oppugnant NGOs."[86] As such, there was no political pressure for banks or other US private firms to cut ties with Equatorial Guinea—if anything, the reverse.

Despite the best efforts of his loyal attorneys, Obiang had even more trouble obtaining insurance for the Malibu mansion and his fleet of thirty-two luxury cars. Although there was no legal requirement to do so, the insurance companies checked Obiang's background. As a result, only one of eleven companies approached agreed to take the business, despite Nagler's point that the rulers of Equatorial Guinea were "no better and no worse than the Saudi Royal family," which had no problems getting US insurance.[87] Vehicle insurance was secured only thanks to a personal connection with an insurance agent "in return for an outrageously expensive sushi dinner at his favorite place."[88]

An important area of continuing vulnerability is real estate. The Malibu purchase in 2006 was the highest value in California that year and the sixth highest in the country,[89] and on these grounds stood out. The $30 million entered the United States via wire transfers from Obiang's personal accounts in Equatorial Guinea that went to the trust account of the escrow agent, First American, at Wachovia Bank. Like real estate agents, escrow firms were (and are) not covered by anti–money laundering requirements and thus are not obligated to ask questions about the source of funds. Wachovia Bank checked that Obiang was not on the Office of Foreign Asset Control list of terrorists and criminals but otherwise pointed out that it has a legal duty only to do due diligence on its clients (in this case, First American), not its clients' clients (Obiang).[90]

The United States versus Obiang, 2011–2014

A major blow against Obiang Jr.'s assets was struck when in late April 2011 the US Justice Department lodged a non-conviction-based forfeiture action against the Malibu mansion, a development that became public on October 25, 2011. The initial claim was for $70.8 million, comprising the private jet, the mansion, seven cars, and the much-publicized Michael Jackson collectibles.[91] The action accused Obiang of extortion, bribery, fraud, and money laundering.

A common-sense reading of the matter might be that a senior political figure with an annual salary of $80,000, no other legitimate source of income, and $70 million of assets is guilty of corruption, end of story. But as Jennifer Shasky Calvery, at the time chief of the Justice Department's Asset Recovery and Money Laundering section, pointed out: "It is one thing to say someone has a lot of money and is a corrupt leader; it is another thing to prove that money resulted from the corruption."[92] Legally, it was necessary to find the specific incidences of corruption in Equatorial Guinea, the specific assets in the United States, and the specific links between the crime and the assets, at a time when the victim country was doing everything in its power to sabotage the case.[93]

Matters did not get off to an auspicious start. Obiang had had time to fly his jet away, and the government managed to restrain only one of his cars. He was promoted to second vice-president, and the supreme court of Equatorial Guinea declared he had a completely clean record. The judge hearing the case in California was not sympathetic to the US Department of Justice, noting the denial of Equatorial Guinea's government that any crimes had been committed. He stated that the US government would have to present more evidence and threw the case out. In June 2012 the Justice Department responded by filing a new, amended claim. The 106-page document covered much of the same ground as the two Senate reports but added important new details about Obiang's alleged extraction of bribes, extortion, and outright theft from local and foreign forestry and construction firms in Equatorial Guinea. This evidence was drawn from many years of investigation and exchange with law enforcement in France, Spain, and Italy. The Department of Justice directly accused Nagler and Berger of involvement in fraud,[94] something the Senate reports had only implied, though no charges were brought against them. Apart from the five different banks that had closed twelve accounts on discovering the Obiang connection covered in the Senate report, Obiang subsequently used two confederates to set up more shell companies and open accounts, with Wells Fargo in March 2008 and J. P. Morgan in October 2010, which then received wire transfers from his companies in Equatorial Guinea for the upkeep of the house.

Despite the weight of detail, the court proceedings did not favor the government.[95] In August 2014 the judge stated that just showing that Obiang was living well beyond his means was not sufficient proof of criminal activity. This once again illustrated the central difficulty faced by the United States in seeking to make its case: the government had to show that specific corruption offenses in Equatorial Guinea had generated funds that were then used in purchasing the assets in question. The judge encouraged the two parties to settle the case.

On October 10, 2014, the two sides reached an agreement. The US government gained the Malibu mansion and the Ferrari, as well as six "Michael Jackson Neverland Ranch Life Size Statues."[96] The proceeds were to be given to a charity, chosen jointly by both parties, to help the people of Equatorial Guinea. Obiang declared via Facebook, "I am pleased to be able to end this long and costly ordeal. . . . I agreed to settle this case despite the fact that the U.S. federal courts had consistently found that the Department of Justice lacked probable cause to seize my property."[97] Not surprisingly, the Justice Department saw things in a different light: "This settlement forces Nguema Obiang to relinquish assets worth an estimated \$30 million, and prevents Nguema Obiang from hiding other stolen money in the United States, fulfilling the goals of our Kleptocracy Asset Recovery Initiative: to deny safe haven to the proceeds of large-scale foreign official corruption and recover those funds for the people harmed by the abuse of office."[98] Meanwhile the Washington public relations firm Qorvis Communications worked to burnish the Obiang family image, and Obiang Sr. sponsored the \$3 million UNESCO–Obiang Nguema Mbasogo International Prize for Research in the Life Sciences.[99]

To what extent was the result a victory or defeat for the campaign against kleptocracy? The investigation and legal proceedings, lasting from 2006 until the end of 2014, represented an enormous commitment of time and resources, and yet failed to win the day in court. This was despite the spectacular and unexplained discrepancy between Obiang's official earnings and his spending and despite the painstaking investigations by journalists like Silverstein, Global Witness, the Open Society Foundations, the Senate subcommittee, and US and foreign law enforcement agencies. The Justice Department obtained less than half of the funds targeted, which themselves represented a relatively small share of Obiang's plunder. Obiang is of course at liberty to continue to enjoy his profligate lifestyle.

The public and private consensus from expert observers, however, was that the US government had done the best it could in the case under difficult circumstances.[100] The results were not trivial. The US government had in some way held Obiang accountable for his crimes in a manner that was impossible in Equatorial Guinea. Depending on how the money is spent, $30 million may actually make a notable difference in the victim country, given that the majority of its 700,000 people live on under two dollars a day. The investigation and the result (and the no doubt stratospheric costs of Obiang's legal team) sent a signal that the US government is willing to go to great lengths to take action against the proceeds of foreign corruption held within its borders.

In terms of the bigger questions at the heart of this book, the Obiang case is all the more significant for targeting a current senior leader, and likely future president, of a country that had been on good terms with the United States, where there were major American investments, and that had considerable geopolitical importance thanks to its oil reserves. Considering these facts, and that nearly all the money was donated to charity, it is very hard to see a cynical rationale that explains US action here. Similarly, although action may have been belated, it is hard to say that the United States was just going through the motions in pursuing these stolen assets.

Alfonso Portillo of Guatemala

A much less publicized example of action against kleptocracy was that against Alfonso Portillo, president of Guatemala from 2000 to 2004, who was indicted on money laundering charges in the United States in December 2009.[101] As in the African cases, the underlying corrupt conduct occurred in a foreign jurisdiction but the illicit funds were in part located in the United States.

Beginning in 2000, the Republic of China (Taiwanese) embassy had made payments of $2.5 million to fund a "Libraries for Peace" program for Guatemalan schoolchildren, drawing the money on a New York bank account. Portillo endorsed the checks, and the funds were deposited into a Miami account and thence to further accounts in the United Kingdom, France, Luxembourg, Liechtenstein, and Switzerland, some directly in the name of Portillo's wife and daughter. Two further charges that were dropped related to corruption funds of up to $70 million that were again routed through US banks after being diverted from the defense budget and a bank controlled by associates of Portillo.

A 2008 embezzlement case against Portillo in Guatemala collapsed after the disappearance of key witnesses. The former president was later controversially acquitted of embezzlement in 2011.[102] Undeterred, the United States sought to have Portillo extradited to face trial in New York. Portillo's lawyers argued that at the time of the alleged offenses, money laundering was not a crime in Guatemala, and that because retroactive justice was unconstitutional, their client should be released. Furthermore, they claimed, money laundering was not included as a relevant crime in the extradition treaty between the two countries. The response from the judges, however, was that money laundering was a continuing crime as long as the illicit assets were held. The response to the second objection was that the mutual legal assistance provisions of UNCAC superseded the narrow scope of the bilateral treaty.[103] The extradition was finally approved by the Guatemalan president, whereupon the suspect was turned over to the United States in May 2013. This transfer occurred at the same time as genocide charges against another former Guatemalan leader, Efraín Montt, were controversially annulled, leading to speculation that the government had sought to deflect criticism concerning the impunity of former leaders by offering up Portillo.

US authorities alleged that Portillo had converted "the office of the Guatemalan presidency into his personal A.T.M."[104] On March 18, 2014, Portillo pled guilty to one count of conspiracy to commit money laundering. He was sentenced to five years ten months in jail, the forfeiture of $2.5 million, and (strangely) a fine of precisely $100.[105] However, because the court took into account the time already served in Guatemala awaiting extradition and during the trial in New York, Portillo served only a few extra months. This short stay may indicate a deal between the prosecution, which could not find enough evidence to prove the other charges beyond a reasonable doubt and hence was eager for a plea bargain, and a defendant keen to bring the ordeal to a close.

Does this result represent a success? Portillo seems to have held on to most of his wealth and is now at liberty. Yet without the US action it is clear that he would have escaped without any penalty at all, since the prosecutions against him at home had failed and seventy months in prison is hardly a trivial punishment. The fact of a former leader being found guilty of a major crime was almost unprecedented in a country that had suffered near-genocidal human rights abuses and endemic corruption. It is difficult to discern a self-interested motive for the US government's actions. Indeed, some criticized the resources expended in this case exactly because there was no direct US national interest at stake.[106]

Assessing Overall Effectiveness: Current Problems and Prospects

For the cause of fighting grand corruption in the United States, 2014 proved to be a bumper year. Capping the decisions in the Obiang and Portillo cases, in August the US government seized $480 million stolen by former Nigerian dictator Sani Abacha and his associates.[107] Reflecting the European focus of Abacha's laundering schemes (discussed extensively in chapters 3 and 4), the money was seized from accounts in Jersey, France, the United Kingdom, and Ireland. As with the Portillo case, the US claimed jurisdiction because the money had been moved through US dollar-denominated financial networks. An additional $148 million was restrained in the United Kingdom awaiting decision. These funds later became the subject of a settlement between the Nigerian government and the Abacha family (see chapter 3). In the period from the creation of the Kleptocracy Asset Recovery Initiative in 2010 until October 2014 it had won $600 million in fifteen cases involving fourteen countries.[108] Further cases are in train, though the details are secret.[109] Up to 2013, the separate Immigrations and Customs Enforcement Foreign Corruption Investigations Group made eighty criminal arrests, secured 148 indictments, and seized more than $131 million in assets.[110]

Despite these successes, it is important to keep matters in perspective. First there is the nagging issue raised in the Introduction: how many other cases of kleptocrats laundering their money have stayed secret and undetected? Relatedly, what about the conspicuous systemic weaknesses that remain? After all these laws, cases, and initiatives, how hard is it to launder the proceeds of grand corruption in the United States? Compared to the pre-2001 situation in which such conduct was perfectly legal, there has been definite progress, but fairly obvious areas of vulnerability still have not been addressed. The interconnected problem areas are real estate; trust accounts maintained by real estate agents, lawyers, and escrow agencies; and the opacity of shell companies. This final section explains why these connected vulnerabilities create money laundering vulnerabilities, as well as the politics behind the failure to close these gaps.

At a public presentation in New York City in November 2014, the chief of the Department of Justice's Asset Forfeiture and Money Laundering section, Jai Ramaswamy, outlined his views on the most serious obstacles to fighting international corruption. He began by noting that while guesses of the total global illicit economy (whatever they are worth) are in excess of $1 trillion, the United States confiscates only $1.5 billion a year of criminal proceeds, representing a "pin-prick." The number-one problem was said to be beneficial ownership, that is, the ability to find the real person in control of shell companies (Ramaswamy also noted that he couldn't believe such a "nerdy" subject was getting so much political attention). Shell companies were used to try to hide illicit wealth in almost all of the cases referred to above. Although untraceable shell companies pose a problem in many countries, there is strong reason to think that the United States, given its central place in the global financial system and the number of companies involved, is the worst in the world when it comes to regulating shell companies.[111] The sustained failure to fix this problem represents a crucial weakness in efforts to hold kleptocrats accountable by targeting their foreign wealth.

The basic problem with shell companies was illustrated in the Obiang case: his bank accounts and assets were held in the name of companies with no other purpose than to obscure the fact that Obiang controlled this wealth. Unless and until banks and law enforcement could discover the link between the ostensibly unrelated companies and Obiang, his illicit wealth was safely hidden. Those Corporate Service Providers forming companies in the United States are under no obligation to establish the true identity of the client who becomes the company owner. Because the only public documents on the shell company relate to the Corporate Service Provider, and this provider has no idea as to the identity of the real (beneficial) owner, the company is untraceable and thus a perfect means for hiding dirty money.

The United States has repeatedly committed to fixing its beneficial ownership problem in a variety of international fora since 2003, including the FATF, the OECD, the G8, the G20, and the Open Government Partnership, and has then repeatedly failed to honor these commitments. Reform has been stymied by domestic opposition, in particular the National Association of Secretaries of State, the American Bar Association, and the U.S. Chamber of Commerce, which have argued that any new regulation would be excessively burdensome to their members and would fail to stop criminals.[112]

The use of untraceable shell companies in money laundering is often connected with the real estate market. For foreigners looking to launder and then hide money in the US financial system, the door is wide open when it comes to real estate. Dogged and often brilliant investigative journalism has unearthed the modus operandi for such transactions, which closely fit the pattern of Obiang's Malibu property. Simply put, any foreign corrupt official wanting to place dirty money in the United States need only contact one of the specialized one-stop real estate firms that act as agent, attorney, and shell company provider. These firms will receive a foreign electronic bank transfer into their trust account. There the money is commingled with that of other clients, obscuring the trail. In any case, there is nothing inherently suspicious about, say, a $5 million transfer to buy a $5 million property. Banks must know their customer (in this case the real estate firm), but are under no obligation to know their customer's customer (i.e., the buyer). In any case, the buyer will usually send the wire transfer through a shell company and/or law firm in the home country, or more commonly a third jurisdiction (one facilitator noted that at the upper end of the market, "Ninety-nine percent of the time they already have the money outside of their home country"[113]). The American real estate agent then sets up a shell company (or perhaps a trust or a chain of interlocking companies and trusts) to own the property, and transfers the money to the account of the seller's representative.

So common are these types of arrangements that those routinely intermediating such deals have been happy to speak on the record to journalists, regarding such attention as free advertising.[114] Thus one New York agent noted of his foreign clients' payments, "Sometimes they come in with wires, sometimes they come in with suitcases." On being asked about the danger that this money represents the proceeds of corruption from abroad, he continued: "It's something that is never discussed, but it's the elephant in the room. Real estate is a wonderful way to cleanse money. Once you buy real estate, the derivation of that cash is forgotten." Another explained, "Like somebody said, Karl Marx or whatever, if the capitalist is going to see a triple return, he's going to close his eyes."[115] In 2012 foreigners invested $50 billion in US real estate (though it's unclear if this total includes foreigners buying through US shell companies and intermediaries).[116]

A *New York Times* investigation in 2015 confirms that "nearly half of the most expensive residential properties in the United States are now purchased anonymously through shell companies," and that "the real estate industry does little examination of buyers' identities or backgrounds, and there is no legal requirement for it to do so."[117] A Global Witness sting made public in 2016 confirmed this picture of lax standards.[118]

In secretly recorded footage of meetings with Manhattan lawyers, including the then-head of the American Bar Association, an impersonator claimed to represent a minister of mines from a West African country who was looking to buy a $5–20 million property, as well as a private jet and mega-yacht for in excess of $50 million. The impersonator explained that the funds, described as "gray or black money," came from "facilitation payments" that the minister had been given by foreign mining firms and that were well in excess of the minister's salary, blatantly obvious hints that the money represented the proceeds of corruption. Though some lawyers spoke of the need for checks on the source of the money, and though no deal was struck or money transferred, the advice issued by the dozen law firms approached outlines a familiar path for foreign corruption funds entering the United States. The law firms stressed the need for the money to come to the United States via a third country (Britain, Switzerland, Luxembourg, the Isle of Man, and the Cayman Islands are mentioned), because American banks would be wary of taking a large of amount of money from a senior official in a corruption-prone region. They recommended that assets be held in the name of US shell companies to obscure the identity of the true owner, sometimes linked up with offshore companies or trusts. In several cases the lawyers also offered the use of their firms' trust accounts to hide the money trail. In one case the price for facilitating these transactions was put at $40,000 to $50,000.

Lawyers and other intermediaries involved in suspect deals almost always escape scot-free, even after quite glaring sins of omission or commission. In a decision that speaks volumes of lawyers' claims of self-regulation, despite being directly accused by the Department of Justice of involvement in a series of schemes to fraudulently open bank accounts for Obiang,[119] and despite the wealth of evidence presented, the California Bar Association declined to take any disciplinary action against Berger and Nagler, even after a direct request from the Department of the Treasury. When asked about the one-stop lawyer–real estate–shell company provider arrangements, an American Bar Association representative said the association "frowned upon" such conduct but had no means to prevent it and opposed any attempt at outside regulation in this area. The real estate industry is also a very powerful lobby, and is equally opposed to new regulatory requirements.[120] The National Association of Realtors unconvincingly claims, "Any risk-based assessment would likely find very little risk of money laundering involving real estate agents or brokers."[121]

In light of the preceding coverage, to what extent is the United States genuinely and effectively committed to the global regime against kleptocracy? From the Foreign Corrupt Practices Act onward, the United States has had an unusual commitment to the cause of fighting international corruption. Uniquely, after 1977 American business had a strong incentive to push for multilateral anti-corruption standards to ensure that foreign rivals were bound by the same anti-bribery rules. A strong tradition of investigative journalism, vigorous NGOs, and activist legislators exposed important foreign corruption scandals. The tools for combating foreign corruption flows were at hand as an unintended by-product of the war on drugs (the anti–money laundering system) and later the war on terror (the Patriot Act). During the Cold War, however, the overriding priority of the struggle with Communism meant that politically reliable dictators were able to steal, export, launder, and enjoy their ill-gotten gains in peace. Beginning in the 1990s, however, no other country has done more to promote the global regime against grand corruption. Thanks to a series of scandals at home publicized by journalists, NGOs, and the US Senate, hosting the proceeds of foreign corruption became a crime. More important than new laws were public presidential commitments to this campaign and the creation of law enforcement units solely devoted to tracking and repatriating kleptocrats' wealth. The United States has taken action against corrupt rulers in conjunction with victim governments (Peru, Nicaragua) but also even when their home countries have been unable (Guatemala, Ukraine) or unwilling (Equatorial Guinea). In other instances US banks have independently blocked the flow of stolen funds by closing accounts (Angola, Gabon, and Equatorial Guinea). Though some regulatory agencies have failed in their duties for long periods, most notably the Office of the Comptroller of the Currency, others have been energetically applying huge fines to banks that host illicit wealth. As a result, perhaps uniquely, financial institutions operating in the United States have a direct financial incentive to follow the rules, especially foreign firms that enjoy less political protection.

The normative commitment to fighting corruption does not mean that national security considerations have gone away. Sometimes the US government will still choose to ignore blatant corruption among client governments. Powerful domestic lobby groups, from lawyers, to real estate agents, to the U.S. Chamber of Commerce, have blocked reforms vital to a properly functioning anti–money laundering system, leading to widening gaps between commitments made in various summits abroad and those legislated at home. Thus if the effectiveness of the US system to combat kleptocracy has improved since the introduction of the Patriot Act and is in some ways a model for other countries, even US law enforcement admits that only a small fraction of the dirty money entering the US financial system is interdicted.

3

SWITZERLAND

The Unlikely Crusader

Switzerland has played an outsized role in hosting legitimate and criminal foreign wealth, as well as in the campaign to combat kleptocracy and repatriate looted funds. No other country illustrates the shift in this area more dramatically. Switzerland has come from being the most secretive and secure host of illicit money to perhaps the most active and effective practitioner and advocate of asset recovery, exemplifying and accelerating broader global normative and policy change. So pivotal is Switzerland that it is almost easier to list the grand corruption cases that do *not* have a Swiss connection than all those that do. Examples include the three textbook cases of Marcos, Abacha, and Montesinos that often dominate writings about asset recovery. Switzerland has repatriated more money than any country, and in the period 2006–2012 it froze more foreign corruption funds than any other country (though critics suggest that this is because the country has hosted so much dirty money to begin with).[1] Stolen wealth has been returned to Angola, Argentina, Brazil, France, Germany, Italy, Kazakhstan, Mali, Nigeria, Peru, the Philippines, Spain, Ukraine, and Russia.² Once more typifying the cross-border nature of kleptocracy, several of the cases discussed here in connection with Switzerland also spill over into other chapters.

This chapter begins with a brief look at why Switzerland has historically attracted such a huge share of foreign wealth. The coverage of kleptocrats' wealth in Switzerland and the various efforts to recover it is roughly divided into three sections. The first deals with the examples of Marcos of the Philippines, Abacha of Nigeria, and Montesinos of Peru over the period 1986–2005 (with a 2014–2015 postscript on the Abacha case), partial successes that have received a disproportionate share of attention. The second section considers some failures, the more representative outcome, with coverage of "Baby Doc" Duvalier (Haiti) and Benazir Bhutto and Ali Asif Zardari (Pakistan). The third section investigates the Arab Spring cases, with brief mention of others involving incumbents in Uzbekistan and Malaysia, to assess the effects of preventive and remedial policy reforms introduced in response to earlier scandals. The same questions tend to recur across these sections: How was the dirty money first placed in the Swiss financial system? Why didn't preventive measures screen out these funds? How well or badly did efforts to confiscate and repatriate stolen wealth work? To what extent were those policies and actors at fault reformed and punished?

Relating to the gap between rules on the books and actual implementation, a theme that runs throughout this volume, it is important to find out what should have happened, in terms of formal laws and regulations, versus what happened in practice, and the reasons for any divergence between the two. Switzerland has gone further than any other country in passing laws to address the most common obstacles to asset recovery. These laws allow for freezing suspect wealth within hours, relax the requirement to link assets with specific corruption crimes, waive the need for a conviction in the victim country, and can reverse the burden of proof, so that where there are credible allegations of grand corruption it may be up to defendants to prove the legitimate sources of their wealth or else have it confiscated. Yet even with such laws, asset recovery generally requires cooperation between host and victim countries. In several important instances, Switzerland's offers of help in pursuing and returning stolen wealth have been spurned by the very governments it has sought to assist.

Less positively, however, while banks have been quick to report suspicious wealth from political leaders once those leaders have lost power, both banks and regulators have largely failed to answer questions as to how these customers were taken on initially, given that their corruption was an open secret. A related weakness is the consistent failure to sanction banks and other intermediaries for their shortcomings. Regulators seem to have been under the thumb of the finance sector, with the banks also wielding extensive influence over the government. This may mean that Swiss banks are free to host the proceeds of grand corruption (and profit from the accompanying fees) and escape penalties, as long as they cut such clients loose if and when their grip on power slips.

In answer to the basic question of why the Swiss moved so far in adhering to the new anti-kleptocracy norm, government concerns about the country's international standing and image were paramount. While reputation risk for banks exposed as hosting corruption proceeds seems to be largely mythical, sources both inside and beyond the Swiss government consistently indicate that the shifting climate of international opinion led Switzerland to take action against foreign corruption proceeds. In part this sensitivity is because the country tends to see itself as politically isolated. As one official put it to me: "Like you in Australia, we are surrounded by sharks."[3]

It is difficult to think of a commercial or other material economic rationale that can convincingly explain the decision to track down and repatriate stolen wealth. Despite the conventional wisdom to the contrary, dirty money does not scare away legitimate business or imperil the financial institutions that accept such tainted funds. If it did, Switzerland would never have been so successful in hosting so much licit and illicit wealth. In terms of international regulatory politics, Switzerland has been most accommodating to poor and weak developing countries seeking the return of looted assets, but most defiant when it came to the demands of the United States and European Union seeking information on their citizens' Swiss bank accounts.[4]

Switzerland as a Financial Center and Secrecy Haven

In 2013 Switzerland hosted more foreign wealth than any other country, 26 percent of the global total, equivalent to CHF 3.14 trillion in assets under management. Bank deposits from all sources totaled CHF 2.85 trillion.[5]

Switzerland owes its importance in hosting the fortunes of wealthy for-eigners to a range of factors. Politically, its domestic stability and interna-tional neutrality have been central, as has the security of the Swiss franc, Switzerland's long-standing lack of currency controls, its educated and skilled workforce, and, not least, solid backing from the government. Having built up a core of banking, financial, and wealth management ex-pertise early on, Switzerland has long been the natural first port of call when the rich look for a foreign host for their money.[6]

Its famed bank secrecy was first the product of judicial decision, bol-stered in 1934 by federal legislation that made it a criminal offense for the bank information of local or foreign clients to be shared with any govern-ment, even that of Switzerland itself.[7] Subsequently justified as a move to protect Jewish wealth from the new Nazi government, in fact this law was in response to leaked information about Swiss banks' role in a French tax evasion scandal in 1932,[8] a theme that would become all too famil-iar eighty years later. Swiss banks formed "numbered accounts," whereby clients were known only by their account numbers to all but a couple of bank employees. Further corporate secrecy could be provided by a local trust formation industry designed to serve foreigners, or trust-like enti-ties sourced from the neighboring Principality of Liechtenstein, which had developed its own secretive banking and finance center in symbiosis with the Swiss.[9] Equivalent secrecy provisions also apply to Swiss lawyers and notaries, who could hold accounts on behalf of clients without revealing clients' identities to the bank.[10] Finally, Switzerland until very recently did not recognize tax evasion as a criminal offense, and on this basis it has refused to assist foreign tax authorities. In combination, these commercial, legal, and political considerations have meant that although countries from Panama to Lebanon have copied many of these provisions, Switzerland has long been second to none in protecting foreign wealth.[11]

From time to time banking scandals erupted and reforms were made. In 1977 the Federal Council and the Swiss Bankers Association concluded an Agreement of Due Care, under which banks were to refuse transac-tions and sever relations with clients if they knew that the clients' funds derived from activity that would constitute a crime in Switzerland. These provisions were largely abandoned in 1982, with little evidence that they had made any practical difference to banks' operations in the meantime.[12] In the 1980s there were scandals concerning the laundering of billions of francs of drug money.[13] In the following decade the reputation of Switzerland and its banks suffered, particularly in the United States, in line with allegations of being "Nazi Germany's banker" and deliberately blocking access to the accounts of Holocaust victims and survivors. The World Jewish Congress launched a lawsuit that was supported by the New York state and US federal governments.[14] Although a subsequent inquiry headed by former US Federal Reserve chairman Paul Volcker largely supported the Swiss position that the claims were exaggerated and unfair, the media headlines were deeply unfavorable.

By 1990 Switzerland criminalized money laundering, including money derived from acts committed abroad that would qualify as crimes in Switzerland, and the legislation was strengthened in 1997.[15] Banks had already been under an obligation to identify customers since 1977, a provision tightened in the 1990 law.[16] Further regulation in 1994 imposed a duty on banks to report suspicious transactions to the authorities, a requirement that, unlike in most other countries, also imposed an automatic temporary freeze on the funds in question. In 1998 the Swiss Federal Banking Commission issued a directive specifying: "Financial intermediaries should not accept money which they know or must assume comes from corruption or misappropriation of public funds. They therefore need to scrutinize with special attention if they want to enter into business relationships, accept and retain assets owned, directly or indirectly by persons exercising important public functions for a foreign state or individuals and companies, recognizably close to them."[17] Yet until May 2000, bribing foreign officials was not a crime in Switzerland, meaning that foreign corruption did not count as a predicate crime for money laundering, a significant loophole.[18] In 2003 the Banking Commission issued a specific directive criminalizing the receipt of foreign corruption funds and requiring senior bank management approval for accepting business from any foreign political leaders. Aside from criminal sanctions, banks violating this provision were threatened with having their licenses revoked,[19] though particularly with regard to bigger banks there are doubts about the credibility of this threat. As subsequent scandals graphically demonstrate, however, in the 1970s, 1980s, 1990s, and perhaps even beyond, many Swiss banks, like most others at the time, were nevertheless largely open for business with respect to kleptocrats, and were often happy to help in laundering and hiding the proceeds of corruption.

The Textbook Cases: Marcos, Abacha, and Montesinos

The first group of cases examined are the iconic successes of asset recovery, though this success is very much relative. They relate to President Ferdinand Marcos of the Philippines, General Sani Abacha of Nigeria, and Peruvian spymaster Vladimiro Montesinos, right-hand man of President Alberto Fujimori. Although significant sums were recovered from each, over $1.2 billion in total up to 2014 (not including the later Abacha settlement), the suspicion is that much of the stolen wealth was missed. Furthermore, each marks a failure of the systems designed to prevent dirty money from entering the financial system. Although the Marcos money was introduced into Switzerland in the 1970s and 1980s, before anti–money laundering laws, that from Montesinos and Abacha entered in the 1990s. As discussed below, there was a notable lack of accountability for those firms that had received these tainted funds, and so questions about what went wrong in these cases are just as pertinent as what went right.

Marcos

The example of President Ferdinand Marcos of the Philippines was vital in setting the anti-kleptocracy and asset recovery agenda, thanks to both the international media coverage of his plundering and the partial success in repatriating looted wealth held abroad. The Marcos story has been trotted out so regularly as evidence of the potential of asset recovery that further discussion may seem superfluous, yet it is too important to ignore, especially with regard to how this case led to attitudinal and policy change in Switzerland.

Marcos came to power in 1965, entrenching his rule via a declaration of martial law in 1972. He was seen by the United States as a reliable ally against the Communist threat. After a "people power" revolt in 1986, both the army and the United States withdrew their support for Marcos, who was forced into exile in Hawaii, where he died in September 1989. The new government initially claimed that Marcos had looted the country of $1 billion, a figure it quickly revised to $5 billion, or even $10 billion.[20]

Marcos's confederates owned several Filipino banks, meaning that much of the laundering of his looted wealth could be done domestically, at least for the initial stages. Millions of dollars in cash was sent out of the country in bulk to Hong Kong, where it was deposited in local bank accounts and then wired on to other accounts in Switzerland and the United States. Lawyers and financial advisers for the ruling family made extensive efforts to obscure the money trail. Bank accounts and other assets were held in the name of companies from Panama, Switzerland, and the Netherlands Antilles; trusts in Hong Kong and the Cook Islands; and Liechtenstein foundations. Swiss bank accounts that were first held in the name of Ferdinand and Imelda were transferred to a series of sixteen Liechtenstein foundations with signatory powers vested in a Swiss lawyer. The foundations were dissolved from time to time, with the accounts being transferred to a newly created company and then back to a new foundation, in an attempt to further disguise the money trail.[21] Two Swiss bank directors made regular trips to Manila to coordinate the Marcos family's financial affairs.[22] Both the Liechtenstein foundations and the Swiss banks were covered by secrecy provisions under which anyone from either country divulging financial information was liable to criminal prosecution and imprisonment. Furthermore, because the Swiss lawyers intermediated between the Marcoses and the banks, their financial records were covered by another layer of secrecy under legal professional privilege (i.e., attorney-client confidentiality). With the possible exception of the 1977 Agreement of Due Care, this deliberate laundering of the proceeds of foreign corruption was legal under the laws of the day.

Such was the haste of the Marcos entourage in fleeing the Philippines in 1986 that it left behind a good deal of financial information. Furthermore, on the group's arrival at Hawaii, US Customs confiscated more documentation, which was later released to the Philippines. This material was extensively redacted, however, seemingly to hide mention of the theft of US aid and details of donations from Marcos to a variety of US politicians. The last major resource for the asset recovery campaign was that under a 1960 law, all public officials in the Philippines had to lodge a declaration of their financial worth at the time of taking office. On assuming the presidency in 1965, Marcos had declared a total financial worth of only $7,000. The tax authorities calculated that his official earnings in the period 1965–1986 would have amounted to $2.4 million.[23] Under Filipino law, any substantial wealth held in excess of that declared was presumed to be illegal, unless the public official could prove otherwise to a court, and would be forfeited to the state.

Two days after its accession to power, the new Filipino government set up a Presidential Commission on Good Governance to pursue the proceeds of corruption from the previous regime. The commission at first estimated it should have this task wrapped up by the end of the year.[24] In March 1986 the Swiss Federal Council froze funds identified as being controlled by the Marcos family, even before it had received a formal request for assistance from the Philippines.[25] The decision was important in its own right, but also in setting a precedent, because the foreign affairs power had not been used in this fashion before. The Swiss Bankers Association was fiercely critical and attempted to stymie any transfer of bank information to Manila. In the 1970s the Swiss government had refused requests from the Ethiopian and Iranian governments to pursue the assets of their former imperial ruling families, on the grounds that these were "political cases."[26] The Marcos freeze marked the beginning of an epic legal tussle.

The crux of the case in Swiss courts was the gap between the $2.4 million that represented plausible legal earnings and the $356 million found in the accounts controlled by the Marcos family (by the time the money was returned to the Philippines the accumulated interest had raised the total to $658 million). The problem for the Marcos lawyers was to explain the huge difference between these two figures and where the rest of the money had come from. Rather than Ferdinand Marcos or any other individuals being the target of the legal action, the assets themselves were the locus of the case. Unlike a criminal case in a common-law jurisdiction, there was no requirement for the Philippine government to prove its case beyond a reasonable doubt, nor was there a need to link the money with specific corruption crimes.

Even with these unusually favorable circumstances, a somewhat sympathetic Swiss government, and a determined and reasonably well-funded Swiss legal team acting for the Philippine government, the assets were only recovered seventeen years after the initial freeze was put in place. Unable to come up with any rationale for how the money had been amassed, the lawyers for the Marcos family, which still had access to ample funds for legal fees, employed an endless series of procedural challenges and delaying tactics. The money was held in escrow until August 2003, only being released by the Swiss after a decision of the Philippines Supreme Court that the Marcos family had failed to explain how it had legally come by the money.[27]

The logic of the eventual Swiss court decision distills the essence of the anti-kleptocracy norm:

> With reference to the presence of the Marcos estate—it is contrary to the interests of Switzerland, if this country turns into a haven for fugitive capital of criminal monies. . . . It is the primary duty of the legislator, the banks and the banking organizations to ensure that the heads of dictatorial regimes cannot—as happened in the present case—deposit millions of obviously criminal monies in Swiss accounts, if such monies nevertheless are discovered in Switzerland and their restitution requested by the aggrieved foreign state, the mutual assistance administrations and the courts are required to make a decision.[28]

Notwithstanding the fact that Switzerland clearly was a haven for fugitive capital at this time, the court statement laid out the nub of the norm: it is not acceptable for one country to host wealth stolen by the leaders of another country, and that to the extent such wealth is discovered, it should be handed back to the victim country.

Despite this result, the Swiss lawyer hired by the government in Manila maintained that the Swiss authorities had "done only a bare minimum" by soft-pedaling the implementation of laws on the books.[29] In particular, he faulted the decision not to take action against Swiss banks and other intermediaries actively and knowingly involved in laundering corruption funds, a point that comes up again and again in subsequent scandals. For example, Credit Suisse had created false identities for Ferdinand and Imelda.[30] The host government's willingness to either excuse or hold accountable local financial institutions is a crucial determinant of the regime's overall effectiveness. Nevertheless, the Swiss government had all the legal grounds it needed to abandon the case had it wanted to: the Philippines never managed a criminal conviction against any member of the Marcos family, and there was no Mutual Legal Assistance Treaty with Switzerland until 2005.[31] The Swiss government's support for efforts to repatriate the proceeds of corruption from the Marcos regime represents a definite shift toward accepting the anti-kleptocracy norm.

Abacha: "An Extremely Regrettable Case"

Though the money stolen from the Nigerian government by military dictator Sani Abacha and his family during his reign (1993–1998) was spread across more than ten countries, Switzerland was the main destination for the funds (I give more detail on the Abacha affair in chapter 4). The failures of prevention that allowed this money to enter Switzerland are at least as important as the procedure by which funds were later returned to Nigeria. As argued in the Conclusion of this book, if grand corruption is to be significantly reduced, preventive measures must bear more of the weight than the remedial action of asset recovery. With this in mind, it is important to closely examine the performance of Swiss banks in hosting hundreds of millions of dollars stolen from Nigeria to get some general sense of how well or badly the system was working. Rather than being "just one case," an isolated one-off, the Abachas and their henchmen had dealt with a substantial fraction of Switzerland's banking sector, including some of its biggest banks. At least 130 Swiss banks turned out to have accepted Abacha money, with three accounts being held by Abacha personally, the rest by his associates and sons.[32] Subsequent investigations found that over half of the funds had come through banks in London and over a third from the United States,[33] though even when money was deposited direct from Nigeria, apparently no red flags were raised.

Although it is impossible to tell for sure, as such reports are confidential, most if not all reports of suspicions from Swiss banks came in not just after Abacha had died, but only after a public announcement from the Geneva cantonal prosecutor Bernard Bertossa urging banks to examine their accounts.[34] Had anyone bothered to check, the president's official annual salary in Nigeria was around $20,000.[35] The scope of failure to apply the Know Your Customer rule can be gleaned by the fact that Abacha's twenty-six-year-old son could deposit $214 million with Credit Suisse without arousing suspicions about the source of the wealth[36] or even causing the bank to establish its new customer's true identity until almost a year after Abacha Sr.'s death.[37] Abacha's sons had given "Sani" as their family name on their accounts, showing a clear failure of the banks to properly identify their customers,[38] a tactic the Abachas also employed in setting up their UK and Jersey accounts.[39]

A report from the Swiss Federal Banking Commission, "Abacha Funds at Swiss Banks," published in 2000, gives an invaluable, if also incomplete, picture of what had gone wrong. The report begins by outlining what ought to have happened in terms of banks' legal duties. Banks had been required to properly identify their customers since 1977, had been liable for money laundering since 1990, and had been required to report suspicious transactions since 1994. These baseline rules are important for assessing other contemporaneous cases (e.g., Montesinos) but also those that came later (such as the Arab Spring).

Nineteen banks were named and investigated for their dealings with the Abachas.[40] While six were found to have deficient controls, the regulator judged that "individual shortcomings and weaknesses . . . were not sufficiently serious to justify radical measures,"[41] presumably referring to prosecutions or revocations of banking licenses (importantly, then and now, the regulator cannot fine banks). A further three banks, Credit Suisse, Crédit Agricole Indosuez, and Union Bancaire Privée, showed more serious faults, including "gross misjudgments." As the report elliptically put it, the investigation "caused the banks concerned to part company with certain persons in leading positions."[42] Reportedly, the practice of discreetly firing bank employees for compliance failures continues, with such individuals then taking jobs in London instead.[43] In accepting $147 million in three accounts held by Abacha relatives, Crédit Agricole established their true identity and relationship to the dictator but did no further checks on the source of funds.[44] An internal due diligence review mandating that the accounts holding $73 million of Abacha wealth at Union Bancaire Privée (which was also sanctioned for its handling of Arab Spring accounts) was simply ignored.[45] As noted above, Credit Suisse had failed to properly identify the Abacha sons, even after they deposited over $200 million.

After describing Swiss banks' involvement in the Abacha affair as "an extremely regrettable case,"[46] the report was keen to end on a positive note. It offered a partial defense of the banks' performance by noting that the only account Sani Abacha had opened in his own name was closed in 1994, and that other banks had also closed other Abacha-related accounts before 1998 (though often the money simply went to the next bank down the road). Furthermore, the report accurately pointed out that many other countries had been at fault too, that these other countries had failed to publicly investigate their banks' involvement, and that Switzerland's due diligence standards on senior public officials were more stringent than those of any other jurisdiction.[47] It encouraged the Swiss government to press other countries to raise their standards in this area.

For all the information the report contained, however, the basic question of how no one could be seriously at fault when more than $600 million of fairly obviously criminal money had passed through dozens of Swiss banks was not answered. The report held that the existing laws were largely adequate and sound, yet failed to draw the conclusion that either many banks had systematically failed to implement the laws, in which case serious penalties were in order, or that the Swiss Federal Banking Commission itself had been consistently derelict in its duty, or some combination of both. It seems that at least some individuals in the three banks identified as making "gross misjudgments" must have been guilty of money laundering, while the decision not to sanction the banks themselves sent a message of impunity and was symptomatic of regulatory capture.

As for the campaign to return the stolen assets, despite huge difficulties, the Nigerian recovery effort started off with some important advantages. The first was strong domestic political support. President Obasanjo, who was a former Transparency International representative, had been one of the most vocal proponents of asset recovery on the world stage. In connection with the Swiss recovery effort, he had stated, "It is morally reprehensible, unjust, unfair and against all established human values to engage in actions that actually encourage corruption in poor nations to fatten your own country. . . . The thief and the receiver of stolen items are guilty of the same offense."[48] Abacha was dead and his family politically discredited (though incredibly in 2014 the Nigerian government posthumously honored Abacha for helping "to defend the integrity and sovereignty of the country";[49] see chapter 4). Abacha and his clique had looted in such a brazen fashion (e.g., stealing truckloads of cash from the central bank, then wiring it out to personal foreign accounts) that it was often relatively easy to follow the money.[50]

The Nigerian government hired a Swiss legal team led by Enrico Monfrini in September 1999, suspect accounts were frozen the next month, and in December the Swiss received a formal mutual legal assistance request. Abacha's son Mohamed Abacha and Abubakar Bagudu (Abacha Sr.'s right-hand man) were indicted for fraud and money laundering. Nigeria was made a party to the criminal case, allowing it to see the evidence produced at the trial. The crucial development was the Swiss authorities' designation of the Abacha family as a criminal organization formed to embezzle Nigerian state funds. The authorizing law, dated to 1994, defined a criminal organization as one that kept its membership secret and was devoted to obtaining income by criminal means. This created the presumption that all assets owned by that organization were of criminal origin and thus subject to confiscation.[51] The law was explicitly designed to remove the need to link specific assets with specific criminal offenses.[52] It had been developed with an eye to expediting international drug-related money laundering cases. The major innovation of the Abacha case was the designation of a former ruler's family as a criminal organization to facilitate the repatriation of corruption proceeds. In August 2004 the Swiss Federal Office of Justice elected to waive the requirement for a local conviction and repatriate $505 million to Nigeria, a decision upheld in court early the next year. Importantly, these funds were released on the condition that they were spent under the supervision of the World Bank for development purposes, reflecting worries that the repatriated money might simply be stolen by another clutch of corrupt Nigerian politicians.[53] This stipulation echoed a more general debate during the negotiations over the UNCAC, with poor countries arguing for unconditional return but many rich countries wanting some strings attached, a division resolved largely in favor of the poorer states.[54]

In a crucial postscript to the Abacha case, in July 2014 the Nigerian government reached a settlement with the Abacha family concerning other looted funds, approved by the Geneva cantonal prosecutor (not the Swiss federal authorities, who found out through the press[55]). The gist of the agreement was that the Abachas would stop blocking attempts to repatriate funds recovered from various countries to the Nigerian government, and in return the government would drop all current and future civil and criminal legal action against the family.[56] The deal may or may not have been connected with the posthumous rehabilitation of Sani Abacha under President Goodluck Jonathan in March 2014. The sums at stake were huge, almost $1.2 billion, representing the largest ever single repatriation agreement, itself the culmination of several independent efforts by the Nigerian and foreign governments. It covered $242 million recovered in Liechtenstein; $628 million seized or frozen by the US government in accounts in France, Britain, and Jersey; and another $370 million from Luxembourg.[57] The banks found holding these tainted funds included HSBC, Standard Bank, Citibank, Deutsche Bank, and Banque SBA, with the accounts generally in the names of shell companies, trusts, partnerships, and Liechtenstein foundations and establishments. The settlement also specified the lawyers' fees for brokering the deal. Enrico Monfrini was paid $5 million plus 4 percent of the funds recovered from Liechtenstein and Luxembourg, by implication around $29 million in total. A second Swiss lawyer, Christian Lüscher, was awarded 2.8 percent, or approximately $17 million (the payment to the Abachas' lawyer, Nicola Boulton of Byrne and Partners, London, is not recorded).

Reactions to the deal were sharply mixed. The Berne Declaration, a Swiss NGO, described the settlement as "catastrophic," first because of the lack of safeguards on how the money was to be spent after being returned to Nigeria, second because ending efforts to prosecute the Abacha family sent a message of impunity, and third because it was "incomprehensible" that the lawyers were paid so much, "as this money belongs to the Nigerian population."[58] These themes were echoed in the relevant Nigerian press coverage and by the Nigerian Network on Stolen Assets.[59] On the other hand, an asset recovery lawyer in London judged that the deal showed Monfrini "was worth every penny."[60] Monfrini had been working for the Nigerian government since 1999 on a contingency basis, according to which he was paid only on recovery of funds, if any funds were in fact recovered.[61] More broadly, the Abacha settlement throws into sharp relief the tension between maximizing the looted wealth recovered, a goal probably best advanced by striking such bargains, and promoting accountability for grand corruption crimes, which is severely undermined by them.

The determination with which the Swiss cantonal and federal authorities pursued the Abacha money inside the country and beyond from 1999 on, and the innovative use of legal doctrine, reflected a genuine commitment to this cause. Given the lack of any convictions in Nigeria and the compromised state of the Nigerian judiciary, which would have been unlikely to meet Swiss mutual legal assistance standards, it would have been very easy for the Swiss government to wash its hands of the matter on the grounds that nothing could be done under existing law. Indeed, this is largely the option the British, French, and other governments chose to take.[62]

Montesinos

Like the Abacha case, that of Vladimiro Montesinos, head of Peru's national intelligence agency under President Alberto Fujimori (1990–2000), relates to laundering conducted in the 1990s. Montesinos had taken kickbacks for arms transfers and extorted money from both legitimate businesses and drug traffickers.[63] In September 2000 the first of a series of leaked videos that Montesinos himself had recorded showing him issuing huge cash bribes was aired on Peruvian television and then around the world. Shortly afterward, CAI Suisse bank lodged a Suspicious Transaction Report in connection with an account connected to Montesinos, quickly sparking a broader investigation and prompting reports from other banks.[64] The case became one of the quickest ever asset recovery cases, taking a lightning-fast two years. The Swiss froze $113 million and invited the Peruvian government to submit a mutual legal assistance request. The Swiss released information about the accounts and account holders even before the request was lodged.[65] Some of those Montesinos associates unmasked by this information struck a deal with the new government in Lima to waive their rights to stolen funds and to provide further information, which was then passed back to Swiss authorities. The Peruvian prosecutor traveled to Switzerland to help coordinate the campaign.[66] In June 2002 a Swiss magistrate decided that $77.5 million represented kickbacks from various arms purchases placed on behalf of Montesinos and should be repatriated (notably, there had been no criminal conviction in Peru).[67] The money had sometimes entered Switzerland directly from Peru but more often via a network of shell companies from the United States and Luxembourg.[68]

The Montesinos case is something of the poster child of the asset recovery community, being a rare instance of the system working almost as smoothly as it is meant to in theory. This includes the progression from initial reports to the quick freeze and speedy exchange of information from host to victim country, first informally and then formally, and the (relatively) rapid decision to seize and return the funds, with no need for a foreign conviction. While the case was a success in terms of remedial action, it was much less of an endorsement of the system designed to prevent such offenses happening in the first place. Although two Swiss banks had closed Montesinos-controlled accounts due to concerns about the source of his funds even before he had run into political problems,[69] many other banks had accepted his custom.[70] The quick freezing indicates that the problem was not so much banks being deceived by the web of shell companies and front men as a failure to do anything more than a perfunctory check on the source of funds or a cynical decision to host funds that banks knew were probably the proceeds of corruption.[71] Because there was no regulatory investigation of banks' performance in this instance, there is less information to go on, but as with Abacha, the fact that no banks were punished despite seemingly serious due diligence faults suggests the low priority accorded to enforcing the rules.

Failures: Duvalier, Bhutto, and Zardari

Critics have argued that judging the success of asset recovery by the three cases above presents a highly misleading picture of (relative) success.[72] The critics are right, in that the defining facts of the anti-kleptocracy regime are the vast amounts of money estimated as being stolen compared with the tiny proportion recovered.[73] The examples presented below, where either no money at all was recovered or a tiny amount after almost thirty years of effort, are much more typical, closely paralleling the contours of the experience with Mobutu, as already described in chapter 1. The cases from the 1990s involving the rulers of Pakistan illustrate problems with effectiveness that are in some ways even more telling: namely, the failing of the preventive system designed to screen out corruption proceeds from the banking system (the Duvalier money entered Switzerland before anti–money laundering rules were in place). These due diligence failures by banks have been reinforced by the regulator's decision not to sanction banks for these shortcomings.

Jean-Claude "Baby Doc" Duvalier

Despite the qualified success of the Marcos decision, the nearly contemporaneous case of Haiti's Duvalier family has shown the limits of the system.[74] Amazingly, the campaign to return the Duvaliers' stolen wealth in Switzerland lasted even longer than that for the Marcos money. It began soon after the downfall of Jean-Claude "Baby Doc" Duvalier in February 1986 and was still not complete thirty years later. Allowing for the costs of the legal fees, financially the recovery was probably a net loss. It throws into stark relief one of the most important obstacles to successful asset recovery: the lack of investigative and judicial capacity in poor and unstable victim countries. In this way, efforts to recover money stolen by the Duvalier regime mirror those of the post-Mobutu governments in Congo. This underlines the fundamental point that if asset recovery is to succeed, rich host countries must be prepared to do most of the work for poor victim countries. This realization, and the frustrations and reverses of the campaign to recover the Duvalier stolen assets, provided the impetus for perhaps the most far-reaching and innovative piece of national legislation on asset recovery, Switzerland's Restitution of Illicit Assets Act of 2011, informally known as the "Lex Duvalier."

After the death of his father, President François "Papa Doc" Duvalier, in 1971, Baby Doc presided over a regime that was probably even more debauched and indifferent to the fate of its citizens than that of Marcos.[75] Like Mobutu, Marcos, and many others, however, the Duvalier family were staunch anti-Communists and thus Western political support and aid kept on flowing, excepting only brief periods of estrangement under Presidents Kennedy and Carter. The Reagan administration helped to evacuate the ruling clique with as much of their loot as they could carry in 1986 in the face of the food riots that forced their departure. Shortly after the change of regime, the new Haitian government requested Swiss help in finding and returning proceeds of the Duvaliers' corruption in Swiss banks. In a now familiar manner, the family had used Swiss and English lawyers to establish accounts held by corporate intermediaries, including a Liechtenstein foundation and Panamanian shell company.[76] A number of relevant accounts were found and the money frozen, yet there was little further progress. A crucial case in France against Duvalier to recover $120 million was lost in 1987. The Haitian government was preoccupied with endemic political instability, and even if its attention had been more focused, the judicial system had been wrecked by decades of dictatorial rule.

In 1988 the government's own US lawyers hired to recover stolen assets expressed their frustration with the complete lack of support or even response from Haiti in a letter to the prime minister: "The behavior of your ministers leaves us no alternative except to conclude that your ministers apparently want our efforts on behalf of Haiti to fail, are not concerned that Haiti will lose the substantial investment it has made in pursuing the Duvaliers, and want the Duvaliers to keep the money they stole."[77]

The government did not recover any money but was stuck with a $1.2 million legal bill. Baby Doc enjoyed a comfortable period in exile in France, unmolested by local authorities who, true to form for the French government, did nothing to bring him to account for either his human rights or corruption crimes, even after he was placed in the sixth spot of

Transparency International's 2004 top ten most corrupt leaders list.[78] Most of the Duvalier family fortune was dissipated by lavish living and then Jean-Claude's divorce in 1993.

In 2007 an attempt to restart the hunt for the missing money (co-sponsored by the newly formed Stolen Asset Recovery Initiative) by pursuing money laundering charges in Switzerland failed. In 2009 the Swiss government attempted to use the same mechanism as had been employed with the Abacha money: declaring that the Duvalier family was a criminal organization. This would mean that because there was no credible account of how the money had been obtained legitimately, the funds would be confiscated and returned to Haiti for humanitarian purposes. At first this seemed to promise a solution to not only the relatively small sum at stake ($5.7 million) but also the generic problem of kleptocracy: when senior foreign officials have vastly more money than can be explained by their legitimate income, when they rule over or have ruled over a country known to have a serious corruption problem, but when no actual criminal conviction has been recorded in either the victim or host country.

Dashing such hopes, however, the Swiss Supreme Court threw out this ruling, deciding that the statute of limitations had expired fifteen years after the initial claim, that is, 2001.[79] The money was once again frozen in place in Switzerland via the intervention of the Swiss Federal Council. After the passage of the Restitution of Illicit Assets Act in 2011, the government finally succeeded in persuading the court of its earlier argument that the funds represented the proceeds of corruption. In September 2013 a Swiss court granted permission to repatriate the funds to Haiti, but at time of writing, the Swiss government had still not found a suitable way of repatriating the money.[80] Baby Doc himself died in October 2014 after having returned to Haiti in 2011, just before the new Swiss act came into force. Observers speculated that this may have been an effort to beat the law by showing he had no case to answer in Haiti.[81] Although he was charged with corruption offenses by the Haitian government, these were later dismissed.[82]

"Lex Duvalier" put Switzerland at the forefront of asset recovery. It was explicitly designed for countries where weak institutions precluded the use of normal channels like mutual legal assistance. In such instances, where the sums at stake are hugely in excess of demonstrated legal earnings for a senior public official and the level of corruption in the country in question is high, the burden of proof is on defendants to show why money should *not* be confiscated and returned. Akin to non-conviction-based forfeiture, it targets assets rather than people as such.[83] The Swiss government won public and private praise for the new law.[84] As one (American) former StAR official put it, "By designing the RIAA legislation, Switzerland has gained a reputation as a world leader in asset recovery, and in many ways, it now serves as a model to other countries."[85] A Nigerian minister involved in the hunt for the Abacha loot similarly noted in 2002 that "Switzerland has been particularly co-operative"[86] (a sentiment the author has heard confirmed elsewhere[87]). Nevertheless, the "Lex Duvalier" does not constitute a silver bullet for the problems of asset recovery. Because the law comes into play only after the conventional state-to-state remedies have been exhausted, it mandates that a formal mutual legal assistance request has to be filed, a significant difficulty.[88] This means the process of asset recovery will still take many years. It is limited to failed states and/or states undergoing a transition, thus excluding incumbent kleptocrats. Any confiscation order can be appealed to the Swiss Supreme Court.[89]

To the extent that there is a positive conclusion to be taken from Switzerland's experience with the Duvaliers, it is the law that informally bears their name. The money recovered may have accrued some symbolic importance, but it was essentially trivial and was unlikely to have even covered the lawyers' bills. As with the Marcos case, the bankers and lawyers who received and hid this wealth before 1986 were almost certainly deliberately aiding and abetting grand corruption, yet by the laws of the day they were not committing any crime.

Benazir Bhutto and Ali Asif Zardari

Benazir Bhutto, daughter of executed Pakistani prime minister Zulfikar Ali Bhutto, was herself elected to power in 1988–1990 and then again 1993–1996, before being assassinated while campaigning for the 2008 election. Her husband, Ali Asif Zardari, served as president after Bhutto's death, from 2008 to 2013. Both were publicly implicated in a range of serious corruption offenses from 1990 onward, with the financial infrastructure centering on the Geneva office of lawyer Jens Schlegelmilch.[90]

An informant sold a sheaf of documents, apparently taken from Schlegelmilch's office, to the Pakistani government for $1 million after Bhutto's second term as prime minister. At this time, she had been replaced by her bitter rival, Nawaz Sharif (himself also the subject of accusations of major corruption[91]). Bhutto had gone into exile while Sharif's government held Zardari prisoner from 1997 to 2004. The documents were later authenticated by the *New York Times* and informed a Swiss money laundering prosecution.[92] The file included letters from prominent Swiss and French firms agreeing to kickbacks of 6–9 percent in return for Pakistani government contracts (bribing foreign government officials was legal in both Switzerland and France at the time). The bribes were paid to Zardari-controlled British Virgin Islands shell companies that had been set up for this purpose by Schlegelmilch and his colleague Didier Plantin. From 1995 on, these companies held accounts with Citibank in Geneva and one in Dubai, as well as another with UBS in Switzerland, all opened with Schlegelmilch's help. He was the signatory on each of the accounts, but Zardari or other members of the Bhutto family were identified to senior officials in Citibank as the real owner of the shell companies.[93] A limit of $40 million was placed on the accounts, though this was later breached without consequences. The bank apparently did not do anything to check the source of funds. By way of context, on their asset declarations in 1996 the family declared net assets of $1.2 million, with Bhutto declaring her income at $42,200 and Zardari $13,100. Both denied holding any overseas property or bank accounts.[94] Citi reviewed the Zardari accounts in 1996 in light of increasing corruption allegations against Zardari and Bhutto but decided that these charges were political smears and took Zardari's claims about the legitimate provenance of the money at face value. In January 1997, however, a new Citi senior official took a different view and ensured the accounts were closed. The money was moved to three other Swiss banks.[95]

The ever-resourceful Schlegelmilch also set up an elaborate corporate structure to hold a property in Britain: the money came from accounts in Geneva held by British Virgin Island and Panamanian shell companies, with the property being held by three Isle of Man companies, owned by two UK trusts, and controlled by a Liechtenstein foundation.[96] The Swiss lawyer's handiwork greatly complicated efforts to link the First Couple to the property until, after years of denial, Zardari admitted he was the owner in 2004, immediately before claiming he was mentally unfit to participate in legal proceedings.[97]

In September 1997 the Swiss federal prosecutor Carla del Ponte launched a money laundering investigation into $12 million in bribes paid to the shell companies' Swiss accounts by two Swiss customs inspections companies.[98] In August 2003 Schlegelmilch, Bhutto, and Zardari were all convicted in a Swiss court of money laundering, awarded four-to-six-month suspended jail sentences, and ordered to pay $11 million in restitution to Pakistan, scant consolation in light of the $2 billion Pakistan had lost in customs revenues as a result of the scam. Bhutto's undoing in the case was her purchase of a £117,000 diamond necklace with funds drawn directly from one of the shell companies' accounts set up to receive the bribe payments.[99] After this conviction was overturned on appeal, a Geneva magistrate began a wider investigation into the affair, leading to the freezing of $60 million of Zardari/Bhutto funds. In the waning days of General Perez Musharaf's regime and immediately before the assassination of Bhutto in December 2007, Musharaf and Bhutto struck a deal whereby the Pakistani government would grant the couple amnesty and withdraw its cooperation with the Swiss investigation. As a result, and following Zardari's victory in the presidential election shortly afterward, the Swiss investigating magistrate dropped the case.

Even with the relatively generous terms of Swiss law, asset recovery almost always takes two to tango, and failures are at least as often the fault of the victim government as the host country. The Nigerian and Philippines governments had doggedly stuck with the drive to recover their assets, while the atypically rapid repatriation of the Montesinos funds imposed comparatively fewer demands on Peru. By contrast, perhaps understandably, Haiti and Congo did not consider this cause a priority, while horse-trading in Pakistan scuttled the chances of holding Bhutto and Zardari accountable.

The Arab Spring and Beyond

In January 2011 the head of the Swiss Bankers Association went on record to assert that "no Swiss bank would knowingly accept money from a corrupt head of state."[100] His timing proved to be unfortunate. In that month the swelling Arab Spring movement spread from Tunisia to Libya, Egypt, and several other countries in the region. This wave of uprisings publicized the kleptocratic nature of the incumbent regimes and the extent to which their stolen wealth was held in Western financial centers, including Switzerland. In response, the Swiss government led the world in the speed with which asset freezes were applied to suspicious funds, coming within hours of key political events. These freezes caught $474 million connected with the Egyptian regime and another $66 million of Tunisian assets (it is difficult to separate Libyan state assets frozen under UN sanctions from those of the Gaddafi family).[101] The Swiss Department of Foreign Affairs also set up a Task Force on Asset Recovery to liaise with victim countries and international partners, and perhaps also with an eye to spreading the word on Switzerland's good behavior in this realm via public diplomacy.[102]

While the early freezing was a positive, and a marked contrast with the United Kingdom, which took weeks to do the same, the familiar question was why the money had been allowed in at all. The key Know Your Customer rules mandating special scrutiny for foreign senior officials and criminalizing the receipt of foreign corruption funds had been in place for years. Though the scale and specifics of corruption among the various ruling families may not have been clear, the basic fact that they were living well beyond their means thanks to misappropriated public money was. Once again, the spur to action was not their corruption per se but their fall from power. This fact is strikingly demonstrated by a jump in Suspicious Transaction Reports in 2011 by Swiss banks concerning clients from affected countries, even though the regimes in question had not become any more corrupt in the space of twelve months and even though these reports related mainly to existing commercial relationships, not new business. From 2010 to 2011 the number of reports rose from 0 to 55 for Egypt, from 0 to 33 for Libya, from 0 to 7 for Syria, and from 0 to 40 for Tunisia.[103] Cherif Bassiouni, an Egyptian American jurist closely familiar with the Egyptian recovery efforts, describes a standard "U-turn" scheme of corruption involving Swiss banks as follows.[104]

Someone from the two hundred or so families that comprised the core of the Mubarak-era elite would come to Switzerland with $10 million and an investment proposal. The money would have been accumulated through corruption over many years, and thus had been at least partially laundered in Egypt, as well as being mixed with legitimate earnings. As such, even a reasonably thorough effort by the receiving Swiss bank to check the source of funds would be unlikely to turn up anything untoward, and in any case banks seem to have taken clients' explanations at face value unless they were obviously implausible.[105] The Egyptian would be paired up with a personal banker, a lawyer, and an investment adviser. This individual would then return the money to Egypt to capitalize a new, locally incorporated company to build a hotel. By offering shares in the new company to bribe officials, the investor would secure the land and necessary infrastructure at well below market price, perhaps even for free, in addition to a generous tax holiday. If the project were now worth $20 million, the investor would take a loan from an Egyptian bank to this value, use half the loan to build the hotel and bring back the other half to Switzerland, together with the original $10 million. The investor would now have a clean $20 million in Switzerland while the Egyptian bank bore all the risk in case the hotel project failed. Much of the Arab Spring wealth held overseas was a sort of "legal corruption": bespoke legislation or regulation was specifically designed to generate windfall profits for favored insiders.[106] Such arrangements were certainly against the public interest, but not technically illegal. However, they were often covered in the Egyptian press and were largely public knowledge, a fact that brings into question how these individuals got access to the Swiss and other Western financial systems.[107]

By comparison, however, not only did banks in Arab countries like Saudi Arabia and the United Arab Emirates accept such money without question (among those in the policy community the UAE and particularly Dubai seem to win an informal straw poll of the leading haven for international corruption funds), but with the exception of Lebanon, they flatly refused requests to assist with tracing corruption funds.[108]

The new postrevolutionary Arab governments experienced many of the same frustrations as victim governments before them in trying to recover stolen wealth. A lawyer acting for the Egyptian government complained that although assets had been frozen in Switzerland, the new Egyptian government was not entitled to find out what they were. They were stuck in the catch-22 situation of having to submit a mutual legal assistance request to find out these details, but in order to lodge the request they needed knowledge of the assets.[109] Egypt was made a party to court proceedings in Switzerland but could only hand-copy evidence, which could not be used in Egyptian trials. Even this privilege was withdrawn in December 2012 with renewed political instability in Egypt. There was a great deal of disorganization and even feuding between the different agencies in the post-Mubarak government responsible for asset recovery (as detailed in the following chapter). Even after Mubarak had been acquitted of nearly all serious charges by 2015 in Egyptian courts, to a large extent pulling the rug out from under asset recovery actions abroad, the government in Cairo maintained that the Swiss should still be handing back assets.

In response to the difficulties exposed by the Arab Spring, in 2013 the Swiss government moved to further strengthen its "Lex Duvalier" with a new "Lex Ben Ali."[110] Once again, the particular problem was dealing with victim countries whose courts and human rights practices do not meet the standard for regular Swiss mutual legal assistance. The new law is designed to ease the exchange of evidence with victim countries, for example to provide more information on assets that have been frozen. Under certain circumstances it would allow for administrative confiscation and repatriation of assets, rather than having to go to court, although there is still a right of appeal. The "Lex Ben Ali" broadens the range of victim countries that may qualify for such treatment, yet there is some debate over whether it would even cover the Arab Spring countries. The requirement to at least attempt a formal mutual legal assistance request may rule out completely failed states like postrevolutionary Libya, whereas the Tunisian judiciary may ironically be working too well to qualify.[111]

As was the case after the Abacha affair, the bank regulator (since renamed the Swiss Financial Market Supervisory Authority, FINMA) conducted an investigation into the role of Swiss banks hosting Arab kleptocrats' money. It audited twenty banks and took enforcement action against six.[112] The regulator emphasized that in general the system had worked as it should, with most shortcomings being minor and only a few more serious lapses. These included failing to independently verify clients' explanations for the source of their wealth, missing spelling variations of the same name (e.g., Mohamed and Mohammed), defining Politically Exposed Person too narrowly, and in two cases failing to apply enhanced due diligence even though account holders were found to be high risk. The Swiss Bankers Association unsurprisingly saw the report as an endorsement of its members' probity, while NGOs were critical of both the lack of specifics and the lack of action. Mark Pieth, who was chair of the OECD's anti-bribery committee and had worked on the Lex Duvalier, noted, "The report says that in two cases they [banks] were aware and helping to hide the money, if that's the case, it's money laundering and they will have a criminal case to answer."[113] No prosecution eventuated, however. Swiss sources suggested to me that an earlier draft of the report had contained significantly stronger condemnations of many more banks' performance but that these judgments were watered down in the final version.

Certainly there had been no shortage of other dubious behavior at Swiss banks during this period in the form of conspiring with thousands of Americans and almost certainly other foreigners to evade taxes in their home jurisdictions.[114] Until beaten down by US pressure, Switzerland refused to cooperate with investigations into such behavior on the grounds that tax evasion was an administrative but not a criminal offense under Swiss law and hence did not trump bank secrecy.

A final point relates to the question of pursuing incumbent kleptocrats rather than those who have recently fallen from power, like the Arab Spring rulers or Yanukovych in Ukraine. As discussed in the preceding chapter, both politically and legally it is one thing to go after former heads of state and their families, but quite another while they are still in office. Here Switzerland has a relatively good record, as two recent examples attest. Both cases are yet to be completed, but they illustrate the trend toward current leaders increasingly finding themselves in the crosshairs of the campaign against grand corruption.

The first of these cases is that of Gulnara Karimova, part-time diplomat, professor, pop star, fashion designer, businesswoman, philanthropist, but especially daughter and at one stage heir apparent to Uzbekistan's dictatorial ruler Islam Karimov. In June 2012 Karimova's personal assistant, Gayane Avakyan, sought to withdraw money from an account held in the name of a Gibraltar shell company Takilant with Swiss private bank Lombard Odier. Avakyan was not an authorized signatory and was refused, but her attempt and several subsequent efforts to retrieve the money led the bank to report the matter to the Swiss anti–money laundering agency.[115] The resulting investigation led to a freeze on over $900 million linked to Karimova that was suspected to be bribes from Scandinavian and Russian telecommunications firms.[116] Sparked by the Swiss moves, the investigation soon spread to Sweden, the Netherlands, and the United States, leading in February 2016 to a $795 million bribery settlement. Inquiries turned up a financial trail involving Citibank in London, Standard Chartered in Hong Kong, and two Latvian banks, Parex and Aizkraukles, as well as real estate worth more than $50 million in France and Hong Kong.[117]

Karimova fled Geneva after her diplomatic immunity as a UN representative was withdrawn and later fell out of favor in Uzbekistan, though the foreign financial investigations continue.[118]

The case of Malaysian prime minister Najib Razak illustrates the diplomatic tensions inherent in investigating kleptocracy. As well as being prime minister and finance minister, Najib chaired Malaysia's 1MDB national wealth fund, launched in 2009. By mid-2015 it became apparent that 1MDB was massively in debt to the tune of $10 billion; at the same time, reports surfaced that $680 million had been moved into Najib's personal account shortly before the 2013 Malaysian election. An investigation in Malaysia into whether 1MDB's losses and the transfer to the prime minister were linked was quickly shut down when Najib's government gutted the country's accountability mechanisms. The bizarre explanation of the Malaysian attorney-general in January 2016 was that the $680 million represented a personal donation to Najib from a Saudi royal, that all bar $61 million had been returned, that there was no connection to 1MDB, and so there was nothing to investigate.[119] Najib declared his satisfaction that "the matter has comprehensively been put to rest." Spoiling any sense of closure, however, the next week Swiss attorney-general Michael Lauber announced that his investigations suggested that $4 billion had been misappropriated from companies connected with 1MDB by unnamed Malaysian state officials. The Malaysian government was not amused. Its communication minister, Salleh Said Keruak, responded in the press, "It's very unusual, and against normal protocol, for a senior official of one country to speak publicly on the internal matters of another country."[120] However patently false the minister's subsequent protestations about his boss's innocence were, on this point at least he was right: for one government to effectively accuse another of corruption in this way is a major breach of diplomatic etiquette and of normal interstate relations. It is another illustration of the puzzle as to why Switzerland would seek to take up this cause.

Why Did the Swiss Government Get Religion?

Though the evidence presented above doesn't all point in one direction, Switzerland seems to have come further than any other country with regard to the anti-kleptocracy norm. In popular imagination and in large part in fact, Switzerland was long the default option for corrupt senior leaders and their families looking to hold illicit wealth abroad. Swiss banks, law firms, and other businesses unselfconsciously offered their services in laundering the loot with the tacit knowledge and acquiescence of the government. Corruption in foreign countries was seen as completely irrelevant to the Swiss reality, despite the dense financial networks centered on Switzerland.

By the time of the Arab Spring revolutions, however, things had changed. The Swiss government had become one of the most enthusiastic and committed proponents of the global normative and policy shift against hosting the proceeds of foreign grand corruption. Not just rhetoric, this shift was reflected in innovative new legislation that made it less difficult (if still not easy) for victim countries to recover stolen wealth. In important instances from 1986 onward the Swiss had taken a highly flexible reading of their own laws to facilitate repatriating assets. The result is that more corruption funds have been repatriated from Switzerland than any other country. What explains this turnaround?

Concerns about the country's reputation seem to have been central.[121] It was not just that the successive scandals built up an accumulating picture of criminal complicity—the normative goalposts were shifting. "Swiss bank account" had become a shorthand for dirty money at a time in the 1990s when transnational crime and money laundering were moving to the forefront of the global political agenda (even if objectively banks in countries like Britain and the United States were little better).[122] Switzerland's unique stigma in this regard is unlike the case of major international banks, which have by and large been tarred with the same brush when it comes to corruption, meaning that reputational concerns are not a lever for reform. For the reasons discussed in chapter 1, having received the proceeds of foreign corruption, Switzerland could no longer say that this was a foreign problem. As the government noted after the Abacha scandal, "The mere fact that significant assets of dubious origin, from people close to former Nigerian President Sani Abacha, were deposited at Swiss banks is highly unsatisfactory and damages the image of Switzerland as a financial center" (though there was no evidence of any loss of deposits).[123] While the Swiss report of June 2015 on national money laundering risks emphasizes the need to be "a morally sound, attractive and efficient financial center," the rest of the world has been skeptical. US officials recount with some sympathy the Swiss being routinely pilloried at the UNCAC negotiations by other delegations as a haven for stolen wealth, even though the Swiss were very supportive of the asset recovery provisions of the treaty.[124] An official from the Swiss anti–money laundering unit recounted to me how his French in-laws scoff at the idea of Switzerland turning away dirty money and expressed his dismay concerning James Bond films in which the criminals always stash their money in Swiss banks.[125]

In interviews some members of the financial services industry indicated their consternation that the Swiss government was sincerely seeking to push out illicit money, rather than just going through the motions, as they had hoped. These financiers were gloomy about the implications for the industry, though commercially the loss of tax evasion money was seen to be more of a concern than corruption funds per se (not that the two are necessarily exclusive).[126]

Arguing that the Swiss government changed course to safeguard the country's reputation raises as many questions as it answers, however. Reputational concerns might reflect heartfelt individual or collective feelings of shame or guilt, or an entirely cynical calculation that the financial center would make more money conforming to changing standards than defying them. There are many points between these two extremes, and different actors, and perhaps even the same individuals, in all likelihood were prompted by mixed motives, especially in such a decentralized, confederal system. In narrowing the range of uncertainty it may help to start with the most hard-nosed presumption first, that is, that it was all about the money. This style of reasoning appeals both to the standard social science presumption of self-interested actors and to common sense. Yet it is hard to see the monetary payoff for the Swiss actions.

As discussed in chapter 1, the countries that are most prone to suffer from grand corruption tend to be those that have the least political and economic clout in international politics. Switzerland could have safely ignored the requests for help from the Philippine, Nigerian, and other governments with little fear of meaningful material sanctions, especially as these governments have often had an intermittent and ambivalent commitment to the cause of fighting high-level political corruption. Switzerland has been far more willing to defy the will of rich and powerful actors like the United States and the European Union when it came to bank secrecy on tax matters than poor, weak victims of kleptocracy.[127] The argument that if

Switzerland had developed a reputation as a haven for criminal money this would frighten off legitimate business is not convincing; Switzerland had long had this reputation without negatively affecting business. As chapter 5's case study of Australia illustrates and the 2014 StAR report *Few and Far* on asset recovery confirms, many OECD countries like France have done little or nothing to tackle foreign corruption proceeds without experiencing any souring of business sentiment or international sanctions.

A more nuanced account reasons that the Swiss banking industry is about 4 percent of GDP.[128] Of the banks' business, around half is domestic, half foreign. If half of the foreign money is problematic, representing corruption, tax evasion, or other crimes, then this share of the financial sector represents about 1 percent of Swiss GDP, and roughly the same share of employment and taxes.[129] The Swiss government increasingly seems to have come to the conclusion that holding on to this 1 percent of the economy was not worth the trouble and embarrassment, especially as inaction was only going to make the situation worse. Private estimates are that Switzerland might lose something like a quarter to a third of its banking industry as a result of determined efforts to root out both tax evasion funds from the United States and the rest of Europe and corruption funds from the rest of the world, though so far declines are much more moderate.[130] Once the decision was taken to flush out corruption proceeds, it was then in Switzerland's interest to take the lead on this cause, and to do so in a very high-profile manner to stanch the bad publicity and reap whatever reputational dividends there were to be had at home and abroad. Hence perhaps the "Lausanne Process," a series of practitioner workshops on asset recovery hosted by the Swiss government since 2001 that have brought together officials from host and victim countries.[131]

Even this somewhat Machiavellian analysis depends on a social logic of the Swiss government being sensitive to embarrassment, ostracism, and shaming rather than a pecuniary logic. Overlaid on this means-end calculation, the broader international changes of attitude toward corruption and policy learning on development aid seem to have significantly affected Switzerland. Although there is a temptation to think that "the real reason" things happen in politics is because of the pursuit of money or power, this belief should be a guide in the consideration of evidence, not a substitute for evidence.

Remaining Vulnerabilities

What overall judgments can be reached about the effectiveness of the anti-kleptocracy regime in Switzerland, aside from the positive change over time described above? The Swiss have perhaps the most "victim-friendly" asset recovery laws of any state. When governments of victim countries have been willing to persevere, Switzerland has shown the political will and technical skills to make its asset recovery laws work. Yet when we compare the system in practice with the rules on the books, both domestic law and international standards, the verdict is less flattering, especially when it comes to the effective enforcement of preventive measures. Thus the general rules of asset recovery still apply: for every dollar or franc of funds recovered, there are almost certainly many more that have been safely laundered.

In some cases these failures occur because offers from Switzerland to victim countries simply are not taken up. As well as the public rebuke of the Congolese government for failing to take action to recover the fragments of the Mobutu loot referenced earlier, Kenya declined an offer of assistance from the Swiss government in shutting down an investigation of top-level political corruption after 2003.[132] As noted, an amnesty deal in Pakistan swiftly ended a long-running Swiss money laundering investigation of Benazir Bhutto and Ali Asif Zardari. Although in some instances the Swiss were prepared to meet the requesting country more than half-way, even with the enhanced asset recovery provisions put into law in 2011 a minimum of support from the victim country was essential.

Kleptocratic elites from Africa, the Middle East, central Asia, and eastern Europe continue to use Switzerland as their playground and home away from home. Swiss bankers maintain that even if many or perhaps even most of the nouveaux riches from the former Soviet Union first made their fortune through criminal activities, the 1990s are now ancient history, and hence this money is legitimate.[133] Earlier, one of the perverse consequences of the desire to assist victim countries was to help the politically motivated persecution of Mikhail Khodorkovsky by the Kremlin in freezing Yukos assets before they were seized by the Russian government.[134]

The most consistent problem concerns the preventive failures to stop dirty money from entering the Swiss financial system and the related failure of the authorities to hold banks and other intermediaries accountable for these lapses. In the wake of the Arab Spring, well after the reforms occasioned by the Marcos and Abacha cases, the chair of the OECD Anti-Bribery Committee, Mark Pieth, remarked that the Swiss banks' system of reporting money suspected to be the proceeds of corruption "does not work. It is quite obvious that the rules exist, but they are applied with insufficient care. This also means that regulators are not doing their job."[135] In this judgment Pieth echoed the verdict of other Swiss observers in drawing a distinction between the law on the books and how it has been applied in practice.[136]

The incentives for Swiss bankers are similar to those for bankers elsewhere: more business for the bank means more money for the individual. Relationship managers in private client banking are awarded bonuses for extra custom but seldom if ever for the stringent application of Know Your Customer rules.[137] As noted in previous chapters, this creates a bias to bend the rules in favor of not-quite-clean money (though as one banker reasonably put it, how else would you expect a bank to reward its staff if not for generating more business?). Once again, Swiss banks use the same commercial databases of senior foreign officials as banks in other countries, and hence are vulnerable to their shortcomings. The same jokes about those in compliance units being "business prevention officers" are in circulation (or variations such as "bankers get the business, lawyers complicate the business, and compliance officers lose the business").[138] A further parallel is the sentiment that banks and other financial firms engage in anti–money laundering measures to assuage regulators and prevent fines and sanctions, not to screen out or detect criminal money.[139] In this sense, the means have become the ends. Unlike the country as a whole, there is little evidence that banks suffer from the reputation effect, whereby they are supposedly deterred from taking tainted funds for fear of compromising their public image and relations with customers, shareholders, and other third parties.

A partial defense from the banks is that they routinely close high-risk customer accounts but that no one beyond the bank, the client, and perhaps the Financial Intelligence Unit knows about this. If banks do the right thing one hundred times but the wrong thing once, only the last will be publicized.[140] In recent cases like that of Uzbekistan's First Daughter, bank reports have been crucial as the starting point for investigations. But even if many or most banks are doing the right thing in screening out suspicious clients behind the scenes, the Swiss government and in particular the regulator FINMA have in effect given a free pass where banks have not enforced the rules, leaving banks able to turn a blind eye to the inward flow of dirty money from abroad. Because prevention is a far more effective means of combating corruption than the long, expensive, and uncertain path of asset recovery, this gap constitutes a crucial flaw, even if we take into account the amounts of stolen wealth returned from Switzerland.

4

The United Kingdom

Development, or Sleaze and the City?

On April 29, 2014, the British government hosted the Ukraine Forum on Asset Recovery, a multilateral gathering to aid the new government in Kyiv in its search for the money stolen by former president Yanukovych and his cronies, who were overthrown after widespread popular protests the month before. At the same time as the demonstrations in Maidan Square that presaged the fall of Yanukovych, a small group of Ukrainians picketed the most expensive private residence in London.[1] A penthouse at One Hyde Park had been bought by Ukrainian oligarch Rinat Akhmetov for £136 million in April 2011. Some journalists and scholars have linked the highly litigious Akhmetov to the corruption that is endemic in the interlinked business and political circles of Ukraine,[2] accusations Akhmetov has strongly denied.

The tension between the British government's efforts to take the moral lead in countering kleptocracy while also hosting spectacular wealth from all over the world, some alleged to be of dubious provenance, symbolizes the conflict between principle and pragmatism at the heart of this book.

In the very same 2015 speech, Prime Minister Cameron declared that "London is not a place to stash your dodgy cash" but also admitted that "we know that some high-value properties—particularly in London—are being bought by people overseas through anonymous shell companies, some of them with plundered or laundered cash."[3] Britain has a particular importance in the campaign against kleptocracy. The City of London exerts a magnetic influence on much of the world's wealth as a financial center and a playground for "ultra-high net worth individuals" from abroad. A commercial report listed London as the world's leading luxury real estate market.[4] The United Kingdom is more dependent on its financial sector than any other G20 economy, imbuing this industry with considerable power over the government and regulators.

The Blair and Cameron governments both came to office firmly in favor of more support for the good governance agenda (including anticorruption), as discussed in chapter 1. From 1997 onward the Blair New Labour government trumpeted an ethical foreign policy, reflected in the creation of the Department for International Development (DfID) and by the United Kingdom's persistent moves in a variety of multilateral fora to advance development by internationalizing the fight against corruption. This was more than just rhetoric: the British government more than doubled its foreign annual aid budget under Blair from £3.2 billion to £7 billion.[5] Seeking a kinder, gentler image for his Conservatives, David Cameron continued this support by exempting DfID from sweeping austerity measures. Both Blair and Cameron seemed to have had a strong personal commitment to overseas development, at the same time pushing the related campaign against illicit financial flows to the front of the G8 agenda.[6] For example, Blair established the Commission for Africa in connection with the development-themed G8 meeting hosted by the United Kingdom in Gleneagles in 2005. At the 2013 G8 summit Cameron made better regulation of untraceable shell companies, perhaps the most commonly used mechanism for laundering corruption proceeds,[7] the centerpiece of the event. The prime minister had reportedly been greatly influenced by Paul Collier, a development economist critical of the West's role in hosting stolen wealth.[8] Somewhat to the puzzlement of viscerally left-wing anticorruption NGOs, the Conservative prime minister seemed determined to make this cause a legacy of his premiership, including a major summit on the topic in 2016.[9]

This chapter looks at the experience of the United Kingdom in hosting, tracing, and returning the proceeds of grand corruption from abroad. Much of the evidence comes from investigations of several exemplary cases. The chapter begins with the "before" picture of kleptocrats laundering with impunity, then moves to later cases that illustrate some progress in attacking the proceeds of foreign corruption in the United Kingdom, while also analyzing continuing serious shortcomings. Public top-level political commitment to the anti-kleptocracy norm has translated into only very partial policy effectiveness. The first case examined, representing a spectacular failure of accountability, demonstrates the ease with which the Nigerian military dictator Sani Abacha and his family were able to launder their loot in the UK financial sector, and the difficulties experienced by the Nigerian government in trying to recover this money after Abacha's death in 1998. Perhaps reflecting in part their discomfort concerning the Abacha debacle, the British government took a close interest in the issue of asset recovery subsequently at home and in multilateral settings. It instituted a program that may serve as something of a model for other countries to follow, whereby development aid money is used to track down looted assets in London. This program led to successful investigations of three Nigerian governors and a former Zambian president.

At the same time, however, indications of dangerous vulnerabilities remain, both in targeting looted wealth in Britain but even more so in the preventive measures designed to screen out illicit funds. The problems that the Libyan and Egyptian governments experienced in the wake of the Arab Spring in seeking to reclaim assets belonging to the Gaddafi and Mubarak clans starkly illustrate that, despite reforms, the odds are still stacked against successful asset recovery. Once again, the question of corruption funds that are never investigated looms large. An effective policy against foreign corruption proceeds, or any other sort of illicit finance, relies on prevention much more than response. Yet key reports on the British banking and real estate sectors in 2011 and 2015 strongly suggest that rules on the books, in theory considerably stricter than those in the United States, are ignored in practice, thanks to weak or nonexistent enforcement by regulators. In general, this chapter concludes that a sincere normative commitment by successive prime ministers to development-related campaigns against international corruption has led to important and innovative policies to track foreign kleptocrats' wealth in Britain. Nevertheless, overall effectiveness remains quite low. While laws are relatively favorable toward confiscating foreign illicit wealth compared with the United States, a lack of enforcement of preventive measures to screen out dirty money means that the results overall are if anything more modest.

The Abacha Case

As with most of the other examples examined in this book, the Abacha case tends to sprawl across a variety of jurisdictions rather than being a strictly bilateral affair between the United Kingdom and Nigeria. Significant judicial actions took place in Switzerland (as discussed in the previous chapter), Jersey (associated with the British Crown but outside the United Kingdom), and later in Liechtenstein and the United States. But it is important to consider the effect of the Abacha affair in the United Kingdom, both for its own sake and because of the policy responses to asset recovery that tended to flow from it. In terms of the absolute amounts and the proportion of funds recovered and repatriated from different host jurisdictions, the Abacha case is the most successful instance thus far of tracing and returning the proceeds of kleptocracy (though it is noteworthy that these repatriated funds have come from the United States and Switzerland, not the United Kingdom). This case starkly showed up the failings of the British system in both blocking and recovering foreign corruption proceeds, thus acting as a spur for later reforms.

Nigeria had long been plagued with rampant corruption by the time that General Sani Abacha seized power in a military coup in November 1993. Despite huge oil revenues, most of the population had actually become poorer during the oil boom.[10] The Nigerian anti-corruption agency estimated that since independence in 1960 up to $400 billion has been lost thanks to corruption.[11] The relative success of the efforts to recover Abacha's stolen wealth may be a product of his relatively short tenure in office (he died in June 1998, reportedly while cavorting with prostitutes), as well as the lack of sophistication in his corruption. Most of the funds looted were simply taken from the Central Bank of Nigeria on the pretext of responding to vague national security emergencies, often in truckloads of cash. The requests were drawn up for Abacha by his national security adviser, Ismaila Gwarzo. Almost thirty such memos netted Abacha just under $2 billion.[12]

It is estimated that from the country's $3 billion annual oil profits, a total between $500 million and $1 billion were taken each year by Abacha and his family,[13] with much of this money being wired to foreign banks in Britain, Switzerland, Luxembourg, and Liechtenstein, though destinations range as widely as Brazil, Lebanon, Dubai, Hong Kong, France, the Bahamas, Libya, and Canada.[14] In most cases, "the members of the families involved did not hide their true identity and bank officials found no impediment in accepting their funds."[15] Additional thefts took place from (among other sources) money earmarked for an immunization campaign, funds connected with the sale of debt from a failed steel plant, and bribes paid by foreign companies in return for inflated government contacts.[16]

During the brief period of transitional military rule immediately after Abacha's death, the new Nigerian government set up a Special Investigative Panel to recover the looted wealth. The former dictator's wife, Maryam Abacha, was stopped at the Lagos airport with thirty-eight cash-filled suitcases, while son Mohammed was found to have the incredible sum of $100 million in cash in his Lagos residence (weighing close to a ton).[17] The new government offered amnesties to those officials providing information on the missing money. Among those accepting were the aforementioned Mohammed Abacha (in jail facing a murder charge since 1999) and Abubakar Atiku Bagudu, one of Abacha Sr.'s closest confidants. These two volunteered information on the location of $670 million and £50 million of looted wealth. Facing a long and uncertain legal struggle, the newly elected President Olusegun Obasanjo reluctantly opted for a deal with the Abacha family. The family would allow $1.4 billion frozen in Switzerland, Luxembourg, and Liechtenstein to be transferred to the Nigerian government, while the Abachas would be allowed to keep $100 million for themselves. After being acquitted of murder and released from jail, however, Mohammed repudiated the deal (though, as discussed in the previous chapter, a very similar deal was eventually concluded in 2014).

Both the actions of British banks in receipt of the looted Abacha wealth and the subsequent limp response by regulators put Britain in a very poor light. An investigation by the Financial Services Authority (FSA) indicated that £900 million controlled by Abacha, his family, and associates had passed through forty-two accounts held at twenty-three banks in the United Kingdom.[18] Most of the money had gone through fifteen banks that were said to have had serious deficiencies in their anti–money laundering procedures. The FSA director referred to these lapses as "disappointing." Evincing a talent for British understatement, the investigation noted that these weaknesses included an "inadequate understanding of the source of the customers' wealth." No banks or individuals were prosecuted, fined, or even named. According to the FSA, it was barred by law from either penalizing or naming the banks in question. Press coverage indicated that Barclays, NatWest, UBS, and HSBC were among the banks at fault.[19]

These banks would seem to have had no excuse for banking Abacha and members of his family, as their corruption was well known at the time. It was a clear indication that banks in one of the world's major financial centers could launder what were obviously proceeds of grand corruption, and that even when they were discovered, absolutely no sanctions were imposed. Under these conditions, accepting the proceeds of kleptocracy made excellent business sense for banks. Later investigations revealed that US and Swiss banks had been just as accommodating, and presumably the same applied to financial institutions in the other jurisdictions also. In contrast to the British, however, the United States and Switzerland did at least name the banks at fault.[20] This sort of conduct undermines the assurances of banks that, quite apart from any legal sanctions they might face, their inherent sense of morality and their sensitivity to bad publicity and reputational damage give them strong incentives to turn away criminal funds.[21]

The US Senate investigation of Citibank's involvement in the affair was far more hard-hitting than the pusillanimous and ineffectual FSA nonresponse, and provides some detail on what this bank's "disappointing" performance actually entailed. Mohammed and Ibrahim Abacha first opened accounts with Citibank Private in London in 1988 (and later in New York as well). By the 1990s these accounts held as much as $60 million at one time. The London account manager, Michael Matthews, was reportedly unaware that Abacha Sr. had become the ruler of Nigeria for three years after the fact.[22] Internal reviews at Citibank had twice found that the Abacha accounts were not compliant with the bank's own Know Your Customer procedures, but no action had been taken. Internal e-mails from Citibank London as far back as 1995 indicated some reservations, with one staff member writing, "I just do not feel right about this deal. It has 'typical' characteristics of a 419 [advanced fee fraud] . . . sound like a rum one to you?"[23]

Was the laundering of Abacha money in the United Kingdom a result of not having the right laws in place or not enforcing the laws on the books? Foreign corruption became a predicate offense for money laundering only after 2002.[24] At this time, banks did not have a duty to identify the real owner of shell companies.[25] However, many of the banks had failed to determine the true identity of the Abacha sons or apply the proper "risk-based approach" to their activities.[26] While some had reported suspicious transactions, other banks had not when they should have, though given the inaction of the authorities even when they received reports, this seems more of a technical than consequential failing. A general review of the UK anti–money laundering system at around the same time noted that law enforcement had little familiarity with or interest in the laws designed to confiscate the proceeds of crime.[27] More broadly, this period was the heyday of "light touch" regulation of the financial sector, a philosophy that permeated the British approach to financial crime also, with authorities emphasizing guidance rather than legally enforceable rules.[28] Thus although there were some significant gaps in the law, the main problem was that regulators and law enforcement were largely uninterested in foreign corruption funds. Although the UK government had espoused a firm commitment against corruption in the developing world, it had not yet made the connection whereby the proceeds of these crimes ended up in Britain. The end result was that there were few obstacles to keep even the most egregious kleptocrats from laundering their ill-gotten gains in Britain.

These facts threw a harsh light on the frequent admonishments from the United Kingdom and other rich countries calling on poor countries to improve their governance and take stronger action against corruption. British police giving advice on fighting corruption abroad recall being told, "It would be a damn sight easier if you [Britain] weren't laundering all the money."[29] The UK government has come to a clear realization that if it seeks to take a global lead in the fight against corruption and illicit financial flows, it must put its own house in order. Officials like President Olusegun Obasanjo and Finance Minister Ngozi Okonjo-Iweala frequently pointed to the complicity of Western financial institutions and governments in facilitating corruption. Nigeria became a particularly strong advocate for the asset recovery focus of the UNCAC and the Stolen Asset Recovery Initiative.

The resistance of Abacha's surviving family members and close accomplice Abubakar Atiku Bagudu in English courts greatly hindered efforts to track down the missing money. Although never able to present anything like a convincing explanation for how they had legally acquired the assets in question, by contesting every step they were able to slow down the proceedings, much like the Marcos family in Switzerland. They could afford a top legal team, as the law allowed the Abacha family and Bagudu to draw on the very funds that were at issue, though most had been moved out of the United Kingdom before legal action commenced. By October 2001 the Abachas had spent $8 million on their British lawyers,[30] later spending another $20 million on legal fees in Britain.[31] Aware that they were in for a long fight with regard to the mutual legal assistance request they had lodged with the British government in June 2000, in May 2001 the Nigerians opened a civil case against the banks that had maintained Abacha accounts, as well as their associates and companies under the Abacha clan's control. This action targeted eight banks, and although the ultimate aim of recovering the stolen money was not successful (most of the money had already been transferred elsewhere by this point), the effort secured financial documents and information on the Abachas' doings.[32] The Nigerian government's Swiss lawyer referred to this evidence as "mostly useless," however, because of the British government's failure to freeze assets.[33] Another lawyer working for the Nigerians commented that the UK Home Office "did not want to know" about the mutual legal assistance request.[34]

The conduct of the British Crown Dependency of Jersey strikes an interesting contrast. Though Jersey is commonly stigmatized as a tax haven, its response was notably more effective than Britain's. After a money laundering investigation, the authorities concluded that "several hundred million" pounds connected with the Abachas was the proceeds of crime, and the funds were frozen. At the same time, the Jersey government sought to have Abubakar Bagudu extradited from Texas to face money laundering charges. Bagudu instead agreed to a deal with Jersey and Swiss authorities, under which agreement he returned $150 million to the Nigerian government.[35] In 2010 the Jersey courts convicted Raj Bhojwani of laundering proceeds of corruption in the local branch of the Bank of India, handing down a six-year sentence. Bhojwani had sold trucks to the Nigerian military at up to five times their real worth in return for $100 million in bribes paid to Abacha and his associates, while Bhojwani himself took $49.3

million.[36] In 2011 Bhojwani was further ordered to pay £26.5 million.[37] This money laundering conviction is highly significant, in that Bhojwani had never been convicted or even charged in connection with these offenses in Nigeria or any other court. Often the lack of convictions or ongoing investigations in the victim country has been seen as precluding the successful criminal prosecution against those involved in laundering the funds in the host jurisdiction, especially in common-law countries, where a case must be proved beyond a reasonable doubt.

In March 2014 the US Justice Department obtained an order freezing yet another $313 million alleged to represent part of the Abacha loot, as well as $145 million in France and over $100 million in Britain. These funds were held with banks, including HSBC, Deutsche Bank, and Banque SBA, in some cases through shell companies formed in the British Virgin Islands. Once again, Mohammed Abacha and Abubakar Bagudu were prominently named.[38]

Much less positively, at around the same time, the Nigerian government conclusively lost the moral high ground when the government of President Goodluck Jonathan conferred posthumous honors on Abacha in 2014 in a ceremony attended by Maryam Abacha (she of the many suitcases), preceding by a few months the $1.2 billion settlement deal struck between Nigeria and the Abacha sons.[39] Meanwhile, former national security adviser Gwarzo was never charged in Nigeria, while Bagudu had been elected to the Senate in 2008 with the ruling People's Democratic Party. Ever one with a talent for being on the winning side, Bagudu changed his allegiance to the rival All People's Congress immediately before its 2015 election victory.

DfID's International Corruption Group

The bad publicity about the laundering of Abacha funds in Britain was particularly embarrassing given the government's very public commitment to assisting Africa's development by fighting corruption. Thus the UK Commission for Africa, set up to coincide with Britain's hosting of the G8 Gleneagles summit, released a report in 2005 reiterating the conventional notions that development efforts had largely failed to bear fruit in Africa and that poor governance (along with geography) was the most important explanation of this failure: "The corrosive effect of corruption undermines all efforts to improve governance and foster development."[40] The report estimated that stolen wealth equal to half of African states' total foreign debt was held in overseas bank accounts (though as is customary no evidence for this figure was presented),[41] again raising the implication that these looted funds were the obverse of African poverty.

In line with the priority of combating such corruption, a novel anti-kleptocracy initiative was launched in 2006. This involved setting up a dedicated International Corruption Group drawing on the City of London Police, the Metropolitan Police, and the Crown Prosecution Service, later centralized under the National Crime Agency. Like the US anti-kleptocracy groups launched around the same time, this new team was specifically responsible for tracking down foreign corruption proceeds within the domestic financial system. Unlike in the United States or any other country, however, the initiative was funded by international development aid money from Department for International Development. The department had successfully made the argument that because corruption was one of the greatest obstacles to development, and because rich-country havens enabled kleptocracy in poor countries, the initial £6 million transferred to the police in 2006–2009 to track down foreign corruption proceeds in London was a legitimate development expense.[42] The premise was that by repatriating the stolen wealth as conventional development aid, the program would more than pay for itself. In practice, DfID had in fact been supporting efforts to trace foreign corruption funds in Britain for several years beforehand on an ad hoc basis. For example, it paid $2 million toward the legal costs for the civil case against former Zambian president Chiluba in London.[43]

These police forces had the necessary skills to pursue stolen wealth from developing countries in London, but because this was a low priority, under normal circumstances little could be expected. The police were under pressure to combat local crime, not chase foreign criminals. This bias was accentuated because asset recovery involves long, expensive court actions, with most of any money recovered then being given away, unlike domestic asset recovery, in which the funds stayed in Britain. Both police units and DfID confirm that absent dedicated funding, foreign corruption would simply not have been investigated.[44] Britain is hardly the exception in this parochialism. The DfID initiative had two components: one unit of eleven staff investigating UK firms engaging in bribery abroad (led by the City of London police) and the six-person Proceeds of Corruption Unit, concentrating on foreign senior political figures' corruption funds in London (the responsibility of the Metropolitan Police until relocated within the National Crime Agency in 2015).[45] In 2015 the combined numbers had expanded to thirty-five staff, with plans for an additional fifteen members.[46] Both units cooperated closely with the Crown Prosecution Service and more distantly with a variety of ministries and other law enforcement bodies.

The Proceeds of Corruption Unit could not succeed without at least some support from the victim country government. Preliminary moves to investigate how money stolen by senior Kenyan politicians was laundered in London were abandoned after the Kenyan government either refused to provide evidence or destroyed it.[47] Indonesia was completely indifferent to suggestions it might pursue wealth stolen by the Suharto family.[48] Although the cooperation from Nigerian authorities was variable, it was enough to land some major successes.[49]

By 2013, when the International Corruption Group was renewed with £8.4 million for another three years, the Proceeds of Corruption Unit had eight successful prosecutions and had seized or frozen over £100 million.[50] Money repatriated was counted as development aid, with the attendant media attention to a "good news story" making the program very popular with the minister.[51] Although difficult to verify, there were also claims that deterrent effects of this program had significantly reduced the flow of illicit assets from Nigeria into the United Kingdom.[52] The head of the Nigerian Economic and Financial Crimes Commission estimated that $15 billion held overseas was voluntarily repatriated to Nigeria as a result and that the first-class section of the Abuja-London flights was noticeably emptier.[53] The sections below provide some specifics of this program in action.

Three Nigerian Governors: Dariye, Alamieyeseigha, and Ibori

The three Nigerian state governors examined below, Joshua Dariye, Diepreye Alamieyeseigha, and James Ibori, were elected in 1999, the first elections after the downfall of Abacha. They represented the ruling People's

Democratic Party, which held power federally until 2015. All three engaged in unrestrained plunder immediately on attaining office, moving
significant sums of this illegal wealth to the United Kingdom. Their cases
are instructive as to the failings that allow dirty money to enter the British financial system, especially in banks' due diligence. But they also illustrate the partial success of the responses taken by Britain and Nigeria, in
that some funds were recovered from each. The British government's decision to devote dedicated resources to this cause was crucial. Cooperation
from the Nigerian authorities was also vital, yet in the end the governors
were able to escape accountability at home and neuter the Nigerian anti-
corruption campaign.

Joshua Dariye moved £2.85 million of corruption proceeds into the
United Kingdom through accounts held by him and his wife with Barclays and NatWest (where they often made large cash deposits), as well
as through an associate, Joyce Oyebanjo.[54] Despite the fact that Oyebanjo
worked in Britain for very moderate pay as a housing tenancy manager,
she was able to deposit over £1 million of Dariye's money through her
NatWest account in a single year, apparently without further questions
being asked. British police stumbled onto Dariye's illegal activity when
an investigation into credit card fraud led back to Dariye's suspicious pattern of cash, bank accounts, and London real estate.[55] He was arrested in
London in 2004 but fled the country while on bail. Once back in Nigeria he
was immune from prosecution as a governor, and attempts to impeach and
prosecute him failed. The Nigerian Economic and Financial Crimes Commission (EFCC) did, however, pass on much useful evidence to its British counterpart.[56] In 2006 the Nigerian government launched civil asset
recovery proceedings in London and British authorities convicted Joyce
Oyebanjo of money laundering. Though Dariye was never convicted of
any offense in Nigeria, the court in London found that he had failed to explain the source of the funds and thus they were confiscated and returned
to Nigeria.[57] The decision apparently did not damage Dariye's political
career overmuch, as he was elected senator in 2011.

On his inauguration as governor, Diepreye Alamieyeseigha declared
total assets of £286,000 and an annual income of £6,000, while his governor's salary was approximately £16,000. Although it was illegal for
Nigerian governors to hold foreign bank accounts, in September 1999 Alamieyeseigha opened an account with UBS London (well after the extensive

media publicity about Abacha's corruption). He was identified as being a governor but claimed that he was already wealthy from private business and that his account would quickly rise in value from the small opening balance. In 2001 Alamieyeseigha received a $1.5 million bribe into this account from the contractor selected to build the governor's lodge. UBS persuaded Alamieyeseigha to hold the money via a Bahamas trust and associated company, while the Corporate Service Provider Fiduciary International set up a British Virgin Islands and a Seychelles shell company to hold his property.[58] From 2001 onward, further bribes were received via Royal Bank of Scotland and HSBC accounts. At this time Nigeria was on the FATF's money laundering blacklist, so banks were meant to be devoting extra attention to transactions from this source, but in practice little scrutiny was applied. The fact that Nigerian politicians are barred by law for maintaining foreign bank accounts also should have been known to UK banks post-Abacha.[59]

From 2003 onward, however, the governor's luck began to change, as an investigation got under way in Nigeria into his foreign bank accounts, with the Nigerian EFCC later making contact with British authorities.[60] Internal correspondence shows that UBS at least knew of this investigation,[61] and thus by extension knew that its client's account was illegal under Nigerian law, but opted to retain the account, though the bank may have lodged a Suspicious Activity Report.

In September 2005 British police raided one of Alamieyeseigha's properties to find almost £1 million in cash heaped on the floor.[62] He was arrested at Heathrow Airport shortly afterward and charged with three counts of money laundering. Like Dariye, however, he skipped bail and returned to Nigeria, forfeiting a £1.3 million bond (presumably British courts will think twice before granting bail to Nigerian governors again).[63] Dismissed from office in 2006, Alamieyeseigha lost his immunity and was convicted of money laundering and making a false asset declaration in a Nigerian court in July 2007. In January 2006 the Nigerian government again launched a civil case in London to recover cash, bank accounts, and property, drawing on evidence earlier collected by the Metropolitan Police.[64] The British judge noted that Alamieyeseigha "had a lot of explaining to do" about the source of his wealth.[65] Soon after the conviction in Nigeria, the civil action was successfully completed (though it probably would have succeeded even in the absence of this conviction). Despite this conviction and the recovery of funds, it was a mixed picture in terms of accountability. Alamieyeseigha was released on time served immediately after the decision and was pardoned by Goodluck Jonathan (who had been Alamieyeseigha's deputy governor) in 2013.

The last and most important action against a Nigerian governor was that aimed at James Ibori. Although the Ibori case was the most successful in terms of convictions and assets frozen, it provoked a purge of the EFCC and a sharp decline in the cooperation between British and Nigerian authorities, as Ibori was close ally of the Nigerian president Umaru Yar'Adua, in power 2007–2010.[66] Though Ibori's financial network reached into Switzerland and the United States, the United Kingdom (and particularly London) was central.

Immediately on being elected in 1999, Ibori set about extorting bribes and embezzling state funds, by some estimates as much as two-thirds of the total budget.[67] Estimates of his total take run to about $250 million (according to charges laid in Nigeria), of which about £20 million passed through the United Kingdom.[68] Some of the transfer and laundering of these funds was done in the name of Ibori's wife, sister, and mistress. But the London lawyer Badresh Gohil became increasingly important to the laundering of Ibori's loot, creating a chain of shell companies incorporated in Nigeria, Gibraltar, the British Virgin Islands, and Mauritius (one of which listed the four-month-old child of Ibori and his mistress as director).[69] Gohil also used his law firm's trust account to disguise the true origin of the funds.

The Metropolitan Police and EFCC began investigating Ibori, possibly with the assistance of the Miami-based US Foreign Corruption Investigations Unit.[70] The breakthrough in the case came when one especially observant police officer spotted a disguised cavity behind a heater in Gohil's office that held an external hard drive with all the details of the scheme. In 2007 £17 million of Ibori's assets were frozen in Britain, and Ibori was arrested and charged in Nigeria for corruption and money laundering. After initially beating these charges, Ibori fled to Dubai in 2010, after which the charges were reopened. There he was arrested on an Interpol warrant and extradited to face trial in Britain. Meanwhile, his sister and mistress had been convicted of money laundering in Britain, and in March 2011 his lawyer, Gohil, was convicted of fraud and money laundering. In February 2012 Ibori himself pled guilty to money laundering and fraud, and was sentenced to thirteen years' imprisonment.

The criminal cases of Ibori and his associates hinged on the juries in each case drawing the "irresistible inference" from the discrepancy between Ibori's legally declared assets and those under his control that this wealth represented the proceeds of corruption.[71] Ibori's defense, however, argued that the prosecution had to prove the specific crimes in Nigeria and then link these with the specific wealth in the United Kingdom in order to win the case: "A robber must be proved to have robbed."[72] The judge hearing the case explicitly disallowed the defense's logic; only the general class of criminality that gave rise to the proceeds had to be established.[73] This decision contrasts with the Obiang case in the United States, where the judges held US authorities to this second, higher standard of linking specific assets with a specific crime in the victim country. Yet this same problem recurred in later efforts to seize Ibori's assets.[74] Although approximately £6 million was confiscated as part of the money laundering conviction, another £90 million was only frozen, pending further proceedings. In 2013 Ibori's defense lawyer argued that his client's guilty plea the year before was not an admission he had personally profited from these crimes and thus the money could not be confiscated.[75] This rather audacious line of reasoning, the best legal logic that £2 million of someone else's money can buy,[76] was enough to delay the confiscation well into 2016 (not to mention substantially raise the legal costs still further). With Ibori eligible for early release in September 2016 thanks to time served and time off for good behavior, it is possible he might return to Nigeria a rich and politically influential man.

With each of the three governors, the performance of British banks raises serious questions. Though it seems that at least in some instances banks reported their suspicions to the authorities, there is little evidence of attempts to block transactions or close accounts in the way that American banks had done in relation to the examples from Equatorial Guinea and Angola, even after Nigerian investigations against these individuals began to be reported in the press. The media attention surrounding Abacha's kleptocracy was an obvious indication of Nigeria's corruption problems. Banks were supposed to be applying enhanced scrutiny to transactions from Nigeria due to the FATF blacklisting in 2001–2006. Banks knew (or ought to have known) that the governors' salaries were completely out of proportion to the size of the deposits they were making, especially as these obviously high-risk clients should have attracted extra scrutiny. Unlike in the earlier Abacha case, after 2003 foreign corruption was a predicate crime for money laundering. Ensuring that senior foreign officials were subject to enhanced customer due diligence in their financial affairs had supposedly been a priority area for British regulators,[77] and was stressed as a vital international anti-corruption measure in the UK-hosted 2005 G8 summit.[78] Yet the Financial Services Authority did not take any action against any of the banks, presumably because it thought they had fulfilled their obligations by reporting. Given how many reports are lodged by British banks and how few are actually investigated, however, this is not a strong argument for effectiveness. A much better approach would be to refuse to accept suspected corruption proceeds in the first place, or to close accounts once such suspicions arose. Together with the other evidence considered in this chapter, this pattern of behavior suggests a continuing poor performance of British banks and regulators with respect to screening out corruption funds from abroad. Until at least 2010 the Financial Services Authority had never taken enforcement action against a bank for handling corruption proceeds.[79]

Nigeria is a key country in the campaign against kleptocracy, for several reasons: the sheer scale of corruption, the massive damage wrought to the nation as a result, the spectacular looting by Abacha, the relative success of recovering much of this money, and the pivotal role played by Nigerians like President Olusegun Obasanjo and Finance Minister Ngozi Okonjo-Iweala in pushing the anti-kleptocracy agenda on the world stage. Yet the Nigerian example also underlines another basic point: that for all the sins of omission and commission of rich-country governments and financial institutions (in this case Britain), the group most at fault for grand corruption in Nigeria is that country's political elite. A depressing reminder is the fate of central bank governor Lamido Sanusi.

In February 2014 Sanusi provided detailed evidence showing that $20 billion was missing from the accounts of the notoriously corrupt Nigerian National Petroleum Commission. He was immediately suspended, and state security moved to charge him as a financier of terrorism.[80] Evidence of a rotten Nigerian political system extended to Alamieyeseigha, pardoned by President Goodluck Jonathan in 2013; Dariye, who became a senator with the ruling party; and Ibori, protected in Nigeria by President Yar'Adua. As noted earlier, Abacha himself, the arch-villain, was rehabilitated in 2014. While referring to Nigeria as a victim state of grand

corruption is tragically true when it comes to the Nigerian people, it is
highly misleading if applied to the government.

Chiluba of Zambia and Missed Opportunities

Perhaps the most senior foreign public official subject to asset recovery
proceedings in the United Kingdom before the Arab Spring was Zambian president Frederick Chiluba. Chiluba ran afoul of the law thanks to
two serious miscalculations. First, in the time before the end of his second term as president in 2002, Chiluba brought charges of criminal libel
against journalists accusing him of corruption. Surprisingly, the journalists managed to win the case after obtaining bank records substantiating
their claims that the president had diverted state funds to the Zambia National Commercial Bank in London for his own consumption (e.g., buying
hundreds of designer monogrammed shirts and shoes).[81] Chiluba's second
mistake was to support the succession of his vice-president, Levy Mwanawasa. Once elected in 2002, Mwanawasa revoked Chiluba's legal immunity and set up a task force to prosecute Chiluba and his allies, as well as
recover the stolen wealth.[82] The task force's efforts to obtain evidence in
London were directly supported by DfID, providing the inspiration and
model for the DfID-funded International Corruption Group discussed
above.[83] In 2009, just after the death of Mwanawasa, Chiluba was acquitted of all charges in Zambia after strong pressure was put on the presiding
judge.[84] The task force had more luck in parallel civil proceedings filed in
London in 2006, winning a $58 million judgment against Chiluba (whose
official annual salary was $10,000) and associates in 2007. Because a local
judge refused to recognize the decision in Zambia, however, Chiluba's assets there remained safe until his death in 2011. This underlines the danger in assuming that a judgment of a certain amount translates into that
amount of money actually being recovered. In the initial judgment Chiluba's lawyer, Iqbal Meer, was singled out for his complicity in laundering
the proceeds of the scheme through the familiar expedients of setting up
shell companies in Luxembourg and the British Virgin Islands and using
the law firm's trust accounts. Meer managed to have this decision reversed
the following year, however, when another judge declared that the lawyer
had been negligent rather than complicit.[85]

There are further cases of corruption proceeds in the United Kingdom that should have been pursued but weren't. This inaction may be more representative than the efforts to recover the Nigerian governors' and Chiluba's wealth. At least in some cases this was squarely the fault of the "victim" government. The Kenyan Anglo Leasing scandal (nicknamed "Anglo Fleecing" in the Kenyan press) is one such example. The scandal involved eighteen fictitious companies, including Anglo Leasing, that were awarded $857 million in security-related government contracts in 1997–2004 despite providing hopelessly substandard goods and services or none at all.[86] The money was subsequently kicked back to key ministers, as well as being used to finance the reelection campaign of the government of Mwai Kibaki (which had come to power in 2002 on an anti-corruption platform). The fictitious companies were ostensibly based in the United Kingdom, and because some of the payments went through Britain, the Serious Fraud Office began an investigation in July 2007. The Kenyan government under Kibaki and Attorney-General Amos Wako, however, resolutely stymied all efforts to investigate the affair, at home and abroad. The government ignored Commission of Inquiry reports and drove its own head anti-corruption official, John Githongo, into exile. When the Kenyan Anti-Corruption Commission repeatedly tried to make mutual legal assistance requests to gather evidence overseas, the parliament removed its authority to make such requests. The Kenyan government refused offers of assistance from Britain, the United States, Switzerland, and France to trace the funds.[87] Facing a complete lack of cooperation, the Serious Fraud Office canceled its investigation, as did the DfID program described above. The only manifestation of accountability was that several of those ministers at the heart of the scandal were barred entry to the United Kingdom. In 2015 the new Kenyan Ethics and Anti-Corruption Commission revived the case and laid criminal charges against private individuals in Kenya, but it remains to be seen how the matter will be concluded.[88]

The Indonesian government has similarly been completely indifferent to recovering the assets of the Suharto family (the highest-grossing kleptocracy ever, according to Transparency International).[89] This indifference is illustrated most conspicuously with reference to the former president's son, Tommy Suharto, who owned a golf course and a number of luxury apartments in the United Kingdom as part of a personal fortune valued at $800 million.[90] The family had held property worth at least £11 million in

London, going on gargantuan shopping binges before the British government refused them entry from 1999.[91] Tommy Suharto had sold a stake in car maker Lamborghini and moved around $70 million to Guernsey, where it was frozen. When asked how he had originally obtained this money, Suharto claimed to have forgotten and to have failed to keep any financial records. Although the money is still frozen, the Indonesian government has never sought to follow up or make enquiries.

The 2011 Financial Services Authority Report

While the Nigerian and Chiluba cases provide some examples of the laundering of foreign corruption proceeds in the United Kingdom, and the varying effectiveness of efforts to counter it, what about the bigger picture? Here a survey of British banks' performance published by the Financial Services Authority in June 2011 is invaluable. Coming ten years after the failures revealed by the Abacha case, the report, *Banks' Management of High Money-Laundering Risk Situations*, paints a scathing picture of general ineffectiveness when it comes to screening exactly the sort of foreign senior public officials (Politically Exposed Persons) most likely to be engaged in grand corruption. The report concludes:

> Despite changes in the legal and regulatory framework a number of the weaknesses identified during this review are the same as, or similar to, those identified in the FSA report of March 2001 covering how banks in the UK handled accounts linked to . . . Sani Abacha. Serious weaknesses identified in banks' systems and controls, as well as indications that some banks are willing to enter into very high-risk business relationships without adequate controls when there are potentially large profits to be made, means that it is likely that some banks are handling the proceeds of corruption or other financial crime.[92]

Rather than the usual homilies about a couple of bad apples, the report presents a picture of systematic failure. Over half of the twenty-seven banks surveyed failed to apply any extra scrutiny to high-risk clients, while less than a quarter took steps to properly verify the source of clients' wealth, in both cases direct violations of banks' legal responsibilities.[93] Often the box

on the forms relating to source of wealth was left blank or simply completed "not known."[94] Wire transfer safeguards are easily beaten, as when
transferring banks identified the sender only as "one of our customers."[95]
Even when banks had good anti–money laundering rules on the books
(and many did not), they often failed to implement them. Some banks provided visiting inspectors with their training material, but it turned out that
these banks had never provided this material to their staff. At one bank
high-risk countries were reclassified as low risk if the bank derived a lot
of business from them. Some banks claimed to be unable to find information on customers linked to corruption when it was readily discovered by
a simple Google search. "In other cases, banks appeared to take the view
that the proceeds of crime became legitimate after a certain, and in some
cases a very short, period of time. Examples included where customers had
acquired substantive wealth by allegedly corrupt means, but subsequently
invested the proceeds in more legitimate ventures."[96] The bias whereby
relationship managers were rewarded for enticing new business rather
than asking sensitive questions was very much in evidence. For example,
even persistent and credible accusations of corruption were dismissed in
the absence of a criminal conviction or because the client was "very nice" or
"from a respectable family."[97] Relationship managers sometimes prevented
Suspicious Activity Reports from being lodged on their clients.[98] Banks
tended to worry not so much about money laundering risk per se as about
the risk of getting caught for money laundering.[99]

Though there were also many examples presented of banks doing the
right thing, in combination the findings completely puncture any mood of
complacency that most banks can be relied on to do the right thing most of
the time. The great unanswered question in the report, however, is that if
the banks' performance had been so poor over the preceding decade, what
did this say about the competence of the FSA itself as the regulator responsible for ensuring compliance? Like the Abacha report a decade earlier,
the report takes care not to name any banks and thus there was no reputational fallout for any of the banks caught flouting their responsibilities.
Subsequent enforcement action was modest. Coutts Bank, owned by the
bailed-out Royal Bank of Scotland, and bank of Queen Elizabeth II, was
fined £8.75 million in March 2012. The FSA described the bank's deficiencies as "significant, widespread and unacceptable," especially in failing to
establish the source of funds from wealthy clients from eastern Europe and

the Middle East, at a time when its staff were paid large bonuses for taking on new clients. Coutts's parent bank had already been fined in 2010 for customer due diligence failures.[100] The FSA's comment was that "the size of the financial penalty demonstrates how seriously we view its failures."[101] However, given the modest size of the fine, this might be read as meaning that the FSA did not take these deficiencies seriously. In the absence of any substantial financial penalties, and given the squeamishness over naming and shaming, it is very difficult to see why British banks' performance would have improved since 2011. The broader significance is that the crucial preventive elements of the United Kingdom's anti-kleptocracy regime do not seem to work.

The Arab Spring

The Arab Spring revolutions illustrate the new expectation that stolen assets held abroad should be returned to victim countries, as this search came to the fore of the international agenda. It stimulated the greatest effort so far to hold kleptocrats accountable by targeting their ill-gotten wealth abroad. This included a range of unilateral and multilateral responses, for example, United Nations asset freezes and financial sanctions; the asset recovery and corruption focus of the G8 after its summit in Deauville, France, in May 2011; and the creation of the G20 Anti-Corruption Working Group at around the same time. High hopes that the Arab Spring would lead to a general transition to democracy were dashed by the outbreak of civil wars and the return to authoritarianism. In part as a result of these broader political reverses, the hunt to find and return Arab kleptocrats' loot has also proved a disappointment. The obstacles and frustrations encountered are highly instructive in showing the limited effectiveness of any global regime premised on returning stolen wealth from overseas hiding places, as opposed to preventing such wealth from entering foreign financial systems in the first place. While part of this story has been told in the chapter on Switzerland, Britain's experience crucially illustrates both its importance as a host for corruption funds and how the government responded to earlier failures in attempting to strengthen measures to counter kleptocracy.

In the immediate aftermath of the demonstrations that led to the overthrow of the Tunisian and Egyptian regimes in early 2011, many foreign governments applied a series of unilateral and multilateral asset freezes. These governments sought to restrain both public and private funds, though the distinction between the two was often somewhat arbitrary, recalling the tendency of the ruling families and their cronies to privatize state assets. In Britain the freezes reflected sanctions decided at the EU and UN level.

Following these initial asset freezes, the first round of requests for legal assistance from Egypt were an early indication of the problems to come. The attitude of the Egyptian government was that the Mubarak family and its close associates were manifestly guilty of corruption, and so foreign governments like the United Kingdom, the United States, and Switzerland should quickly find these assets and hand them back.[102] The heady rhetoric from British and other governments in support of asset recovery may have contributed to the impression that the process could be this easy, much like the hopelessly optimistic estimate of the Philippine government in 1986 that recovering the Marcos assets should be possible within twelve months.[103] While beginning trials against Mubarak and some of his closest associates for corruption and human rights abuses at home, the Egyptian government fired off requests to foreign governments for help in tracing, freezing, and repatriating stolen wealth. Evidencing the usual tendency for unsubstantiated estimates about the sums at stake to escalate almost without limit, guesses as to the Mubarak clan's stolen wealth ranged from $1 billion to an incredible $70 billion (compared with guesses of $3–5 billion for those associated with Ben Ali and $30–80 billion for Gaddafi).[104] It did not take long for mutual disenchantment to set in between the Egyptian government and those foreign governments fielding its requests for assistance.

Interviews in the United Kingdom identify problems similar to those encountered in the United States.[105] At the most basic level, transliterating names from Arabic script to English meant that there was potentially a wide variety of spellings for many names, a situation worsened by the commonness of some names (especially Mohammed). For electronic searches of financial records and for law cases, names generally had to match exactly. More seriously, there was often little or no evidence supporting the claim that the suspect had acquired assets through corruption. Similarly, there was often little guidance as to where assets might be found. As interviewees are quick to point out, mutual legal assistance does not work on the basis of receiving governments trawling through the records in relation to every bank in their jurisdiction, every company, and every property in order to find if, for example, some member of the Mubarak family holds an interest. Instead, requesting governments are expected to provide most of the information to their foreign counterparts, allowing for a very narrow, targeted search and at least suggesting why these assets are likely to be the proceeds of corruption (as discussed in chapter 5, China is now experiencing many of the same frustrations in its hunt for corrupt officials and stolen assets abroad). From the point of view of foreign respondents, Egypt had earlier done itself no favors by consistently failing to cooperate with foreign counterparts. For example, Egypt had never once granted a US mutual legal assistance request. The treaties in question were often hopelessly out of date—the one in force with the United States had originally been concluded with the Ottoman Empire.[106] In the particular case of individuals like Gamal Mubarak (Hosni's son and at one point heir apparent), the situation was complicated still further because he had amassed legitimate wealth in London through an earlier job in the finance industry.

Given the volatility of the political situation in Egypt, it was anything but business as usual for its judges, officials, and investigators, who were now facing their most complex ever foreign legal case. Judges and many senior officials had been appointed by the same kleptocratic regime that was now in the dock, unsurprisingly leading to divisions and mutual suspicion. These divisions were reflected in the number of separate agencies tasked with repatriating looted wealth held abroad: the Public Prosecution Department, the Illicit Gains Department, the Asset Recovery Judicial Committee, the Department for International Cooperation at the Ministry of Justice, the Ministry of Foreign Affairs, and the Financial Intelligence Unit.[107] British officials complained about what they saw as the tendency for one Egyptian agency to berate (or sue) them for failing to hand over information that they had in fact already passed on to another, separate agency in Cairo. Questions about the fairness and impartiality of the Egyptian legal system and the extent to which human rights were respected complicated not only any process of extradition but also the recognition of decisions taken in Egyptian courts. Beyond this was the seemingly self-contradictory idea of "legal corruption," as when the Mubarak government passed legislation or decrees that deliberately enriched its members at the expense of the national interest, for example in granting monopolies or overpriced contracts to political insiders.[108] How could countries return wealth that was lawfully acquired according to the Egyptian law of the time? The final indignity was that after what felt like a huge effort in London, Mubarak was acquitted of all charges in Egypt after the military coup that overthrew the Muslim Brotherhood government, meaning the whole effort had been for naught (in fact there is technically a danger that Mubarak could successfully sue UK authorities for damages[109]).

For all these complaints about Egypt's handling of the asset recovery campaign, it is very important to consider the other side of the story. As far as the Egyptians were concerned, they were caught in a catch-22: they needed to find the specific location and nature of stolen assets abroad in order to recover them, yet the very countries that hosted these assets would cooperate only once the Egyptians had located these assets. In some cases the money in question had never touched Egypt, as for example if a foreign firm bribed a member of the Mubarak family with a payment into a foreign bank account. As one Ministry of Justice official put it: "The British government is obliged by law to help us but it doesn't want to make any effort at all to recover the money. It just says: Give us evidence. Is that reasonable? We're in Egypt. How can we search for money in the UK?"[110]

Western countries like the United Kingdom and Switzerland had frozen assets as a result of the Arab Spring, but they then refused to give the details of these assets to the victim governments concerned.[111] The British law firm taken on by Cairo, Stephenson Harwood, ran up millions of pounds of legal fees without returning any funds.[112] Lectures on the sanctity of the rule of law failed to impress, in view of Britain's and other Western countries' seeming willingness to ignore their own laws in accepting the corruption funds in the first place. Mubarak himself came from humble beginnings and earned an official annual salary of under $25,000, with ministers and other government officials earning far less,[113] so presumably banks would not have had to think too hard as to how most of the Mubarak family came by its vast wealth. In 2012 the Egyptian government sued the UK Treasury for its failure to cooperate, and claimed that of twenty-five requests for mutual legal assistance, fifteen had been denied.[114]

Nor was it just the government in Cairo that was dissatisfied concerning the British response. A BBC documentary, "Egypt's Stolen Billions," was harshly critical. It pointed out that thirty-seven days elapsed between the announcement of the freeze on key officials' assets in the United Kingdom and its implementation, allowing plenty of time for these funds to be spirited away.[115] At a time when Gamal Mubarak was on trial for money laundering in his home country, journalists looking through publicly available corporate and property records found that his £10 million Knightsbridge mansion had not been included in the freezing order, a year after it was first issued. Naglaa el-Ghazarley, the wife of a minister imprisoned for corruption and herself on the freeze list, was nevertheless able to open a new business in London eight months after being listed. Mark Pieth, chair of the OECD's anti-bribery committee, speculated that rather than just oversights, this pattern of omissions might reflect London's desire not to burn its bridges with the old elite.[116]

The British government was stung by this critical media coverage, particularly given its ambitions to lead the anti-kleptocracy cause on the world stage. As a result, in September 2012 it set up a new Arab Spring Asset Recovery Task Force, comprising representatives of the Crown Prosecution Service, Metropolitan Police, and Serious and Organized Crime Agency (now the National Crime Agency), to focus and reinforce its efforts. The British government also posted liaison officers in Cairo to assist asset recovery efforts and energetically supported multilateral initiatives through the G8, G20, EU, UN, and other groups.[117]

Not all efforts to hold Arab kleptocrats accountable by targeting their UK assets ended in disappointment. An early success was the freelance effort of British lawyer Mohamed Shaban in winning back a £10 million London mansion bought by Saadi Gaddafi, Muammar Gaddafi's son.[118] The Hampstead house had been acquired by Saadi via a British Virgin Islands shell company, Capitana Seas Limited, in 2009. Saadi had done little to conceal his ownership of the company and through it the house (appearing on the public records as Capitana's director). The initial purchase was reported in the media at the time, and hence the property was frozen as part of the sanctions against Libya. On March 9, 2012, Shaban, acting on behalf of Libya, won a private civil case against Capitana. The case was straightforward in that it was uncontested. Six months after the outbreak of the uprising against his father in March 2011, Saadi escaped from Libya to Niger, from where he was extradited back to Libya in May 2014. In the meantime he had failed to pay the $500 annual company registration fee in the British Virgin Islands for Capitana, which was thus no longer in good standing, complicating any effort on behalf of Capitana to contest the case. Given the disparity between Saadi's official salary and the value of the house, and because there was no defense to argue this point, the judge decided on the balance of probabilities that the property represented stolen assets and hence should be transferred back to the new Libyan government.[119]

This success indicated what can be done to repatriate assets in a relatively cheap and easy fashion. As a civil case, it did not depend on a prior criminal conviction or investigation in Libya, or going through lengthy government-to-government mutual legal assistance procedures. Again because it was a civil case, Saadi's absence was a bonus rather than an obstacle, and the case was decided on the balance of probabilities instead of the criminal threshold of beyond a reasonable doubt. Saadi's failure to do much to conceal his ownership, coupled with his notable false economy in neglecting to keep his shell company registration up-to-date, meant that there was little detective work to be done. Finally, Shaban's personal initiative and willingness to work without any up-front payment greatly helped.

What are the general lessons of these attempts to target Arab kleptocrats' British wealth? The first is the recurring failure of banks in Britain and elsewhere to screen out foreign officials who were not only extremely corrupt but also quite obviously corrupt. Aside from the persistent press reports on corruption and the terrible rankings of these countries in Transparency International's Corruption Perceptions Index, a simple comparison of Arab kleptocrats' tiny official salaries and their huge fortunes should have made their misconduct plain. While some of these individuals went to elaborate lengths to hide their ownership of assets, many others did not. In turn, the banks' failure reflects a failure of the regulators. The debacle of the Abacha case, the Nigerian governors and Chiluba, the damning 2011 FSA report, and the Arab Spring wealth all paint a consistent picture of British banks' putting profit above their anti–money laundering responsibilities, and regulators consistently letting banks get away with it. The unwillingness to even name guilty banks, let alone actually impose meaningful sanctions, speaks volumes of the failures of prevention.

Two Views on Oligarchs from the
Former Soviet Union

Aside from the specific difficulties of repatriating stolen wealth in the aftermath of the Arab Spring revolutions, the most important unanswered question was how such tainted wealth had entered the British and other foreign financial systems in the first place. Why hadn't the laws and regulations designed to screen out criminal money worked? Furthermore, how much more looted wealth was parked in Britain from other areas of the world? Perhaps the single greatest risk area concerned persistent rumors of vast sums of stolen assets looted from the former Soviet states.

With the collapse of Communism and the USSR, the new post-Soviet states embarked on wrenching political and economic transitions. Ostensibly aimed at producing law-ruled democracies with market economies, in the 1990s this process often degenerated into a corrupt free-for-all. The major winners from this process were a new breed of oligarchs, businessmen who had come by huge wealth through picking up former state assets and who often wielded enormous political influence. Closely related to this outcome were rulers who often engaged in grand corruption, especially in Ukraine, Russia, Azerbaijan, and central Asia.[120] Though much of this new wealth was spent locally on conspicuous consumption, and even more so on the side payments and patronage necessary to maintain power, tens of billions of dollars were also sent abroad. This new elite has been acutely aware of the essentially precarious nature of their power and wealth. The prospect of losing either or both (not to mention life and liberty) to revolution or purge has loomed large. Thus just as kleptocrats from developing countries have moved their illicit funds into the host countries examined here, so too have the new class of post-Soviet oligarchs and rulers. Beginning in the 1990s, Russian billionaires like Boris Berezovsky and Roman Abramovich occupied a prominent place in British public life.[121] Other Russians, Ukrainians, Azerbaijanis, and central Asians of slightly more modest but still substantial means have had a huge impact on the market for high-end London real estate (discussed below), as well as luxury goods and financial services.

It is an open secret that much of this new wealth from the former Soviet Union is at best of uncertain origins, if not outright criminal money. Besides David Cameron's admission in his 2015 Singapore speech quoted earlier, a senior officer from the British National Crime Agency stated in a documentary on Russian criminal money in London real estate that the amounts laundered through Britain were in the "hundreds of billions" of pounds.[122] Given their responsibilities to prevent the laundering of foreign corruption proceeds, how have the British authorities reacted? So far, there has been no major corruption case brought against an oligarch in London and hence no instance of repatriating stolen assets. Does this gap indicate that the accusations of corruption against the oligarchs are just so much innuendo or that there has been a massive and ongoing failure by the UK government to prevent London from being used as a haven for money laundering? It is hard to see a middle position between these two extremes.

The more pessimistic view might be as follows. It is a safe bet that almost every oligarch who got rich in the 1990s in the former Soviet Union did so by committing serious crimes, at the very least fraud, corruption, and tax evasion, and possibly crimes of violence as well. Then and now, governments like those of Russia, Ukraine, Azerbaijan, and the central Asian republics are basically criminal conspiracies, whereby the elite clubs together to plunder the countries they rule, with most of the wealth then placed in havens in the West. Though various rival factions may displace one another, even revolutions like those in Ukraine in 2005 and 2014 and Kyrgyzstan in 2005 and 2010 do not change the fundamentally kleptocratic nature of government. The same is true of African countries like Nigeria and Kenya, and of many, perhaps even most, developing country governments too. Corrupt officials are the norm, clean ones are the exception.[123]

The British government, like most other Western governments, knows this full well, but for diplomatic reasons would never say so in public. On this basis the British government knows, or at least strongly suspects, that a very large portion of the money in the United Kingdom from elites from such countries represents the proceeds of corruption. The government does little about this, partly because of a realistic appraisal that there is nothing it can do to turn these fundamentally corrupt regimes into anything approximating the "good governance" ideal that the international community insincerely professes to believe in, partly because the status quo provides financial rewards for Britain. Here proponents might point to the document secretly photographed on the way into the prime minister's

Downing Street residence stressing that Britain's response to the Russian invasion of Crimea should take care not to harm the City of London by barring Russian customers.[124]

The more optimistic view might counter as follows. Following the law during the chaos of the transition period in the decade after the fall of Communism was difficult even for the best intentioned; governments themselves barely knew what the laws were. People in the East made their fortunes as unscrupulously as those in the West had done at an earlier date, but such individuals now make most of their money through legal pursuits and have a self-interested commitment to the rule of law. The massive capital flows into London and elsewhere are not a gigantic money laundering scheme but rather an understandable effort by those from countries traumatized by financial crises, depressions, and hyperinflation to seek security abroad. Western critics of this "capital flight" demonstrate a parochial ignorance and arrogance in seeking to deny access to the stable, rule-governed systems that they themselves profit from and take for granted. As a matter of practicality and priorities, there are definite limits to what Western governments like Britain can do to combat corruption, but they are putting significant effort into the anti-corruption campaign, for little or no reward. Expropriating property outside the law and handing individuals back to countries where they are unlikely to get a fair trial, on the basis of little or no hard evidence, does not serve justice.

These contrasting pessimistic and optimistic scenarios were on stark display during the court battle between Boris Berezovsky and Roman Abramovich in London in 2012.[125] They suggest very different views of a highly relevant 2015 report of suspicious wealth invested in London real estate. As with the 2011 Financial Services Authority report on banks, the main finding is that laws on the books do not work in the absence of enforcement.

London Real Estate

The United Kingdom attracts more foreign real estate investment than any other country, with 44 percent of the purchases over $3.6 million going to foreigners.[126] According to the 2015 Transparency International UK report, *Corruption on Your Doorstep*, 90 percent of newly built luxury dwellings (i.e., those selling for more than £2,000 per square foot) are bought by foreigners, in declining order individuals from eastern Europe and the former Soviet Union, the Middle East and North Africa, and China.[127] Figures compiled by the DfID-funded Proceeds of Corruption Unit within the Metropolitan Police show that current investigations of foreign corrupt assets involve 120 London properties worth a combined £180 million. In London as a whole, 40,725 properties (commercial as well as residential) were owned by foreign companies, with the British Virgin Islands, Jersey, and the Isle of Man being the most popular jurisdictions of incorporation.[128] Because the property records indicate only the name of the company, and because the company owners are not listed in offshore company registries, this arrangement conceals the identity of the real owner.

The report draws the common inference that offshore companies from "secrecy jurisdictions" are a prima facie indicator of money laundering, and makes much of the fact that Jersey property holding companies are the most commonly represented among investigations by the Proceeds of Crime Unit. The solution for this is said to be company registries that include real (beneficial) owners. Yet the report also notes that Jersey already has such a registry,[129] whereas like the rest of the G8, at the time the report was written Britain did not (though it has committed to do so in the future). So here the "secrecy jurisdiction" in fact has more corporate information than "normal" countries. In practice, there is convincing evidence that the other "secrecy jurisdictions" mentioned in fact collect more information on shell company owners than the United Kingdom and United States.[130] What a local UK company did not do, however, was confer the notable tax advantages and limited liability that probably have much more to do with the prevalence of foreign companies than money laundering as such.[131]

Unlike in the United States, the UK anti–money laundering regulatory net covers the key intermediary professions involved in these sorts of high-end property dealings, most notably lawyers, Corporate Service Providers, and real estate agents, and of course banks are covered in all countries. Additional scrutiny is mandated for Politically Exposed Persons. These professionals also have a duty to establish the identity of the real owner when the property is to be bought in the name of a company or trust. What difference do these due diligence requirements make in practice? A prominent gap in the law is that real estate agents must perform due diligence only on sellers, not buyers. Real estate agents are forthright in admitting that in practice establishing the real owner of a foreign company is too hard.[132] Real estate agents submit only a tiny number of Suspicious Transaction Reports (179 of 350,000 lodged in the United Kingdom[133]). Although lawyers are certainly more scrutinized in the United Kingdom than anywhere in the EU or North America, British lawyers regard most of the reports they submit as a waste of time (e.g., reporting clients for not having an asbestos policy).[134] Before 2014 there had never been an anti–money laundering enforcement action against a real estate firm, and when fines were imposed in that year they were lower than the commission an agent might expect from a single sale.[135] The British tax agency is the regulator responsible for those forming shell companies, but because this agency concentrates on activities that will actually bring in revenue, Corporate Service Providers are effectively unsupervised.[136] Regulating lawyers and real estate agents in Britain has apparently done little to screen out dirty money. While this does not mean that properly enforced regulation cannot work, it should serve as a caveat to the nearly reflex action of demanding more and more regulation.

The UK government has been one of the most enthusiastic promoters of the new global anti-kleptocracy norm. Prime Ministers Blair and Cameron in particular personally took the initiative on this issue in international summits and in their budgetary support of DfID. At the turn of the twenty-first century Britain completely failed to translate this political support for the anti-kleptocracy agenda on the international stage into effective policy at home. The ease foreign kleptocrats had in placing their money in the British financial system was exceeded only by the difficulty of victim governments in trying to recover these assets, as exemplified by the Abacha case. The decade leading up to the Arab Spring revolutions saw a number of successful asset recovery cases, in part because the United Kingdom introduced stronger laws than the United States in repatriating stolen wealth (e.g., a lesser requirement to link a specific asset to a specific crime), but more importantly because of the creation of a unit dedicated to tracking down overseas corruption proceeds.

Yet even when host country agencies are reasonably committed to the cause of asset recovery, as bodies like DfID and various British law enforcement agencies have been, the legal and political obstacles are daunting.[137] Leaving aside the problem of governments that energetically connive in sabotaging investigations, like Kenya, or those that are completely indifferent, like Indonesia, there are long odds against success. For all the developments like the UNCAC, the multilateral initiatives by the G20 and StAR, and national legislation, basic tasks like obtaining information on stolen assets remain serious obstacles. Host countries still do not regard it as their job to do most of the investigative spadework in hunting for stolen assets, and so victim governments must do so. Problems of looking through shell companies, and the fact that the funds in question may never have touched the victim country, greatly complicate this task. Host governments may not even share the information they do have, as was the case with the Arab Spring asset freezes. When kleptocrats or their families can contest efforts to confiscate their wealth, they can hold up proceedings for years, even when they fail to offer any explanation of how they came by their money. The strong suspicions that much of the wealth from Russia, Ukraine, and the other former Soviet republics in London is also of dubious provenance reinforce the impression of the limits of effectiveness.

The most notable failures relate to prevention. Such is the difficulty of recovery that by the time tainted funds have entered the system, it is almost too late to do anything about it. While the United Kingdom (like Australia) has stronger preventive regulations on the books than the United States (e.g., Corporate Service Providers, lawyers, and real estate agents are at least partially covered by the anti–money laundering system), the lack of effort to police and enforce these responsibilities among banks and other intermediaries means that the actual effect is weaker. The regulators in question are concerned with other priorities. This underlines one of the central conclusions of the book: enforcement and implementation, not laws on the books, are the key to effectiveness. Weak laws and strong enforcement do more good than strong laws and weak enforcement.

Australia

In Denial

It is much harder to write about things that don't happen than those that do. At most times and in most places, kleptocrats have stolen and laundered without action being taken against them. Nevertheless, even where the trail of money from grand corruption has not attracted much attention or provoked countermeasures, it may still be possible to glean enough evidence to establish its presence. This chapter on Australia as a host for the proceeds of foreign grand corruption helps to address the selection bias noted earlier: the neglect of the common instances in which inward corruption flows have attracted scarce publicity and little or no investigation, and where the host country government has been resistant to the idea of tracing, freezing, and returning looted wealth from abroad. In this regard, Australia is almost certainly more typical than the United States, Britain, and Switzerland. Even the most enthusiastic anti-corruption activists admit that a large majority of serious corruption crimes are never publicized or investigated.[1] Including a "negative" case, characterized by more inaction than action, thus serves as a partial corrective to the bias created by the fact that most instances of grand corruption that we know about through detailed media coverage and formal investigations are almost by definition unrepresentative. Too often we only hear about the atypical anti-corruption success stories, while the more typical stories of corrupt leaders being able to enjoy their loot undisturbed are overlooked.

I concentrate on the flow of illicit funds into Australia from two main sources: China and Papua New Guinea. The Chinese economy has experienced explosive growth since the 1980s and has become increasingly internationalized; the same is true on both counts for corruption among China's elite. Fearing for its continued rule, in 2014 the Communist Party leadership embarked on a cross-border campaign to track down and return thousands of fugitive officials accused of corruption, and the tens of billions of dollars of state assets they are said to have taken with them. Beijing has identified Australia as one of the top three host countries for this looted wealth (along with Canada and the United States). But the first case considered here is Papua New Guinea, a South Pacific example of the resource curse, and a country that has seen up to half its national budget stolen by politicians and senior bureaucrats, with Australia the favored host destination for the resulting criminal funds.[2] Papua New Guinea also demonstrates the unintended consequences of even insincere adherence to anti-corruption norms. In 2014 the body set up in Papua New Guinea to recover corruption funds issued an arrest warrant for the very same prime minister who had created it only a few years earlier.

There is evidence of illicit funds from other countries in Australia as well. A 2015 Financial Action Task Force review concludes, "Australia is seen as an attractive destination for foreign proceeds, particularly corruption-related proceeds flowing into real estate, from the Asia-Pacific region."[3] This attractiveness reflects in part the lure of a stable economy and banking sector, in part the personal ties offered by a multicultural society with close familial links to many countries within and beyond the region, and in part the lack of any deterrent, thanks to the supine response to inflows of dirty money.[4] Around 2012 the Indian government began to make behind-the-scenes inquiries about Indian corruption funds in Australia.[5] Further afield, Australia has been identified as one of the main hosts of oil wealth stolen from South Sudan.[6] More generally, a December 2013 report from the OECD ranking its members' measures to counter inward illicit financial flows placed Australia in the second-worst position, behind only

Poland[7] (the governments of Australia and Canada, also poorly ranked in the report, unsuccessfully tried to cut out this unflattering verdict[8]). From 2010 onward, no foreign corruption proceeds have been returned from Australia, with the grand total of assets returned being only $4 million.[9]

The desire to look beyond the iconic kleptocracy cases (e.g., Marcos, Abacha) raises the question of how to get evidence. The positives of looking at the typical cases of impunity rather than the exceptional instances of accountability come at a cost in terms of how robust the conclusions can be. To address this dilemma, the material here relies heavily on confidential interviews, supplemented by investigative journalism, impersonating a would-be bribe giver and secretly recording conversations with facilitators, and analysis of property and corporate databases provided by a private investigator I employed. By necessity, the greater dependence on these kinds of sources means a somewhat tighter focus than in the other three case study chapters. The advantage of this concentration is seeing the dynamics of a government and financial sector in denial about their role as a corruption haven up close, observing this complacency under attack, and witnessing the partial, halting, and very incomplete moves toward matching international rhetorical and legal commitments with concrete action at home. As discussed at the end of this chapter, these dynamics raise more general questions about the nature of norms in international politics.

More than in the other three cases, lack of effectiveness has been the result of a lack of willingness to take action rather than a lack of capacity. Australia has some of the most powerful applicable laws in the world, more stringent than those available to its American, Swiss, and British counterparts, but the authorities have lacked the inclination to apply them. Regulators have had ample opportunity to get banks to take the danger of foreign corruption funds seriously but have instead signaled that this is not a priority. While authorities in the United States and United Kingdom, for example, frankly admit that vastly more corruption money flows into their countries than is intercepted,[10] the Australian government has tended to brazen it out, denying that there is a problem. It has argued that Australia is not a haven for significant foreign corruption proceeds, a conclusion said to be supported with the circular logic that no such looted wealth has been found.[11] Moreover, the official position is that even if there were foreign corruption funds in Australia, the victim country must win the key early legal battles in its own courts and then formally request legal assistance from Australia.[12] As the cases examined in the previous chapters repeat-edly show, if there is any approach sure *not* to work in asset recovery, it is this one of leaving most of the work to the victim country. Growing outside pressure, in concentrated form from China but also through more diffuse channels, may, however, change this stance in the future.

In backing up these claims, I first look at the general problem of klep-tocracy in Papua New Guinea, then show how this stolen wealth flows into Australia, with reference to some specific examples as well as broader analysis of real estate and corporate data. The section on China begins with evidence indicating a massive outflow of corrupt funds and officials, with Australia being one of the main destination countries. It then examines overlapping global campaigns waged by China since 2014 to repatriate cor-rupt officials who have fled to Australia and many other countries, as well as their loot. There are some common patterns in the channels through which illicit funds flow into Australia, in particular laundering in the real estate sector, but banks and law firms also play important roles. Finally, I discuss the reasons behind the gap between words and action in combat-ing kleptocracy, and the prospects for change, with reference to parallel developments in Australia's stance in countering foreign bribery. The gap between words and action in combating kleptocracy is a result of Austra-lia's insulation from the iconic cases, the lack of a major domestic scandal on this topic, and the fact that the relevant victim country governments have previously had little interest in asset recovery.

Looting Papua New Guinea, Laundering in Australia

Papua New Guinea achieved independence from Australia in 1975 and now has a population of around seven million. The country is a democracy, but thanks to a lack of consolidated political parties and strong regional and clan identifications, governments have been chronically unstable and based on patronage.[13] Recent strong economic growth is based on a miner-als and energy boom, with a huge liquid natural gas project said to double the country's GDP and triple its export revenues.[14] Unfortunately, there are pronounced signs of the "resource curse" or "paradox of plenty" ex-perienced by other developing countries, specifically in the coincidence of rapid growth and endemic corruption.[15] This situation is apparent from the mismatch between the expanding GDP and government revenue, on the one hand, and stagnant or declining social, health, and governance indicators, on the other. Corruption has become endemic.

A 2009 report from Papua New Guinea's Parliamentary Public Accounts Committee gives some indication of the scope of the problem: "By 2006, the Constitutional and statutory scheme of accounting and accountability for the management of public monies, had collapsed. The Committee respectfully advises the National Parliament that this collapse of accountability and responsible, lawful and competent fiscal management was, and remains, a direct threat to the viability and civil stability of the Nation and the health and welfare of our citizens."[16] Another report into the Department of Finance revealed the systematic corruption of this body, which had stopped paying any attention to the wishes of parliament or cabinet as to how government revenue was spent.[17] The report was suppressed thanks to the efforts of the figure at the center of the scandal, Paul Paraka (of whom more later), and its recommendations ignored. In an indication of how little had changed, in 2013 Prime Minister Peter O'Neill threatened to sack every member of the Department of Finance. The local anti–money laundering unit estimated in 2010 that up to half of the taxes owed to the government were not collected, due to corruption-enabled tax evasion.[18] Furthermore, estimates from local police officials in 2014 suggested that up to half of the government's revenue that was collected had then been stolen by senior public officials.[19] In June 2014, Task Force Sweep, a new anti-corruption body set up by Prime Minister O'Neill in 2011, issued a warrant for O'Neill's arrest, endorsed by the country's top judge and police officer. In response, O'Neill took refuge under armed guard in parliament, replaced the police commissioner with a more pliable candidate, and cut off funding to the task force.

Corruption in Papua New Guinea fits many of the patterns of kleptocracy elsewhere. Although there are problems with corruption at all levels of government, including the police force, it is the corruption of senior public officials that poses the greatest threat. Previously it seems that most stolen funds were spent domestically, in cash, on consumer goods, and especially to buy favor before elections. However, as the scale of corruption has increased, the country's ruling elite has become more inclined to send illicit funds overseas. Interviews with Australian and other foreign officials working in Papua New Guinea suggest that it is an open secret that corrupt Papua New Guinean officials hold their illicit wealth in Australia, a suggestion supported by the evidence presented below.

As a result of former colonial ties, Papua New Guinea enjoys close links with Australia. The country's law is based in part on Australian law, and most air routes from Papua New Guinea to third countries pass through Australia. Cabinet ministers and other senior officials have often been educated in high schools, universities, or military institutions in Australia, a pattern that is replicated among their children. Many current and former ministers have established second homes in Australia, and indeed their families may spend as much time in Australia as in Papua New Guinea. Although Australia does not host a global financial hub like London or New York, it is the world's fourteenth-largest economy and the largest financial center in the South Pacific. The nearest rival is Singapore, which has also enjoyed some popularity with Papua New Guinean elites, though it is geographically and culturally more distant.

Unlike the cases of host countries taking the initiative while the "victim" country remains indifferent (e.g., Equatorial Guinea, Kenya, Indonesia), here the dynamic is more akin to Nigeria's dogged and unrewarding effort to recover Abacha proceeds from Britain. In 2011 the head of Papua New Guinea's newly created anti-corruption Task Force Sweep referred to Australia as "another Cayman Islands," a haven for dirty money.[20] The same official, Sam Koim, later gave a high-profile controversial speech on the problem to an audience of Australian bankers. After referring to his own country as a kleptocracy and noting that Australia had never repatriated so much as a single cent of Papua New Guinean corruption funds (still true as of mid-2016), Koim spoke of the activities of corrupt officials from Papua New Guinea in Australia: "They have bought property and other assets, put money in bank accounts and gambled heavily in your casinos and have never been troubled by having their ill-gotten gains taken off them. . . . Be under no illusion, these people have chosen Australia as their preferred place to launder and house the proceeds of their crimes because it is easy. Cairns is only a short flight and property can be bought off the plan without permission. The financial system is stable and, it has been, up until now, extremely easy to get their money into your system."[21]

This verdict is supported by earlier testimony before the Australian Senate by AUSTRAC (Australian Transaction Reports and Analysis

Centre, the financial intelligence unit), which stated: "AUSTRAC considers the Pacific a priority region for regulatory engagement and information exchange given the large number of Australian financial institutions operating branches across the Pacific and the level of money laundering, crime and corruption in the Pacific. *Australia is a significant destination country for funds derived from corrupt activities within the region.*"[22] In May 2013 the Australian Federal Police senior liaison officer in Port Moresby, Steve Mullens, stated that "half a billion" kina (approximately $200 million) of corruption funds flows from Papua New Guinea to Australia each year.[23] This unintended revelation caused great discomfort in the Australian law enforcement and government agencies, contradicting as it did the official line that Australia does not have a problem with foreign corruption proceeds.[24]

Despite these sporadic admissions, senior Australian government officials have consistently maintained that talk of foreign corruption proceeds is mere "gossip and innuendo" and that there is no "hard evidence" of foreign corruption proceeds in Australia.[25] The formulaic response is that "Australia has a robust anti–money laundering and counter-terrorism financing (AML/CTF) framework, based on international Financial Action Task Force (FATF) standards, to deter and detect money laundering. Australia is committed to ensuring that Australia is not a safe haven for the proceeds of corruption."[26] The government maintained this position during a Financial Action Task Force review of the country's anti–money laundering system in 2014–2015 (with officials complaining that questions about Papua New Guinean corruption proceeds in Australia reflected the undue influence of NGOs and academics[27]). In order to contest this position, we must look at some more specific evidence.

The Wartoto and Paraka Cases

The case of Eremas Wartoto is a rare example of action by the Australian government against Papua New Guinean corruption in Australia, an exception that proves the rule of general indifference.[28] Wartoto was charged in 2011 with misappropriating A$30 million in collusion with former minister Paul Tiensten (who was sentenced to nine years in jail for corruption offenses in Papua New Guinea in March 2014) and several senior public servants. Learning that the charges were pending, he fled to

Australia in August 2011. He used a car rental company he owned to sponsor him for an Australian work visa. On August 24, 2011, the Papua New Guinean government asked that the visa not be issued, given the criminal charges and outstanding warrant for Wartoto's arrest. The request was ignored and the visa granted in September. The Papua New Guinean government then asked the Australian government to return Wartoto to face charges. The Australian government agreed with Wartoto's lawyers that he was too sick to travel (suffering "fatigue"), even though during this period Australian government records show him traveling to Fiji, Indonesia, Singapore, Malaysia, and the Solomon Islands. Having compiled this information, two Australian journalists then broke the story during the first day of the Australian prime minister's visit to Papua New Guinea in May 2013 so as to cause maximum embarrassment.[29] The story hit the papers on a Thursday, and the following Monday the Australian foreign minister canceled Wartoto's visa, belatedly endorsing the request of August 2011. Subsequent action showed that Wartoto held four accounts with major Australian banks, five properties in Australia (two held by trusts with a lawyer acting as trustee and one with an outstanding mortgage), as well as the assets of his car rental company.[30]

An even bigger case relates to Paul Paraka, currently charged in Papua New Guinea with thirty-two corruption and money laundering offenses, and accused over his career of corruptly obtaining almost $400 million of Papua New Guinean government funds.[31] Paraka, himself a lawyer, owned Papua New Guinea's largest law firm and controlled several others. A succession of investigations by various official bodies into corruption in Papua New Guinea have named prominent law firms and dozens of individual lawyers, recommending that they be disbarred and/or prosecuted.[32] Often the lawyers in question have been able to win injunctions against the publication of these reports (though they are available online nonetheless), and before late 2013 there was no follow-up. Paraka's influence was such that he had earlier persuaded a judge to grant a court order specifying that the police give him seven days' notice before executing any search warrant on his properties, despite the fact that the legal system did not allow for any such order.

Paraka is a close associate of many past and present cabinet members in Papua New Guinea. Like Wartoto, he has strong links with Australia. Paraka had four separate "wives" in Australia, each of whose accommodation he paid for. This necessitated holding Australian bank accounts, both in a personal capacity and in association with the law firms he owned and controlled. Between February 2012 and February 2013 alone, A\$3 million was transferred directly from Papua New Guinea to Paraka's Australian accounts, the credible allegations of corrupt conduct again proving no obstacle to accessing the Australian financial system.[33]

Though there is no verdict in the case, the key breakthrough in the effort to bring charges was when Task Force Sweep persuaded Paraka's bank in Australia to refuse his wire transfers and close his accounts, a development that occurred just after Koim's speech to Australian bankers in October 2012 quoted above. Other banks in both countries realized that because Paraka had been rejected by one bank on the grounds of corruption risk, if they continued to do business with him, they could be vulnerable to money laundering charges, since banks and individuals can be charged if they reasonably ought to have suspected that funds are the proceeds of crime. This financial interruption created immediate problems for Paraka (aside from loud complaints from his four wives, who were also cut off from funds). In particular, he was unable to pay his way out of trouble when it hit shortly afterward in the form of a huge tax assessment and then the criminal charges in October 2013.

This crisis escalated sharply when Paraka produced a letter from Prime Minister O'Neill authorizing the suspect payments in direct violation of an injunction prohibiting such transfers. O'Neill said the letter was a forgery. However, the letter was certified as a true copy, leading to the issue of an arrest warrant for the prime minister in June 2014, which, as noted above, he evaded through assembling an armed guard and removing the officials who had issued and authorized the warrant. The Australian government's overwhelming priority at this time was to preserve an earlier deal whereby Papua New Guinea had agreed to act as a detention center for refugees trying to reach Australia by boat. "Stopping the boats" had been perhaps the single most important issue in the previous two Australian elections, and Canberra's solution was critically dependent on cooperation from Papua New Guinea. O'Neill (who had also been linked to previous corruption trials) had had his personal bank accounts in Australia closed because of the corruption risk. The bank's decision, occurring at a key point in the negotiations over the refugees, came as a surprise to the Australian government and threw it into a temporary panic about the deal, but O'Neill did not raise the subject. Since this time, the refugee deal has decisively trumped any inclination the Australian government may have had to take action against corruption among senior Papua New Guinean government officials.[34]

Private Investigations

These individual examples to one side, what evidence is there of a general movement of corruption funds into Australia from Papua New Guinea? Many of its senior officials maintain extensive real estate holdings in the Australian state of Queensland, including those named in connection with corrupt activities in various Papua New Guinean government reports, and even those formally charged with corruption and other criminal offenses. To ascertain the size of the problem and test the Australian government's official position that there are no significant corruption funds in the country, I took on the services of a private investigator specializing in financial crime.

Queensland property records are available online in two commercial databases, and for a relatively small fee the records can be searched by the owner's name. As well as the name of the owner, they provide the last sale date and price. Sometimes they also include pictures of the property and scans of the original mortgage documents, showing the name of the relevant bank and the lawyer involved, if any. The first step in tracking suspicious funds in the real estate sector was to draw up a list of names of those individuals charged or convicted of corruption offenses in PNG, as well as individuals and companies named in connection with corrupt conduct in official PNG government inquiries (59 from the Department of Finance inquiry, 28 named by Task Force Sweep), and then match these against the databases to determine property ownership. The second was to search for these individuals on the Australian company registry to see if they featured as directors or owners of companies that in turn held property in Queensland.

The result was that in 2013, individuals and companies charged with or named in connection with corrupt activities in Papua New Guinea owned properties worth A$86 million. Using Google Earth, the investigator could map the physical locations of these properties, showing that many corruption-tainted senior officials own property in the same neighborhoods (sometimes directly next door to each other), use the same lawyers, and buy from the same few property developers. The legal significance is that it is a criminal offense for Australian banks to handle funds where there is a reasonable suspicion that these funds represent the proceeds of corruption. Yet in practice this did not preclude transactions being processed and mortgages being issued, even when the individual was charged with serious criminal offenses in Papua New Guinea and when this information could be found with a simple Google search. The list of properties compiled by the private investigator is unlikely to be the complete record for Queensland, and it does not include property data from the other five Australian states or wealth held in other forms.

In some cases it was possible to spot deliberate attempts to hide ownership. Thus one senior public official sold his property at a loss to a company owned by a trust, which turned out to be controlled by the same official. The wording of the trust deed seems to have been designed to omit the official's name. It specifies that the beneficiary of the trust is the official's wife, who is named, and the wife's spouse (i.e., the official himself), who is not named. Given the capital loss on the sale and the transaction fees, this move makes little sense from a commercial point of view but a great deal of sense if the aim is to hide and protect criminal proceeds.

In conclusion, there is an ironic circularity in the financial flows between Papua New Guinea and Australia: large aid payments of up to A$500 million go north, while large flows of illicit wealth come south. Up to the present, the Australian financial intelligence unit, AUSTRAC, has consistently refused to share financial intelligence with its Papua New Guinean counterpart in a stark illustration of both the lack of priority accorded this problem and the perverse consequences of the international anti–money laundering regime. The official grounds for refusing to share information are that the Papua New Guinean agency is not a member of the international club of financial intelligence units, the Egmont Group. It is not a member of the Egmont Group because Papua New Guinea does not have legislation to counter the financing of terrorism, even though there is no credible evidence to suggest that financial institutions in the country are being misused in this way. The upshot is that because Papua New Guinea has not legislated against a problem it does not have, Australia refuses to help with the corruption problem it manifestly does have.

From China to Australia: A Secret Report
and Naked Officials

China is a second major source of corruption funds flowing into Australia.
This section begins by briefly sketching out the massive international corruption problem faced by the Chinese Communist Party as thousands of
its cadres flee the country with billions of dollars of corruption proceeds.
The second goal is to provide some general background on how investment from China has increasingly flowed into the Australian real estate
sector, with some specific examples of how suspicious or downright criminal funds have followed this path. In keeping with the international nature of the problem, China's responses to this outflow of looted assets have
become increasingly internationalized, and Australia has been targeted as
one of the main host countries.

China has been a glaring anomaly in relation to the nostrum that high
levels of corruption are incompatible with rapid economic growth.[35] The
country's economic success since the beginning of the reform era in 1978 has
redefined the geopolitical order, at the same time marking the most rapid
and widespread reduction in poverty ever. Yet China has been blighted
by persistent corruption, as evidenced by the recurrent anti-corruption
campaigns waged by the ruling Communist Party. These efforts reached
a crescendo under the leadership of Xi Jinping. From Xi Jinping's initial
speech at the 18th Party Congress onward, the regime has identified elite
corruption as a major threat to its continued rule. The internationalization
of the economy has meant that more and more money stolen by Chinese
officials now flows abroad. Australia is one of the major destinations for
these funds, a conclusion supported by the Financial Action Task Force
judgment that "large amounts are suspected to be laundered out of China
into the Australian real estate market. China and other countries within
the Asia-Pacific region were also seen as likely sources of corruption proceeds that are laundered in Australia."[36] This often intertwined movement
of money and people out of China represents a strong financial and personal vote of no confidence in the system.

Though the Chinese government has been quite open in admitting
that corruption is a threat in general terms, important aspects of this problem have been shrouded in official secrecy. Western media coverage of
the extraordinary wealth of senior leaders' families has been vigorously

suppressed. Examples include the *New York Times* investigation of how former prime minister Wen Jiabao's relatives amassed a fortune of $2.7 billion through privileged insider deals, along with similarly lucrative successes for the families of other former prime ministers Li Peng and Zhu Rongji, former president Hu Jintao, and other Politburo members.[37] A Bloomberg investigation revealed that Xi Jinping's own family owns tens of millions dollars of Hong Kong real estate and even more valuable corporate assets in China proper.[38] Grassroots activists agitating for the kind of public registry of officials' assets and conflict-of-interest laws that are standard in other countries have been repressed and imprisoned. Finally, the international dimension of corruption among China's ruling elite has similarly been viewed as too sensitive to see the light of day. Fortunately, however, an official report on exactly this transnational aspect of the problem, accidentally made public in 2011, sheds invaluable light on this subject.

In 2008 the People's Bank of China, the country's central bank, prepared an internal report for the central leadership on high-ranking government officials fleeing abroad with state assets ("A Study on Methods of Transferring Assets outside China by Chinese Corruptors and Monitoring Methods for this Problem"). The report was marked strictly secret. Yet after being awarded first prize in a competition for confidential finance and banking research, it was briefly published online in 2011, at which point it was copied and translated.[39] The estimates contained in the report of the numbers of officials and the sums of money exiting China are staggering. From the mid-1990s to 2008, the number of officials fleeing is put at somewhere between 16,000 and 18,000, taking with them around $120 billion (RMB 800 billion).[40] The most common destinations for these officials are listed as North America, Australia, and Southeast Asia, with the most senior officials favoring the first two areas, often transiting through Hong Kong.[41] After presenting the usual estimates as to the size of international corruption, and citing the usual examples of Marcos, Abacha, and Montesinos, the report briefly summarizes the means by which officials transfer stolen wealth abroad.

The first is bulk cash smuggling, either when the official in question simply carries cash across the border or more commonly when a series of cash couriers make repeated trips to break the transfer into smaller and less conspicuous amounts that are then re-concentrated in the overseas destination.[42] In Australia this has often led to young Chinese on student visas carrying backpacks of A$50,000 into banks for deposit; if challenged, they simply abandon the money and leave.[43] The second path relies on informal remittances, rather like the Islamic *hawala* money transfers. Here a transfer from the official to the remittance agent in China in local currency is balanced by an equivalent transaction abroad, as a confederate of the remittance agent puts an equivalent sum of foreign currency (less a commission) in the official's overseas account.[44] Money is in effect moved abroad without any record and without the risk of physically moving cash. Such is the efficiency of the system that it may be cheaper than a formal international bank wire transfer. Chinese abroad are particularly likely to make even quite large purchases of property in physical cash, though this may reflect culture at least as much as any attempt at money laundering (the Amish in the United States also buy their property in cash; this is unlikely to be a money laundering dodge).

For those senior officials in state-owned enterprises, international trade provides a further set of options, including early or inflated payments for exports combined with late or understated payments for imports, fake international consultancy commissions (a particular favorite among the corrupt worldwide), and manipulating transactions among related domestic and offshore companies.[45] A similar route is through stealing Chinese firms' investments abroad. An example concerns Li Huaxue, entrusted with RMB 27 million for property development in Australia. Li bought land in Sydney with the money but gave the ownership rights to a shell company set up by his brother, an Australian citizen. Li then borrowed money to build from an Australian bank using the land as collateral, again privatizing the proceeds.[46] Finally, officials may accept bribes and kickbacks in cash abroad, real estate, or services like foreign education for their children, without the money ever entering the Chinese financial system.[47]

The report stresses that the process of sending dirty money abroad and officials' own flight are connected, but that the former usually proceeds the latter.[48] More recent is the rise of the "naked official," that is, those who have moved their families and their assets abroad in advance of their own departure. Interestingly, these corrupt officials are said usually to go to a different country from where most of their assets are located, at least in the first instance, to confuse the trail.[49] Another approach is to acquire multiple fake or real passports for corrupt officials and their family members. As discussed below, the rise in investor visas, over 90 percent of which in Australia are awarded to Chinese nationals, may have integrated the process of personal and financial relocation (of 10,000 investor visas granted annually in the United States, recently 8,000 have been taken up by Chinese[50]). The Chinese government came to the same conclusion as anti-corruption activists in the 1990s and those targeting kleptocracy from 2000 onward: because of the inherently transnational nature of the problem, no one country could effectively combat high-level corruption in isolation. One interviewee suggested that the main motivation behind China's joining of the Financial Action Task Force was precisely this priority.[51] The examples below suggest why following the money trail often leads to Australia. After some relevant coverage of Chinese flows into Australian real estate, the next task is to look at the Chinese government's international campaigns, beginning in 2014, to recover both corrupt officials and their wealth.

In 2012 Australia was the single largest recipient of aggregated Chinese global direct investment, falling to second just behind the United States in 2013–2014.[52] China has become the number-one source of investment into the Australian residential property market, with A\$5.9 billion in 2013 and A\$12.4 billion in 2014.[53] Chinese investment has become so prominent that 18 percent of new homes in Sydney are bought by Chinese nationals, and 14 percent in Melbourne. While local property specialists have speculated about a link between anti-corruption campaigns in China and spiking Chinese investment in Australia,[54] it is important not to give the impression that all or even most of these capital flows from China represent the proceeds of crimes like corruption, tax evasion, or capital control violations. Most of this money is probably legitimate. Nevertheless, some specific instances noted immediately below give cause for concern, as do more general failings in Australia's anti–money laundering system, reviewed in the penultimate section of this chapter.

In 2012 prefecture governor Yang Hongwei was convicted in China of taking bribes and living an "indecent lifestyle." Aside from his opium and alcohol habits, his mistresses and \$2 billion worth of debt-financed prestige projects, the governor invested his plunder in seventeen properties in his home province of Yunnan but also another six in Melbourne.[55] Despite his conviction, and court evidence establishing that a significant portion of the looted wealth was moved to Australia, no action had been taken as of 2016 by either the Chinese or Australian governments to take possession of the Australian properties.[56]

Another recent example of the movement of suspicious funds from China to Australia is the case of Su Shunhu, a Chinese senior Ministry of Transport official sentenced to life in prison for corruption offenses in October 2014. Shunhu explained his corrupt conduct to the court in part by the need to support his son and daughter-in-law. He had earlier paid his son, Su Guanlin, then in his early twenties, A$2 million via an associated company, even though the son had no substantive role in the company. The father wired at least A$1.2 million from China to his son's accounts in Australia in sixteen installments between 2008 and 2010. The son and daughter-in-law then bought A$4.5 million of local real estate.[57] An example of the Sino-Australian corruption link outside the real estate sector came to light in May 2013 when a former deputy director of the National Development and Reform Commission was arrested in China in possession of A$19 million in cash.[58]

In 2007 the Chinese magazine *Caijing* discovered a deal according to which 92 percent of the shares of the state-owned power company Luneng had been transferred to obscure private companies. Although the net assets of Luneng were valued at $9.47 billion, the shares had been sold for only $478 million, meaning that those controlling the private companies had made a windfall profit of almost exactly $9 billion.[59] After the initial story broke, Chinese authorities exerted strong pressure to suppress it and the transfer of shares was reversed. A particularly sensitive aspect of the story was the central role played by one Zeng Wei. Wei was the son of Chinese vice-president Zeng Qinghong, who had been a key ally in Xi Jinping's ascent to the leadership. The next year, the same Zeng Wei bought a A$32 million mansion in Sydney. Wei had earlier been enrolled at the University of Melbourne, though he had never actually taken courses there.[60] In November 2014 the head of a company part-owned by Wen Jiabao's brother bought a property close by for A$39 million. Another nearby A$52 million house was bought by well-connected Chinese businessmen Wang Zhijun using a trust and a local couple to front the deal. Both purchases violated Australian investment law.[61] Among those of more modest means, purchases of A$1–2 million in physical cash by Chinese are said by real estate agents to be relatively common in Sydney. Failing that, Chinese clients often pay off mortgages in cash in A$100,000 or A$200,000 increments at a time in cities such as Brisbane.[62]

Fox Hunt and Sky Net

In mid-2014 the Chinese government launched its first coordinated international dragnet for fugitive corrupt officials, the rather theatrically named Operation Fox Hunt. This campaign was part of a broader anticorruption effort dating from Xi's accession to power in late 2012 that by the end of 2014 had seen 180,000 Party members sanctioned for corruption.[63] Fox Hunt began with an offer of leniency for those who voluntarily returned home with the money they had stolen before the end of 2014. Leading the operation was Wang Qishan, head of the Communist Party's Central Commission for Discipline Inspection and member of the Standing Committee of the Politburo. Being an arm of the Party rather than law enforcement, the commission has no formal law enforcement powers, a legal nicety that is ignored in practice, however, along with suspects' human rights. In combination with China's use of the death penalty for corruption offenses and the lack of an independent judiciary, the commission's extrajudicial status has made it harder for China to secure the extradition of suspects abroad.

By the time this campaign was launched, the Chinese leadership had already clearly communicated to governments, including those of the United States, Britain, Canada, Australia, and New Zealand, that it was set on much more cooperation in the return of corrupt officials and stolen assets.[64] The Chinese government had privately voiced concerns with Australian inaction on this front beginning in 2012. Since that time China has suggested a quid pro quo whereby it will provide more support in fighting Asian drug networks operating in Australia in return for this increased assistance with fugitive Chinese officials. Not long afterward the Chinese government and Australian Federal Police announced that they were seeking the return of a target list of around a hundred officials, topped by Gao Yan, former governor of Jilin province, and the "many hundreds of millions of dollars" of illegal funds that these individuals had moved into Australia over the years.[65]

Multilaterally, at the Asia-Pacific Economic Cooperation (APEC) summit hosted by Beijing in October 2014, the Chinese leadership again made clear that international assistance in fighting corruption was now a priority.[66] The Chinese government estimated that there may be as many as one thousand fugitive officials in the United States, and it presented US authorities a priority list of around one hundred it wanted returned in late 2014.[67] In late 2014 the United Kingdom received a similar "most wanted" list from Beijing of about fifty individuals (France received a list of ten).[68]

Despite a personal visit by Wang Qishan to the United States in March 2015 (at a time when he held no state position), the United States, Britain, Australia, and the other countries could do relatively little to help. In view of China's abysmal human rights record, even if extradition were legally possible via UNCAC in the absence of bilateral treaties, there could still be major political obstacles. Aside from this problem, those fielding the Chinese lists have expressed similar frustrations to those receiving the initial Egyptian requests immediately after the overthrow of Mubarak.[69] Getting a document with dozens of names on it, together with an assertion that these individuals are corrupt, and therefore that the presumptive host country should track down assets belonging to these people and confiscate and repatriate them, is no help at all in either a practical or legal sense. Those in host countries make clear that such open-ended requests would require them to mandate every single financial institution in the country to run dedicated searches and to look through all the corporate and property registries, including intermediating shell companies and trusts, and that there is no chance they will do this. Instead, the Chinese themselves need to amass enough information to make a proper request: locating the assets in question and providing evidence that at least establishes reasonable grounds for suspecting that a crime has been committed. Aside from this frustration, China's anti-corruption campaign may have actually stimulated the flight of officials, if history is anything to go by. In 2003 an anti-graft drive apparently led over eight thousand officials to flee the country.[70]

In April 2015 Fox Hunt was succeeded by a broader initiative going under the Hollywood-esque moniker "Sky Net," which saw the Central Commission for Discipline Inspection joined by the People's Bank of China (which houses China's anti–money laundering unit), the Ministry of Public Security, and the prosecutor's office. Sky Net had similar goals of recovering stolen assets, bringing home corrupt officials, and attacking underground banks. Aside from the financial intelligence expertise of the central bank, enrolling the relevant state bodies might have been a move to ease foreign concerns that the campaign should be conducted in accord with the rule of law, thus encouraging extradition. By this time Fox Hunt had apparently produced the return of 680 corrupt officials (voluntarily and otherwise) from fifty-six countries, including the precedent of an extradition from Italy.[71] However, Beijing's frustration with a lack of cooperation from other governments was indicated in the exposure of undeclared and unauthorized actions by Chinese police in late 2014 and 2015 seeking to "persuade" Sky Net targets in Australia, Canada, the United States, and perhaps other countries as well to return to China. The Australian and US governments both condemned these actions, receiving a promise that they would not be repeated.[72]

Laundering Corruption Proceeds: Banks, Real Estate, and Lawyers

A central concern of this book is whether shortcomings in fighting cross-border grand corruption reflect host governments that are unable or unwilling to stanch the inward flows of tainted funds from abroad. In light of the powerful laws in place to combat criminal money, the Australian government's lack of response in intercepting, confiscating, and repatriating foreign looted wealth clearly suggests that a lack of motivation is more important than a lack of capacity. Here I examine deficiencies in preventive measures that allow foreign criminal money in, with reference to banks, the real estate industry, and lawyers.

Of the three, banking is by far the most regulated sector and thus would seem to provide the best safeguard against dirty money. Australian banks are covered by extensive reporting obligations to AUSTRAC, and they have a strict legal duty to perform Know Your Customer checks with respect to new and existing account holders. Division 400 of the criminal code mandates that banks and individual bankers can be prosecuted for money laundering where they knowingly, recklessly, or negligently accept money derived from crime, including corruption offenses committed abroad. Negligence applies when "the defendant has failed to exercise a reasonable standard of care to ensure that money or property is not the proceeds of crime."[73] In the information gathered by the private investigator mentioned above, banks' willingness to process payments for properties on behalf of those facing charges of corruption abroad without checking the legality of the funds might well qualify as negligent. Australia's banking sector is highly concentrated around four major institutions, each of which spends tens of millions of dollars on compliance and risk management. As a result, Australian government officials interviewed by the author on the record maintain that because any significant flows of corruption funds would have to go through the banks, and because the banks are well regulated, corruption proceeds are not a significant problem for Australia. But confidential interviews, as well as experience from equivalent foreign jurisdictions, suggest that this complacent attitude is fundamentally mistaken.[74]

Some unpublicized examples of failures among junior and senior bank staff bring this complacent attitude into question, as recounted to me in confidential interviews. One wire transfer payment routed through a major Australian bank to New York had an associated message, "This is for the jihad mother-fuckers." When the bank employee in Australia responsible for screening suspect wire transfers for terrorist financing risks was asked why he hadn't flagged this, he replied that he didn't know what "jihad" meant. One customer at a major Australian bank had had over 90 suspicious transactions lodged in connection with his activities without any action being taken by the bank or the authorities to either close his account or begin an investigation. At a presentation to another major bank's board, one board member suggested that international sanctions on North Korea and Iran presented the bank with a highly lucrative commercial opportunity to "play in this space" and sell services to these countries, considering the complete lack of competition. This board member was only reluctantly persuaded to drop the idea on the grounds that deliberately violating UN, US, and Australian sanctions might involve some legal complications further down the track.

Australian bankers earlier indicated privately to me that they believed the federal government did not take the issue of holding the proceeds of foreign corruption seriously, and so the banks took a correspondingly relaxed view of this risk.[75] Similarly, these bankers indicated that they took a tolerant view of accepting the proceeds of corruption in their Southeast Asian and South Pacific subsidiaries and branches (including Papua New Guinea). Once the funds are accepted at an overseas branch of an Australian bank, it is a relatively simple matter to transfer them to Australia. Especially when it comes to their private banking presence, Australian banks suggest that this aspect of their operations would simply be uneconomical if they were to take rigorous precautions to screen out suspect wealth, though this is more a concern in Southeast Asia (where private fortunes are bigger) than in the South Pacific.

In part this vulnerability in the banking sector reflects a bureaucratic disconnect among Australian government agencies. While AUSTRAC is responsible for ensuring that banks implement proper Know Your Customer procedures, the Australian Federal Police are tasked with investigating specific money laundering crimes. When it comes to overseas corruption proceeds, each agency is of the belief that tackling this problem is the responsibility of the other.[76] Since its creation in 1988, AUSTRAC has never sanctioned any Australian bank for money laundering violations. Rather like the case of the UK Financial Services Authority (subsequently replaced by the Financial Conduct Authority), this lack of any substantive enforcement action seems to indicate that the regulator has been captured by those it is supposed to be supervising. One individual with experience of both systems contrasts enforcement in the United States and Australia. AUSTRAC's regulation of banks was said to be limited to monitoring the number of Suspicious Transaction Reports and sending letters to banks when the level was felt to be too low. US regulators would send staff to question compliance officers and audit banks that were suspected of lax enforcement.[77] In view of earlier conclusions about the mythical nature of banks' reputational incentive to comply with anti–money laundering standards, the lack of monetary sanctions is a cause for concern. AUSTRAC does little to audit banks' due diligence in relation to high-risk foreign senior officials and actually tried to block the Papua New Guinean police from distributing a list of such officials directly to Australian banks. Though evidence is very hard to come by, there are some indications in my interviews that those within the Australian police trying to take a more robust line against the banks were vetoed by senior leadership.

Despite these unpropitious circumstances for screening out illicit funds from abroad, somewhat surprisingly, beginning in late 2012, Australian banks have, in some instances at least, independently tightened their standards when it comes to accepting suspicious foreign transfers, perhaps reflecting the sporadic media attention to this issue. As noted above, the key initial move against Paul Paraka was the decision to refuse his wire transfers, and Prime Minister O'Neill had at least some of his personal accounts in Australia closed, to the surprise and consternation of the Australian government. Further indications of a tightening up emerged after May 2014, when an investigator working for Global Witness posed as a foreign investor looking to bribe a Papua New Guinean minister for various investment permits. He went to a law firm in the capital, Port Moresby, to seek advice on the best way to pay the bribe, secretly videotaping the conversation. The lawyers cautioned that one-off large payments of this nature to Australia would now be flagged as suspicious, and that instead "small dribs and drabs are the only way to go," with an ostensibly commercial rationale for the transfers. One lawyer commented wistfully, "The days of banging a million bucks into this secret numbered account in Singapore is over."[78]

The real estate sector is much less regulated than banks, and so it can be an easy and convenient way of laundering money, as per the examples discussed earlier in this chapter. Akin to the situation in the United States, under a "temporary" exemption in place since 2006, real estate agents have no duty to screen their clients or their clients' wealth, or to report suspicious transactions. Despite the prominence of real estate in money laundering generally,[79] AUSTRAC has paid little or no attention to this sector,[80] first because of the "temporary" exemption and second on the assumption that because all real estate transactions must go through banks, all property transactions will be subject to rigorous scrutiny at this stage. This position has been echoed exactly by the real estate industry association, which confidently asserted: "To the extent that we have any money going through a financial institution of any sort, we have anti–money laundering laws—which involves 'know your client' et cetera—so that basically filters out grey money and shadow money."[81] While the examples above indicate how singularly misplaced this confidence is, a November 2014 parliamentary inquiry into foreign investment in Australian real estate only reinforces these doubts, as described below.

In theory, only residents may buy established residential properties (as distinct from those properties built from scratch). In the context of massive increases in inward flows (at A$24.8 billion, investment in commercial and residential property in the first nine months of financial year 2013–2014 was 44 percent higher than the entire preceding financial year), the inquiry noted the complete lack of any enforcement action by the responsible regulatory agency, the Foreign Investment Review Board, since 2006. The report noted that it "defies belief" that there had been no violations in this period.[82] The board has eight people to consider six thousand applications a year, with some individual applications being for buildings that contain dozens of apartments sold to different owners. As a result, the inquiry notes, "No-one really knows how much foreign investment there is in residential real estate, nor where that investment comes from."[83] The following year the board's directors confirmed this, noting that finding out "where the money came from is somebody else's responsibility." A senior law enforcement official responded, "They should lose their job . . . that is an indictment."[84] Yet the police themselves indicate that there is so much Chinese money flowing into real estate that unless there is a specific request from a local or foreign agency relating to a specific individual, they have no appetite to screen for illicit wealth.[85] Investment from Papua New Guinea is similarly waved through.[86]

If banks and real estate are two common channels by which suspect funds enter Australia, the third closely related link involves law firms. Once again, the prominent role of lawyers in laundering the proceeds of corruption is by no means peculiar to Australia, as we saw in the Marcos, Duvalier, Ibori, Bhutto/Zardari, and Obiang cases covered earlier. A particular point of vulnerability is once again the use of law firms' trust accounts. In Papua New Guinea, for example, an official may transfer funds from his personal account to his local law firm's trust account, which then transfers these funds to the trust account of its Australian counterpart office. The funds may then be used to buy property or pay further bribes. In such cases it is very unlikely that the bank transfers would be flagged as suspicious and thus come to the attention of the anti–money laundering system. Law firms' trust accounts often have a high volume of funds from different clients passing through, and therefore even quite large transfers for property purchases are unlikely to stand out, especially in the case of large firms. Many of the law firms represented in Papua New Guinea are originally Australian, and in some cases senior Papua New Guinean officials practiced for these same firms.

The Global Witness secret footage of local and Australian lawyers in Port Moresby discussing the best way to pay a bribe is again instructive. In it one of the lawyers (an associate of Prime Minister O'Neill) refers to the services of an Australian law firm with offices in Brisbane and Sydney that is willing to submit deliberately inflated invoices in order to camouflage money brought into Australia for laundering and illicit payments. It is explained that because the parties are working with a prestigious Queen's Counsel lawyer in Australia, the transfers don't arouse suspicion.[87] Other investigations indicate that there are at least half a dozen other Australian law firms willing to make similar arrangements.[88]

Able but Unwilling, and the Prospects for Change

When it comes to foreign corruption, Australian law enforcement has taken the line that the proper path for stolen asset recovery is for the victim countries to get confiscation orders in their own courts, which can then be enforced in Australia.[89] The other option is for the victim country to lodge a mutual legal assistance request. Either way, the legal system in the victim countries must do most of the work before Australia will take action against stolen assets it is hosting. If this had been the attitude in any of the other countries considered earlier, probably not a single dollar of the proceeds of grand corruption would have ever been recovered. The United States, Britain, and Switzerland are all explicitly committed to taking the initiative in pursuing foreign corruption proceeds, through the US Department of Justice anti-kleptocracy task force and Immigration and Customs Enforcement unit, the British Department for International Development–funded Overseas Corruption Unit, and the Swiss 2011 "Lex Duvalier," the prospective "Lex Ben Ali," and the dedicated asset recovery team in the Swiss Ministry of Foreign Affairs. Australia, by contrast, still maintains the pre-Abacha and pre-Marcos attitude that denies host country responsibility for grand corruption and the associated money laundering. Even when the money in question has been placed and laundered in Australia, foreign corruption is seen as a problem for foreigners, not the Australian government, law enforcement, or regulators.

The paucity of kleptocratic wealth recovered is not because Australia lacks the relevant laws, which actually tend to give authorities stronger confiscation powers than those of the other three countries considered. It is possible to obtain a money laundering conviction when the crime that gave rise to the proceeds is not even mentioned, let alone proven.[90] This and the provisions for reckless and negligent money laundering (i.e., in the absence of intent) mean that the legal hurdles to obtaining a conviction are significantly lower than in other countries, or than is required by the relevant international conventions.[91] Australia has non-conviction-based forfeiture powers that are among the strongest in the world.[92] Furthermore, alone among the states examined here, Australia also has unexplained wealth laws in place. These serve to reverse the burden of proof: respondents must prove the legality of their assets, even in the absence of any evidence connecting them with any criminal activity.[93] The fundamental obstacle that has frustrated action against many kleptocrats, the necessity of linking a specific asset with a specific crime, thus does not apply. The point is not that Australia could quickly and easily confiscate all or most foreign corruption proceeds if the government wanted. Even with these extensive powers, asset recovery is difficult. Rather, it is that inaction is a result of political judgment rather than deficient laws.

If weak laws cannot explain the failure to take action against foreign corruption proceeds in Australia, what can? At a lower level, as with anywhere else, banks operate to maximize profits, while in a phenomenon that is observable in the United Kingdom and Switzerland (and to a lesser degree in the United States), regulators seem to have been captured by banks. Yet this fails to explain why Australia lags these other countries in countering kleptocracy, and why in some instances banks have actually taken independent action to expel suspicious funds while law enforcement and regulators have remained passive. Similarly, other specific failures, like AUSTRAC's view that money laundering in the real estate sector is not its problem, or the career incentives in the Australian Federal Police that favor not investigating potential crimes (because failed investigations are a much bigger career negative than successful investigations are a career positive), are also relevant. However, more important than any of these factors is that the Australian government has decided that taking action against foreign corruption proceeds is not a priority.[94]

The question of why the Australian government has legally and rhetorically endorsed the global anti-kleptocracy regime but so far failed to implement its tenets returns us to the main questions posed in the Introduction. As we have seen in the experiences of the United States, United Kingdom, and Switzerland, there was a significant lag between the initial commitments to fighting grand corruption and concrete action to hold kleptocrats accountable. Change occurred thanks to determined victim governments like the Philippines and Nigeria, interacting with related domestic scandals fanned by the media, NGOs, and activist legislators. Australia has not been connected with any of the iconic instances of kleptocracy, and despite occasional media stories, there have been no major scandals as a result of hosting foreign corruption proceeds. Victim countries in the region either have been indifferent to asset recovery (e.g., Indonesia, Malaysia, and Pacific Island states) or have had a only a recent and sporadic interest in this cause (China and Papua New Guinea). In the absence of sustained foreign pressure and until such a scandal does occur, the decision not to look for foreign corruption proceeds, and hence not to find them, is a self-sustaining excuse that allows rhetorical endorsement of the anti-kleptocracy norm with practical inaction.

An instructive analogue that may illuminate the potential for change is the long delay between Australia's accession to the OECD Anti-Bribery Convention in 1999 and the decision to actually start to enforce its provisions more than a decade later. The shift was a result of outside peer pressure, foreign investigations as part of the UN Iraqi Oil-for-Food inquiry and a resulting political controversy at home, and revelations about the foreign bribery by Australia's central bank in seeking contracts. In a 2012 review the OECD reported that the assessment team "has serious concerns that overall enforcement of the foreign bribery offence to date has been extremely low," with not a single conviction recorded and only one investigation under way.[95] The assessment team was blunt in its criticisms in meetings with government officials across all the relevant agencies.[96] Much like the reasoning behind the inactivity in response to foreign corruption proceeds, the government's line had been that Australian firms simply didn't bribe, and thus that the lack of investigations and convictions reflected an inherent Antipodean honesty.

This insouciant thesis became much harder to sustain, however, when in 2005 the Volcker Inquiry for the United Nations into the Iraqi Oil-for-Food affair revealed that the Australian Wheat Board had regularly and enthusiastically paid huge kickbacks to Saddam Hussein's government. Furthermore, the Australian government had repeatedly ignored public and private warnings to this effect.[97] The terms of a public inquiry into the matter were designed to deflect responsibility from the government, while a police investigation ultimately failed to make any charges.[98]

The negative publicity regarding the Wheat Board affair had only recently died down when another, even more serious case of foreign bribery came into the media spotlight. Whistle-blowers came forward concerning foreign bribery committed by two firms, Note Printing Australia and Securency. The first was wholly owned by the Reserve Bank of Australia (RBA, the central bank), while the second was half-owned by the RBA, which was also responsible for auditing both companies. Jointly they sold Australian banknote printing technology under license to foreign central banks, aided (as it turned out) by bribes of more than A$50 million to officials from up to sixteen countries.[99] The whistle-blowers had made complaints in 2007 to the RBA, which ignored them, and in 2009 to the police, who were similarly uninterested. In 2010, however, the story was leaked to journalists, precipitating extensive media coverage and a near-instantaneous change of heart among the police, who began an investigation. The case blew out to involve Vietnamese president Truong Tan San, two Indonesian presidents (Megawati Sukarnoputri and Susilo Bambang Yudhoyono), and three Malaysian prime ministers (Mahathir Mohamad, Abdullah Ahmad Badawi, and Najib Razak).[100] In response, the Australian government obtained a gag order forbidding all reporting of the case, and also forbidding any mention of the gag order itself on the grounds of "national security" (the order was leaked by Australian Julian Assange).[101]

More positively, however, a task force was assembled from a variety of agencies to investigate not just this case but also several others of suspected foreign bribery. In July 2014 this new priority was formalized with the establishment of a police-led multiagency Fraud and Anti-Corruption Center, which launched investigations into several of the country's largest companies. Though it is early days, in 2015 an OECD follow-up review noted the seventeen new investigations under way and generally acknowledged "good progress on addressing a number of important recommendations" (though the report also faulted the gag order in the RBA case).[102] Though there were some legal and regulatory adjustments, the main difference was a change in political priorities institutionalized in a new, dedicated enforcement unit given scope to begin many investigations, including against large and politically powerful corporate interests.

The parallels between Australian firms bribing foreign officials and foreign officials laundering the proceeds of corruption in Australia can be taken only so far, but the comparison is suggestive. In both cases international legal and rhetorical commitments to fight corruption were left unenforced, a dead letter. The drivers of change in the former were foreign investigations, media scandals leading to political pressure on the government, and a scathing public peer review highlighting Australia's lack of effectiveness in implementing its international obligations. Although as of 2015 there has still been only one foreign bribery conviction, public evidence suggests that there is now something of a real commitment to enforcing the letter and the spirit of the OECD Anti-Bribery Convention. There are only the faintest signs of any such commitment to effectively implementing the anti-kleptocracy regime.

The final, more abstract question is that if Australia's indifference to enforcing the legal and policy emanations of the anti-kleptocracy norm is typical of most other rich-country governments, to what extent is this a norm at all? Can words and paper commitments to a principle comprise a norm if they are disconnected from action? It seems that governments can talk the talk of anti-corruption by subscribing to the norm without necessarily walking the walk, for at least two reasons. First, grand corruption and associated foreign money laundering may be hidden. Second, it is not easy to tell the difference between governments that have tried but failed to recover stolen assets and those that have not tried at all. These two characteristics mean that the peer pressure, social sanctions, and accountability mechanisms that might otherwise be applied against hypocrites and shirkers are attenuated or absent. Although there is a generally shared idea that it is wrong for a country to host money stolen by the leaders of another country, absent high-profile scandals governments are not (yet) pushed to make this principle effective.

Conclusion

Making Them Pay

For the first time in history, there is a public consensus that for a state to host money stolen by an official of another state is morally wrong. Furthermore, an elaborate system of conventions, treaties, laws, and regulations have institutionalized this principle. What we do not have, though, is a good sense of how much difference this system of rules has made in reducing the cross-border flow of plundered wealth. My assessment is that the regime to counter grand corruption is not working well, even where governments are genuinely committed to this cause (many are only going through the motions). Shortcomings in the way the regime is operating reflect obstacles, including the difficulties of international legal cooperation and misaligned commercial and bureaucratic incentives. In thinking about effectiveness more broadly, we may find it useful to reconsider the three original goals of the campaign: to generate funds for development by returning stolen assets, to deter kleptocracy and laundering through increasing the chance of detection and punishment, and to satisfy the desire for accountability in victim countries. I argue that the first goal is unrealistic and that attention should instead be focused on the second and third.

The longer section of this Conclusion suggests some options for improving the effectiveness of the anti-kleptocracy regime. Though many are quite radical, I maintain that none is utopian or completely unrealistic, since the suggested reforms build on, adapt, and extend measures that are already partially in place. Remedies are roughly divided into those in the state sphere and those better suited to private actors. The former include much more robust policing and sanctioning of banks and other intermediaries to boost the effectiveness of preventive measures, exploiting the anti-corruption potential of the tax system, and expanding the use of blacklists against individuals and countries to prevent physical and financial access to key host states. Private actors can exploit the potential of civil and criminal law to bring cases directly against kleptocrats and their assets in host countries. These challenges could be funded by an intergovernmental trust fund, wealthy NGOs, or for-profit firms in return for a share of the proceeds. As a complement to this strategy, it is possible to turn the profit motive from an enemy into an ally by enlisting law firms, legal financing companies, venture capitalists, and vulture funds to hunt down looted wealth.

Implications for World Politics

Though this is not a book about theory, detailed evidence on whether and how global rules work is important even for abstract, big-picture accounts of world politics. There are few more important questions than whether and under what conditions international anarchy can be tempered by global rules. Working out the effect of such rules is much harder than it might seem. Compliance might indicate that rules are shaping states' actions, but it might just as well reflect that states have designed the rules to fit with what they planned to do anyway. Short of the unrealistic notion of using the full experimental protocol of randomly assigning states to control and treatment groups to test for causation, detailed studies tracing the chain of events built on a mix of firsthand and secondary accounts seem like the next best thing.[1]

With regard to compliance with rules, one school of thought suggests that if people say the right words for long enough, their behavior will sooner or later converge. Officials giving speeches denouncing the "cancer" or "scourge" of corruption, extolling good governance, signing treaties, and enacting legislation is not just verbiage, this view holds, but an indicator of minds progressively being changed as part of a process that will later flow through into actual change. The shift may happen either because policy makers are socialized into sincerely adopting new beliefs or because they are pressured into following through for fear that their insincere commitments will be publicly exposed as duplicitous.[2] But can we really say that there is a global anti-kleptocracy norm if most countries fail to implement the provisions of the associated regime? No one publicly challenges the prohibition on hosting stolen wealth, nor do leaders any longer argue the cultural relativist line that corruption is merely a Western framing of legitimate local practices.

But an opposing perspective holds that the connection between words and actions in world politics is almost infinitely elastic and that hypocrisy can endure over the long term. On this basis, cynics would argue that because there are so many powerful entrenched interests threatened by the anti-kleptocracy campaign, all these promises and commitments will amount to nothing. In a world without a central enforcer, states must look after themselves and will not engage in costly altruistic causes.

When it comes to grand corruption, no amount of analyzing speeches or reading legislation will shed light on which of these opposing optimistic and pessimistic perspectives is closer to the mark. Instead, coming to a judgment requires a closer look at whether governments are actually trying to implement commitments, at what cost, and to what effect. The evidence from the four countries analyzed here forms a picture that crosscuts these different theoretical takes. In line with the pessimists' expectations, a majority of states are like Australia, in that they have signed up to the anti-kleptocracy regime but seem to put little or no effort into trying to make it effective. Yet unsettling this view, the three states whose commitment is probably most important for the functioning of the regime thanks to their having the largest international financial centers, the United States, Britain, and Switzerland, have gone to considerable lengths to implement their commitments, despite the lack of a compelling national interest. In these instances, shortcomings do not reflect insincerity so much as limited ability. Furthermore, in response to the pessimistic thesis, it might be asked why states would feel the need to make principled commitments at all if they have no regard for peer pressure, especially because these commitments may leave them vulnerable to unintended consequences down the road. Much of the media embarrassment and political damage suffered by governments in states hosting foreign looted wealth has arisen from the gap between promises and action, or the lack thereof.

Conclusions on Effectiveness

It has now been over a decade since the most important planks of the anti-kleptocracy regime were laid. These include the United Nations Convention Against Corruption, corresponding amendments to national laws to criminalize the holding of foreign corruption proceeds, and perhaps most importantly, political decisions in the United States, Switzerland, and the United Kingdom to devote real effort to hunting down foreign corruption proceeds. Is this soon enough to make any sort of judgment on the regime's potential? When it comes to judging compliance, intergovernmental organizations have often concentrated on asking questions which are easy to answer, like the presence or absence of certain laws, but which are only tenuously related to actual effectiveness. In contrast, I have sought to answer more difficult questions about practical effectiveness. The remainder of this section suggests that hoping that greater effectiveness will come with time is overly optimistic, taking into account current limitations. These limitations spring from the mismatch between the global economy and the sovereign division of political authority, the tensions between holding kleptocrats accountable and the need to preserve fundamental rights, and misaligned incentives that undermine the motivation of banks, other intermediaries, and law enforcement agencies to make the system effective. Finally, before turning to some potential solutions, I ask what effectiveness really means in the struggle against kleptocracy.

One optimistic view of the campaign against kleptocracy suggests that getting a problem on to the policy agenda, breaking the taboo around even talking about corruption, is the first and most important step, and that effectiveness will follow in due course. The world has certainly moved on from the deafening silence about corruption in the 1980s and before. It is now almost a mantra that corruption is morally wrong and a serious impediment to economic development. But will all the rhetorical support for the anti-kleptocracy regime feed through into greater effectiveness in the future? An example that might support this hopeful line of thinking is the experience with foreign bribery, in the United States and with respect to the OECD Convention more generally.

The Foreign Corrupt Practices Act was passed by Congress in 1977, but at least until the 1990s there was little or no effort to apply it, with only 23 enforcement actions up until 1992.[3] In the period 2001–2013, however, there were 189 enforcement actions, and since 1999 there have been 128 cases ending in convictions or other sanctions.[4] A further 21 enforcement actions were under way in 2014 alone.[5] This lag between legislation and implementation is not an American exception. The British Aerospace scandal in the United Kingdom, involving secret payments to leading Saudi officials in return for a £43 billion arms deal, was a tawdry spectacle of successive Conservative and Labour governments sabotaging investigations to protect the guilty.[6] Yet out of this affair came both stringent new anti-bribery legislation in 2010 and, more importantly, a series of robust investigations. As discussed in the previous chapter, the Australian government did nothing to implement its 1999 commitment to the OECD Anti-Bribery Convention until more than ten years later.

Among the signatories to the Convention (who extend beyond the membership of the OECD as such), the period 1999–2006 saw only 49 enforcement actions, while from 2007 to 2013 there were 366 such actions, with 390 current investigations in 2014.[7] This trend may actually understate the improvement, because later enforcement actions have imposed much more severe penalties than earlier ones. Aside from the formal penalties, governments have become more adept in shifting the costs of investigation, which may run into the hundreds of millions of dollars, on to the corporate defendants.[8] As with almost any type of white-collar crime, there are more cases of foreign bribery that escape detection than are exposed. Nevertheless, there is a definite trend toward more countries devoting more effort to improving effectiveness, which is leading to better results. By extension from this example, even if the anti-kleptocracy regime has had limited success so far, might it just be a matter of time?

While it is impossible to rule out a sudden jump in effectiveness, there are reasons to be skeptical. The lag in effectiveness in policies to counter foreign bribery was a matter of governments shifting from introducing laws and ignoring them to then actually trying to implement these laws. Not surprisingly, when governments aren't even trying to enforce rules, the rules are ineffective. This describes the current position of Australia and most other OECD states in relation to hosting foreign corruption proceeds. Yet although a genuine commitment to implementing the rules may be a necessary condition, it is far from being sufficient. When it comes to the United States, Britain, and Switzerland, even committed efforts to hold kleptocrats accountable have more often than not come up short. Though it is impossible to say for sure, even if many other countries began living up to their UNCAC obligations, that might not boost the effectiveness of the regime very much. Social scientists are notoriously poor crystal-ball gazers, but aside from trying to peer into the future, it is possible to discern some of the most important current legal, bureaucratic, and commercial obstacles to effectiveness, even where governments are trying to do the right thing.

Perhaps the first of these hindrances is the simple fact that both dirty and clean funds traverse borders easily, while cross-border law enforcement and international legal cooperation are difficult. International agreements like UNCAC and countless others, as well as asset recovery facilitators like StAR and the International Centre for Asset Recovery, mean that the problem is less daunting than it was, but the basic fact remains unchanged. Together with a second key factor, the weakness of legal systems in victim countries, these problems mean that it is almost impossible to prove kleptocrats guilty beyond a reasonable doubt, either for their original crimes at home or for derivative money laundering abroad. In part thanks to the "war on drugs," governments have lowered the legal threshold for confiscating assets. Some countries have relied on non-conviction-based forfeiture procedures or unexplained wealth rules that obligate those targeted to prove that their wealth is legitimate, rather than the state having to prove the opposite. These types of laws, combined with more traditional civil legal action, have produced most of the asset recovery successes to date. As a result, many policy makers and NGOs have urged that the presumption of innocence be relaxed even further. The dilemma this raises, however, is that the fight against corruption becomes a threat to fundamental liberties. Governments have a wide scope to abuse such far-reaching powers. There is something of an Alice in Wonderland quality to defining corruption as the abuse of government power and then giving governments more power to fight corruption in the hope they won't abuse it.

An illustration of this tension is Transparency International UK's lobbying for unexplained wealth laws in a 2015 report. The report specifies that there should be safeguards to prevent the abuse of such powers but then admits that similar safeguards have failed to prevent the misuse of laws supposedly limited to fighting terrorism.[9] In Britain laws passed to fight the most serious national security threats have been pressed into service to curb existential menaces like littering, dog fouling, putting out recycling bins on the wrong day, and unauthorized pizza sales, as well as to designate Iceland a terrorist state.[10] Of course there have been far worse examples elsewhere, including the authorization of mass surveillance, kidnaping, and torture by the US government as part of anti-terrorism measures.[11] International standards to counter the financing of terrorism and money laundering have unintentionally strengthened the repressive powers of tyrannical regimes to persecute dissidents and destroy independent NGOs, both at home and abroad.[12] The problem with measures like unexplained wealth laws is that lowering legal safeguards sufficiently far to effectively hold kleptocrats accountable would seriously damage the legal system as a framework designed to protect citizens' freedoms against the state.[13] Those studying corruption should be the first to appreciate that governments will often abuse new powers. As long as fundamental legal rights like the presumption of innocence, the right to a fair trial, and the right to property remain substantially intact, the criminal justice system will struggle to deal with cross-border grand corruption, which is why we should look to other policy solutions as well.

The first and perhaps most important line of defense against tainted money is the banks. As described in chapter 1, beginning in the 1980s and 1990s, banks were conscripted to track and screen out drug money. The coverage of these anti–money laundering laws has since expanded to include corruption crimes. Yet considering that banks and individual bankers have a strong incentive to accept money on a no-questions-asked basis, how can they be made to act as unpaid enforcers, against the grain of the profit motive? The conventional answer comes in two parts. The first is that the relevant laws allow the authorities to impose severe penalties on banks and their employees if they are found to be shirking their responsibilities in accepting criminal proceeds. The second is that beyond formal punishment, banks that are derelict in their duty to screen out tainted funds will suffer damage to their reputations, especially in high-profile cases like grand corruption. Exactly what damage to reputation means in terms of specific consequences is seldom made clear. It seems to refer to some combination of damage to the brand and standing of the institution, perhaps flowing on to diminished share price and loss of business. Yet both of these mechanisms look very suspect.

With the singular exception of the United States, regulators rarely if ever impose significant penalties on banks, even when they are caught engaging in serious misconduct. This reluctance seems to be product of regulatory capture, as regulators have come to identify with the interests of banks rather than the general public. With this record of inaction, banks have presumably concluded that regulators' bark is much worse than their bite. The same problem of those laundering foreign corruption proceeds escaping penalties is even more true of other gatekeepers, such as law firms.

What of reputation? Here the trouble is that large international banks have been involved in so many major scandals, reaching well beyond the matter of corruption, that they would appear to have little reputation left to lose. Nearly all of the leading banks making up the Wolfsberg Group, which pledged the highest ethical standards, including fighting corruption, have been exposed as participating in a wide range of criminal conspiracies. Aside from the corruption-related lapses covered already, this criminal conduct includes disguising wire payments to sanctioned regimes and rigging key interest-rate benchmarks and foreign exchange markets, not to speak of the more diffuse failings associated with the financial crisis beginning in 2007. Banks are not indifferent to the negative media coverage and criticism generated when they are exposed as hosting the proceeds of corruption.[14] Yet it is hard to see any actual cost as a result of such adverse publicity, let alone one sufficient to counterbalance the imperative to generate more business.

In fairness to banks, it is important to acknowledge gaps in the evidence. When suspicious clients are turned away or have their accounts closed, and when banks report suspicious transactions, this rarely becomes public. Accordingly, preventive successes by banks are invisible. While many interviewees are critical of banks' performance, arguing that these and other financial firms are only going through the motions of screening out dirty money, they also concede that there has been substantive change since the 1990s. Banks no longer dispute that they have a duty to screen out criminal funds, including those derived from corruption abroad. Large banks spend tens of millions of dollars and employ hundreds of staff in their compliance departments. It also bears stressing that even when banks have a direct incentive to counter crimes (unlike corruption and money laundering cases), such as employee and credit card fraud, these kinds of white-collar crimes more often than not go unsolved.[15] Somewhat surprisingly, both the financial sector and regulators privately agree that the substantial sums of money that banks spend on compliance are oriented toward placating regulators rather than catching criminals or screening out their money.[16]

At the broadest level, the continuing prevalence of grand corruption, and the fact that this money continues to go through the banks, shows that the system is not working well. The obvious profit motive combined with the paucity of sanctions, regulatory capture, and the illusory nature of the reputation effect jointly suggest why this is the case.

If banks face incentives that compromise the fight against kleptocracy, so too do the police. These incentives favor tackling local crimes. As one interviewee put it, "Belgian cops are paid with Belgian taxes to solve Belgian problems." Why should police be investigating crimes committed abroad when there are plenty of unsolved murders and rapes at home? Some law enforcement officers commented to me that many of their colleagues got into this line of work to shoot guns, kick down doors, and get in car chases, not pore over spreadsheets and accounting records (though this temperamental objection to financial investigations seems to be changing). A further impediment might be prosecutors favoring relatively straightforward cases with a high chance of quick success, rather than long, complicated, and uncertain foreign corruption cases. Making a particular agency or unit explicitly responsible for pursuing foreign grand corruption and the associated money flows, as has been done in United States, Britain, and Switzerland, helps to bring these incentives into better alignment.

Three Views of Effectiveness

More broadly, it is helpful to reexamine the question of effectiveness. Fighting kleptocracy via asset recovery is said to be worthwhile for three main reasons: it provides new money for development in poor countries; it deters would-be corrupt officials and associated money launderers; and it satisfies the desire for accountability among those in victim countries.[17] After all the evidence considered, how well do these claims stack up? If something around $5 billion of looted wealth has been repatriated, this might seem to be a substantial benefit in absolute terms, even if it represents only a small fraction of the total stolen.[18] Unfortunately, however, there is much less than meets the eye to this figure.

First, it does not include the legal fees and broader investigative expenses. These figures are rarely made public (the approximately $46 million in legal fees in the 2014 Abacha settlement being a notable exception), but in cases like the Duvaliers, Chiluba, and the Arab Spring, the costs are almost certainly greater than the amounts actually recovered. If generating more development funding was the aim, it would be simpler just to leave the proceeds of corruption in place and give the money that would be spent on lawyers and investigators directly to developing countries. Then there is the painful subject of repatriated assets being stolen again after they have been returned to the victim government. There are indications that at least some of the confiscated corruption funds returned to the Philippine, Peruvian, and Nigerian governments were diverted.[19] A controversial response, much resented by victim governments, has been to set up independent monitoring arrangements to ensure that the money is spent appropriately.[20] While these may be effective, they are also expensive. In the case of $48 million returned from Switzerland to Kazakhstan, monitoring cost a third of the funds repatriated.[21] Thus in view of the costs of recovery and monitoring, and the danger of repatriated funds being stolen by a different government in the same country, the real financial rewards of asset recovery are very meager.

Deterrence, being a counterfactual about what would otherwise have happened, is always difficult to study. Considering the costs and difficulties of the asset recovery process, prevention by deterrence is in principle a much more promising route to tackling kleptocracy. Has the anti-kleptocracy regime dissuaded senior political officials from stealing public wealth and laundering it outside their own country? The evidence simply does not permit an answer, but with the low chances of being caught, it would seem to be a leap of faith to assume it has. It is possible that certain financial centers may have deterred corrupt officials from placing their money there, though even here the evidence is scarce. The mobility of capital could mean a displacement of corruption-related money laundering to a less scrupulous center (Dubai and Latvia being regularly mentioned as such havens among interviewees) rather than a reduction.

The final payoff is said to be political: demonstrating to victim populations that, sometimes at least, there is justice, in that corrupt and tyrannical leaders are sometimes held to account. Experiences from the Arab Spring, to the overthrow of the Ukrainian government in 2014, to contemporary discontent with corruption among the leadership of the Chinese Communist Party certainly suggest that there is a deep and widespread popular yearning for corrupt rulers to be brought to book. From this perspective, if the costs of asset recovery exceed the funds actually recovered, this may not matter. Potential deals struck with past or present kleptocrats to offer amnesty in return for handing over a portion of their loot, as in the Abacha case, may be the most efficient way of recovering assets, but such agreements are the worst in promoting accountability. When corrupt officials are still in power, or efforts to hold them accountable at home have failed, attacking their wealth in host countries may be the only recourse left. Most of the (partial) success stories examined in previous chapters fall into this category, from Marcos to Obiang. The campaign against kleptocracy looks to be on firmer ground when accountability is the main goal, first in setting down a marker that both kleptocracy and accepting the resulting tainted wealth are morally unacceptable, and then in condemning some of those who violate this prohibition. Even so, the question might be whether important symbolic verdicts of condemnation and shaming might be achieved more effectively and far more cheaply, for example in a UN General Assembly or Security Council resolution, or an updated Transparency International top ten kleptocrats list.

Solutions

If the effectiveness of the current anti-kleptocracy regime is low, if the rules fail more often than they succeed, and if the costs too often outweigh the benefits, what, if anything, can be done? Here I argue that there are measures that can improve the rather unhappy status quo. Though jointly radical, each of these suggestions is based on policies that in some form are already in place. These measures are relatively cheap and would improve the effectiveness of the fight against grand corruption. The goal is not so much to boost narrow measures like the number of convictions or the amounts of money confiscated and repatriated. Instead, it is to advance the broader policy goals of making it harder for kleptocrats to launder the proceeds of their corruption in major financial centers and promoting accountability where there otherwise would be none. The logic of this aim is that "corruption will remain a profitable crime in developing countries as long as counterparts in rich countries are willing to hide stolen resources."[22] Though screening out foreign kleptocracy proceeds will not end grand corruption, it will remove one of the main facilitating conditions. Some of the most important innovations suggested here to boost effectiveness revolve around a greater role for private actors, but states still have a vital role to play, first in strengthening preventive measures, second in adapting tax policy, and third in applying blacklists against individuals and states.

Preventive measures are far more cost-effective than remedial action to find, seize, and return plundered wealth. Indeed, in the large majority of cases, once foreign corruption proceeds have entered the financial system, it is too late to address the problem. Even if these funds are detected later, the time and expense of going through the recovery process generally outweigh the benefits of doing so. With a few exceptions, improving safeguards is a matter of better enforcing existing laws rather than passing new legislation or drafting new international standards. Better enforcement means actually checking that firms are following the laws and regulations they should be, and applying substantial penalties to those that aren't. It might be thought that this point is too obvious to mention, but the material presented earlier shows that regulators often do not check on compliance, or they do so by simply asking firms whether they are complying. Even when regulators check performance independently, outside the United States they almost never apply meaningful sanctions for those violating the rules. Where foreign corruption proceeds are found, typically after a regime has fallen, authorities should conduct a full inquiry to find out how illicit funds entered the financial system and punish those private parties at fault. Because the preventive aspects of the anti-kleptocracy regime (drawn from anti–money laundering policy) are the most important, the pattern observed in previous chapters in which banks and other gatekeepers are almost never held accountable for not preemptively screening out illicit funds creates a standing incentive to turn a blind eye to suspicious funds.

One tool that has been remarkably neglected in the fight against cross-border corruption is tax policy. While anti–money laundering and countering the financing of terrorism are new priorities, states have long had very powerful means of looking into individuals' and firms' financial affairs and coercively extracting money from them in order to raise revenue. A campaign to improve international tax enforcement has proceeded in parallel with but in isolation from the campaign against corruption.[23] Traditional domestic tax powers and new international tax agreements have great potential for tracing and seizing illicit funds, but this potential has generally been overlooked. For example, if a kleptocrat has a foreign bank account, it probably earns interest, and failure to report this interest may constitute tax evasion. Tax laws also commonly require that foreign bank accounts, assets, and income are declared in the home country, a requirement that corrupt officials seldom meet. Most of the corrupt officials covered in this book are likely to be guilty of some such tax crime. Because tax evasion is increasingly a predicate crime for money laundering, these laws may be brought into play as well. It is often much easier to apply criminal or administrative sanctions for these kinds of simple tax crimes, such as failing to declare foreign assets or interest income, than for complex corruption cases. This action could be taken by either the victim or host state, or both. Tax authorities can often confiscate assets without having to go to court through raising tax assessments directly against individuals and companies, and, unlike the case for police forces, financial investigation and confiscating wealth from tightfisted owners are tax agencies' core functions.

As well as shoring up the regulatory framework to better ensure that private gatekeepers are applying the rules, and pressing the levers of tax compliance into service, there are several related, more direct state approaches. These include visa denials, blacklisting, and targeted financial sanctions. Denying entry to senior foreign officials on the grounds of suspected corruption was pioneered in the United States by presidential decree before being legislated in 2008. Since that time, visa denials for officials suspected of corruption have been endorsed by the G8 and the G20. Visa denial lists are not public, but in 2013 the United States apparently banned sixty to seventy individuals, Britain at least some officials from the

Kenyan government, and Australia some from Papua New Guinea (Swiss authorities firmly reject this "very Anglo-Saxon" approach).[24] Despite the importance of electronic, intangible financial flows, visa bans are important in cramping kleptocrats' proclivity for conspicuous consumption and high living in rich countries. Such bans can isolate these officials from their real estate abroad. Visa denials are cheap and legally easy to enforce, so it is eminently practical to use them more often.

From drawing up a list of those barred from entering a country, it is only a short step to a more comprehensive blacklist of suspected kleptocrats, or even whole governments. These lists would be public and could augment the visa ban by blocking access to a country's financial system. There are many precedents. Governments have long used economic sanctions as an instrument of statecraft.[25] Increasingly, these are targeted at particular individuals rather than whole countries.[26] Especially since 2001, individuals and organizations suspected of involvement in terrorism have been subject to both unilateral and multilateral blacklisting. In December 2012 the US Congress passed a law blacklisting eighteen Russian government officials for corruption and human rights abuses connected with the death of Moscow lawyer Sergei Magnitsky.[27] How might a more extensive and systematic blacklist of kleptocrats work? A 1995 US presidential executive order, later legislated as the Foreign Narcotics Kingpin Designation Act, provides a relevant template. Drawing on powers in place since 1986,[28] this act prohibits all US entities from doing business with designated individuals, their families, and any companies connected with these individuals, on pain of up to ten years' imprisonment.[29] The list is jointly compiled by the Departments of Treasury, State, Justice, and Homeland Security and other agencies, based on open-source and classified information leading to a "reasonable basis" to believe that an individual is in fact a drug kingpin.[30] Designating drug kingpins in this manner arose from similar frustrations as have been experienced by those looking to bring kleptocrats to account.[31] These individuals are untouchable in their own countries and can rarely be extradited, and even if their assets were in the United States, it would be difficult to attack them using conventional anti–money laundering laws, thanks to the lack of evidence from the foreign jurisdiction. In contrast, blacklist designations are cheap, practical, and effective and could be easily adapted to list suspected kleptocrats, their families, and associated business interests.

Though such a list of kleptocrats would be most effective if adopted multilaterally, there are good reasons to think that even US unilateral action would pay dividends. The United States sits at the center of global financial networks, the dollar is the world's default currency, and the US government has taken a very expansive view of its jurisdiction over the international financial system. Furthermore, because foreign private entities like major banks quickly adopt such US lists, they effectively become multilateral. The companies that design customer screening software for banks and other financial firms are voracious consumers and reproducers of data, especially listings backed by the imprimatur of the US government. Thus, as in the earlier example, in practice being designated a drug kingpin has meant ejection not just from US banks but from risk-averse local banks as well.[32] It has also severely hindered the ability of designated individuals to obtain visas to third countries.

A related, more encompassing tactic would be to blacklist whole governments as systematically corrupt, or at least the senior echelons, rather than working on an individual basis. Once again, there are related precedents in the way that countries have been blacklisted for money laundering purposes, either unilaterally by the United States thanks to the Patriot Act or multilaterally through the Financial Action Task Force. Perhaps the simplest route would be to use these existing mechanisms to designate kleptocracies "jurisdictions of primary money laundering concern" under Section 311 of the Patriot Act and/or "High Risk and Non-Cooperative Jurisdictions" under FATF provisions. Even if not formally required to acknowledge such a designation, banks are likely to be wary of dealing with those from blacklisted jurisdictions, especially senior public officials.[33] One former US official explains the logic as follows: "This approach work[s] by focusing squarely on the behavior of financial institutions rather than on the classic sanctions framework of the past. In this new approach, the policy decisions of governments are not nearly as persuasive as the risk-based compliance calculus of financial institutions."[34]

If individual and collective blacklisting represents a cheap, practical, and effective solution, why isn't this measure being used already? Two objections might come to mind, one diplomatic, the other a principled concern about due process. The first one reasons that blacklisting violates notions of acceptable diplomatic practice and would be a gross breach of protocol. Yet since 2000 the Financial Action Task Force has labeled whole countries "uncooperative in the fight against money laundering," in doing so raising the risk profile of every single financial institution, business, and individual in that jurisdiction. If it is politically and practically possible to declare whole countries delinquent in fulfilling their anti–money laundering responsibilities, there seems to be no reason why states couldn't be listed as systematically corrupt. As noted above, even a unilateral US listing would probably become de facto global, thanks to private risk raters. It may even be possible to have an effective global kleptocracy blacklist of states without any government involvement at all. Transparency International's Corruption Perceptions Index has achieved wide acceptance as a credible and authoritative measure of corruption (rightly or wrongly) among a wide range of intergovernmental organizations, governments, and private actors. Banks already use this index when assessing client risk.[35] Considering the demand for risk-rating information, a kleptocracy blacklist by Transparency International could enjoy wide currency and impact among crucial private sector intermediaries.

The second objection, a lack of due process, is more serious but still not fatal. The process of blacklisting individuals and organizations accused of supporting terrorism has become controversial because those included often have had no way to clear their name or even see the evidence against them. A series of legal challenges in Europe and the United States by individuals and businesses included on various terrorist lists found that the listing process was often based on scanty evidence and violated basic human rights.[36] Reforms have allowed those accused to see at least some of the evidence against them and have provided an opportunity for a right of reply. Presumably the same could be done for those listed on corruption grounds. In the response to this point about due process, however, it is important to point out the dangers of the alternative. After all, the current system has led to a steady weakening of the presumption of innocence for all citizens, not just a restricted class of foreign senior officials, with the growth of non-conviction-based forfeiture and unexplained wealth laws, as well as governments' ability to preemptively freeze assets. It has also produced a massive system of surveillance which has ended any financial privacy that citizens may have had vis-à-vis the state and which authoritarian regimes have exploited to crush dissent.[37]

A final, hybrid state-international organization response is suggested by something like the International Commission against Impunity in

Guatemala. At the invitation of the government, in 2006 the United Nations established an international investigative and prosecutorial unit that nevertheless works within Guatemalan law and in tandem with local institutions.[38] Though the commission was primarily intended to safeguard human rights and prosecute murders by paramilitary forces in league with the police, it has proved highly effective in holding senior political leaders to account for serious corruption crimes. The commission was pivotal in corruption investigations that forced the resignation, arrest, and imprisonment of the country's vice-president and president in 2015.[39] In early 2016 Honduras set up a similar hybrid anti-corruption body involving the Organization of American States and United Nations.[40]

Private Solutions

So far the solutions have depended on government action. Other options involve private actors taking the initiative in the fight against grand corruption. This might take the form of an alliance of "Baptists and boot-leggers,"[41] that is, NGOs and other actors motivated by principle joining with private firms engaged in asset recovery for profit. The fact that victim governments have found private civil legal action to be preferable to criminal law and state-to-state mutual legal assistance indicates the legal possibilities for private actors.[42] Groups like Global Witness as well as journalists have often played a vital role in investigating and publicizing instances of grand corruption in such a way as to spark formal action by the authorities. These groups are unconstrained by the diplomatic and national security concerns that sometimes stay governments' hands. Their commitment to justice over the long haul is unlikely to waver in the way that victim states' often does, as the examples of Nigeria, Haiti, the Congo, Pakistan, and others discussed earlier attest. These groups can also carry out NGOs' now traditional role of "accountability politics," creating pressure for governments to live up to commitments they have made but not yet honored.[43]

While these roles are important, a more innovative strategy is for NGOs to take direct action to attack kleptocrats' wealth. A variety of French groups have publicized the plundered wealth Francophone African leaders have placed in France but then successfully used the court system to challenge the French government's inaction and bring criminal charges themselves: "In French law, victims can launch criminal proceedings by filing a private complaint before an investigating magistrate."[44] Spanish law has similarly allowed an NGO to bring a money laundering action against the Obiangs' wealth.[45] Common-law systems are somewhat less hospitable for these kinds of actions, but even here there are precedents. After the UK government dropped a bribery investigation into British Aerospace Systems in late 2006, the NGOs Corner House and the Campaign Against the Arms Trade took court action to force the government to reopen the investigation. Dismissed as a "hopeless challenge brought by a group of tree-hugging hippies," the case was won by the two groups in 2008, though it was later overturned on appeal.[46]

A powerful option in the United States is private actors using the Racketeer Influenced and Corrupt Organizations (RICO) Act.[47] While RICO has been used by the US government to target corruption, as in the case of FIFA from 2015 onward, it is now more often used by domestic and foreign private actors, potentially including NGOs.[48] It can be used in foreign cases as long as there is some connection to the United States, such as a US dollar bank account. In common-law jurisdictions, private parties from victim countries may also be able to sue banks that receive and disburse corruption funds for breach of constructive trust. This opportunity may arise if banks have knowingly or recklessly accepted the proceeds of corruption or can be shown to have been willfully blind, circumstances that would seem to cover many of the examples discussed in the previous chapters.[49] More speculatively, a public interest or class action lawsuit on behalf of the victims of kleptocracy might be mounted to seize stolen assets. Thus even if states are deterred by the expense and complexity of taking action against stolen wealth themselves, they can modify their legal systems to allow greater scope for NGOs and others to take private legal action or to bring criminal charges on their own initiative.

Private legal action is extremely expensive, so how could these strategies be funded? Both of the French and Spanish actions have been substantially funded by the Open Society Foundations. A StAR trust fund to support such efforts, proposed by the Dutch government in 2006 but never adopted, could be another source of money.[50] Some private foundations are extremely wealthy (e.g., the Gates Foundation), while the huge fines and deferred prosecution agreements levied against banks may provide a further stock of support if a fraction of these were to be diverted to anti-corruption NGOs. For example, a 2009 settlement with the German company Siemens included a payment of $100 million over the next fifteen years for a range of anti-corruption activities, explicitly including assisting asset recovery efforts.[51] Questions about how to fund private efforts to hold kleptocrats accountable by targeting their foreign wealth raise the topic of those engaged in anti-corruption for profit.

The profit motive has conventionally been seen as an obstacle in this cause, because banks and other financial firms are tempted to turn a blind eye to dirty money. Yet law firms working on a contingency basis, private firms that fund legal challenges like class action lawsuits, or even venture capitalists may provide an answer. In essence, these kinds of arrangements mean that a private firm, whether the law firm taking the case or a third-party litigation financing firm or venture capitalist, pays the up-front costs, and bears the risk of losing the case, in return for a large share of whatever money is recovered. This share might be in the range of 30–50 percent.[52] Predictably, such firms take on cases on a contingency basis only when they believe they have a fair chance of winning. Transparency International refers to such a split as "an unacceptably high proportion for most states to contemplate,"[53] but this judgment makes little sense. Although legal fees are not made public, it would seem that even in many successful civil asset recovery cases, lawyers' costs would equal at least this proportion of the stolen assets recovered. But of course, asset recovery cases often fail, leaving victim governments worse off than they were before. Deciding what is an acceptable division of spoils returns us to the question of what asset recovery is for. As discussed above, it is an extremely inefficient way of generating funds for poor countries to achieve development goals. If there is value to chasing kleptocrats' loot, it is to create a deterrent effect and promote accountability through public judgments against previously invulnerable leaders. For the purposes of deterrence and accountability, it is better to have more cases taken by private actors, even if less money is returned to victim governments, than fewer cases taken overall but a higher proportion of funds repatriated. Pushing this principle to its logical limit, where none of the recovered funds are handed back to the victim government, brings us to the final form of private actors: vulture funds.

More politely known as distressed securities funds, vulture funds buy up debt for a small fraction of its face value in cases in which the original creditors believe they have little chance of being repaid, and then sue the debtors for repayment. The debts in question may be owed by individuals, companies, or states. An example of the relevance to action against kleptocrats concerns Denis Christel Sassou-Nguesso, son of the president of Congo-Brazzaville, and the fund Kensington International. Kensington purchased $121 million of Congolese debt and sought to force repayment by making a claim against payment for oil from the Congo in 2005.

The crux of the claim was that money paid by Western firms for the oil to various shell companies really belonged to the Congo, and hence was due to creditors, because the only real purpose of the shell companies was to disguise the link with the Congolese state.[54] Kensington showed that the shell companies and their bank accounts were controlled by Sassou-Nguesso and one Denis Gokana, director of the state oil company and special adviser to the president. Not only did the case establish the true ownership of the shell companies, it also revealed financial documents indicating that proceeds of the oil sales were corruptly diverted, including the heir-apparent's credit card statements, which detailed spending vastly beyond his legitimate means. Kensington obtained a judgment for $59 million (it later tried to seize Belgian aid money to the Congo in partial repayment).[55]

Global Witness published the relevant documents from the court proceedings on its website, leading to a lawsuit by Sassou-Nguesso in England. Not only did the effort to force the removal of the online documentation fail, but the judge was moved to remark that the information, "unless explained, frankly suggests" that the plaintiff was "unsavory and corrupt," and that the Congolese oil profits "should go to the people of the Congo, not those who rule it or their families."[56] The vulture fund's suit did not do anything to help achieve this last goal, but it indicated a new threat for kleptocrats holding wealth abroad and promoted accountability by investigating and publicizing the misconduct of the ruling clique.

Rather than being a one-off, this type of case came up again when a vulture fund launched a pursuit of money corruptly taken from the Argentine government. Elliott Management bought $2 billion of Argentine sovereign debt after that country defaulted on its international creditors in 2001. Elliott accused Lazaro Baez, a close business associate of Presidents Nestor and Cristina Kirchner, of stealing $65 million in state funds, following up on allegations first broadcast on the Argentine Clarin television network (the Kirchner government later tried to close Clarin).[57] The media exposé suggested leads to Nevada and the Seychelles, where in 2014 Elliott took legal action to force Corporate Service Providers to provide details on shell companies suspected of being controlled by Baez.[58] In February 2015 the same journalist who had initially broken the story won the right to access the US court records, bringing them into the public domain. The actions are far from finished, and Elliott Management has yet to recover any funds, but the interaction between Elliott Management and Argentine journalists, like that between Global Witness and Kensington International, gives an indication of what is possible were these unlikely bedfellows to combine their efforts more systematically.

Following up on this logic, a recent judgment against the Russian government in connection with its actions against oil company Yukos may present enormous possibilities for a similar Baptist and bootlegger coalition to pursue and seize Russian kleptocrats' wealth abroad. Until 2003 Yukos was Russia's largest oil company, and its owner, Mikhail Khodorkovsky, was Russia's richest man. In that year the Russian government presented Yukos with a series of massively inflated tax bills, and arrested and convicted Khodorkovsky for fraud, tax evasion, and money laundering.[59] A series of later court decisions outside Russia concluded that the tax demands were an excuse to appropriate Yukos for a fraction of its real worth and that the charges against Khodorkovsky were politically motivated. A 2014 arbitration court decision awarded the former owners and managers of Yukos the staggering sum of $50 billion in damages (although they had originally asked for $114 billion).[60] The Russian government has refused to pay, so how might it be possible to collect even a portion of this money (and the interest now accruing)? In line with the Kensington International and Elliott Management examples above, it may be possible for litigants to look for money properly belonging to the Russian state that has been misappropriated and transferred to a third country, and then sue to take these assets. Anti-corruption NGOs and journalists could help those seeking the Yukos money, and vice versa.

As with any Baptist and bootlegger coalition, pairing activists, journalists, vulture funds, and other private litigants has none of the moral clarity and purity of the usual anti-kleptocracy story. Because no money would be returned to the original victim countries, there would be no asset recovery as such. Yet those opposed to such a solution should think hard about the failings of the current approach, even according to some of its most fervent supporters. Thus Transparency International passes the following harsh verdict on asset recovery policy at present: "This approach is allowing the corrupt to steal with impunity; enabling only a tiny proportion of assets to ever be seized, let alone repatriated; creating considerable difficulties in recovery and return, even in prominent cases with guilty pleas; failing to deter those who have laundered their money through their financial or professional institutions; and, ultimately, facilitating the severe harm caused by corruption, often directed at the most vulnerable citizens around the world."[61] Rather than seek to cancel out and override the profit motive, governments and campaigners may have to harness it in the effort to pursue and confiscate (if not return) kleptocrats' ill-gotten gains.

The Future of the Anti-Kleptocracy Regime

If the cause of fighting grand corruption came on to the agenda thanks to a confluence of unanticipated events and trends, its future is correspondingly hard to predict. Yet in a world where most states are ruled by thieves and thugs, holding individual leaders accountable for corruption crimes committed in office is a revolutionary idea that undermines centuries of accepted practice and conventional wisdom. It has the potential to transform international diplomacy and world politics more broadly. Even the most avid supporters of this campaign have failed to appreciate how radical the potential of the new regime really is. Many and perhaps most state leaders would become fugitives outside their home state, or at least would be cut off from the international financial system. To be sure, it is possible, perhaps even probable, that we will see a continuation of the status quo: most governments rhetorically and legally endorsing but failing to implement the rules, and those that are really trying to target kleptocrats and their wealth continuing to be frustrated by the obstacles discussed above. Cynics would predict that fine words will be matched with little action, and the cynics may well be right. Yet it is nevertheless worth considering the alternative that the new global regime really will effect a fundamental change, especially over the medium and longer term.

In establishing the global regime to counter grand corruption, governments have put in place a system they do not control, certainly individually and perhaps even collectively. Governments commonly misunderstand the consequences of their actions, as even a casual survey of international

200

 Conclusion

financial regulation forcefully demonstrates. It would be surprising if the campaign to counter grand corruption were any different. Governments' lack of ability to forecast, let alone control, the development of the anti-kleptocracy regime is exacerbated by the extent to which powers have increasingly been delegated to or taken by transnational nonstate actors, particularly financial firms, but also non- and intergovernmental organizations.

Both scholars and policy makers struggle to understand the complex interaction of public and private authority in global governance. The upshot is that even if governments first agreed to anti-corruption rules in a purely hypocritical way (which is not my argument), this does not mean that the regime will necessarily stay a dead letter. Intentions do not determine outcomes. This is especially true because global rules legislated "from above" are now meeting a powerful upsurge of demands for accountability "from below." People across every continent are less and less likely to see elite corruption as either acceptable or inevitable. Many regimes have been brought down by corruption, and even powerful autocracies like China and Russia fear the depth of popular discontent with a ruling class intent on feathering its own nest. The combination of these two forces, from above and below, could mean that over the long term the anti-kleptocracy regime may have greater significance than either its most enthusiastic supporters or most critical detractors currently anticipate.

Notes

Introduction

1. Author's interview, Asian Development Bank Institute, Tokyo, Japan, October 13, 2011.

2. Robert Klitgaard, *Tropical Gangsters: One Man's Experience with Development and Decadence in Deepest Africa* (New York: Basic Books, 1990).

3. African Development Bank, "African Economic Outlook: Equatorial Guinea" (Tunis, 2012), 2.

4. African Development Bank, "Equatorial Guinea," 11.

5. US Department of Justice, United States Court for the Central District of California, No. 2 CV 11:3582-GW-SS June 11, 2012, 44–47.

6. See http://www.unesco.org/new/en/natural-sciences/science-technology/basic-sciences/life-sciences/international-prize-for-research-in-the-life-sciences/.

7. Jennifer M. Hartman, "Government by Thieves: Revealing the Monsters behind the Kleptocratic Masks," *Syracuse Journal of International Law and Commerce* 24 (1997): 157.

8. Bruce Buchan and Lisa Hill, *An Intellectual History of Political Corruption* (London: Palgrave, 2014).

9. Jon Elster, *Nuts and Bolts for the Social Sciences* (Cambridge: Cambridge University Press, 1989).

10. Stephen D. Krasner (ed.), *International Regimes* (Ithaca: Cornell University Press, 1982).

11. Sarah Chayes, *Thieves of State: Why Corruption Threatens Global Security* (New York: W. W. Norton, 2015); Tom Burgis, *The Looting Machine: Warlords, Oligarchs, Corporations, Smugglers, and the Theft of Africa's Wealth* (New York: Public Affairs, 2015).

12. Hun Joon Kim and Kathryn Sikkink, "Explaining the Deterrence Effect of Human Rights Prosecutions for Transitional Countries," *International Studies Quarterly* 54 (2010): 939–963; Kathryn Sikkink, *The Justice Cascade: How Human Rights Prosecutions Are Changing World Politics* (New York: W. W. Norton, 2013).

13. "US Door Stays Open in Face of Swirl of Corruption," *New York Times*, November 16, 2009.

14. The Wolfsberg Group, "Wolfsberg Anti-Corruption Guidance," 2011, 1.

15. Ethan A. Nadelmann, "Global Prohibition Regimes: The Evolution of Norms in International Society," *International Organization* 44 (1990): 479–526; Peter Katzenstein (ed.), *The Culture of National Security: Norms and Identity in World Politics* (New York: Columbia University Press, 1996); Richard Price, "Reversing the Gun Sights: Transnational Civil Society Targets Landmines," *International Organization* 52 (1998): 613–644; Alexander Wendt, *Social Theory of International Politics* (Cambridge: Cambridge University Press, 1999); Wayne Sandholtz, *Prohibiting Plunder: How Norms Change* (Oxford: Oxford University Press, 2007).

16. Edward Keene, "A Case Study in the Construction of International Hierarchy: British Treaty-Making and the Slave Trade in the Early Nineteenth Century," *International Organization* 61 (2007): 311–339.

17. John Mueller, *Retreat from Doomsday: The Obsolescence of Major War* (New York: Basic Books, 1989); Steven Pinker, *The Better Angels of Our Nature: Why Violence Has Declined* (New York: Viking, 2011).

18. Martha Finnemore and Kathryn Sikkink, "International Norm Dynamics and Political Change," *International Organization* 52 (1998): 887–917; Richard Price, "Transnational Civil Society and Advocacy in World Politics," *World Politics* 55 (2003): 579–606.

19. For contrary studies of failed would-be norms, see Charli Carpenter, *Lost Causes: Agenda-Vetting in Global Issue Networks and the Shaping of Human Security* (Ithaca: Cornell University Press, 2014).

20. Timur Kuran, "Sparks and Prairie Fires: A Theory of Unanticipated Political Revolution," *Public Choice* 61 (1989): 41–74.

21. Paul Pierson, "Big, Slow-Moving, and . . . Invisible: Macrosocial Processes in the Study of Comparative Politics," in *Comparative Historical Analysis in the Social Sciences*, edited by James Mahoney and Dietrich Rueschemeyer (Cambridge: Cambridge University Press, 2003), 177–207.

22. "Peddler's Martyrdom Launched Tunisia's Revolution," Reuters Africa, January 19, 2011, http://af.reuters.com/article/libyaNews/idAFLDE70G18J20110119?pageNumber=3&virtualBrandChannel=0).

23. Monday, July 27, 2009, Secret Tunis 0000516, SIPDIS, REF: TUNIS 338, http://www.theguardian.com/world/us-embassy-cables-documents/218324?guni=Article:in%20body%20link.

24. See http://www.theguardian.com/world/us-embassy-cables-documents/217138.

25. George M. Downs, David M. Rocke, and Peter N. Barsoom, "Is the Good News about Compliance Good News about Cooperation?" *International Organization* 50 (1996): 379–406; Jana von Stein, "Do Treaties Constrain or Screen? Selection Bias and Treaty Compliance," *American Political Science Review* 99 (2005): 611–622.

26. Beth Simmons, "International Law and State Behavior: Commitment and Compliance in International Monetary Affairs," *American Political Science Review* 94 (2000): 819–835.

27. Von Stein, "Do Treaties Constrain or Screen?"

28. StAR, *Few and Far: The Hard Facts on Asset Recovery* (Washington, D.C., 2014).

29. United Nations Office on Drugs and Crime, "Estimating Illicit Financial Flows Resulting from Drug Trafficking and Other Transnational Organized Crimes" (Vienna, 2011).

30. United Nations Office for Drug Control and Crime Prevention, *Financial Havens, Secrecy and Money Laundering* (Vienna, 1998), 56.

31. Michael Levi and Peter Reuter, "Money Laundering," in *Crime and Justice: A Review of Research,* edited by M. Tony (Chicago: University of Chicago Press, 2006), 289–375.

32. Global Witness, *Undue Diligence: How Banks Do Business with Corrupt Regimes* (London, 2009), 45–47.

33. "France Impounds African Autocrats' 'Ill-gotten Gains,'" *Guardian,* February 6, 2012.

34. Emma-Kate Symons, "A Fight inside Gabon's Kleptocratic Dynasty Exposes the Complicity of French Business," Quartz, May 1, 2015, http://qz.com/395572/a-fight-inside-gabons-kleptocratic-dynasty-reveals-the-complicity-of-french-business/; "Life in the Fast Lane: The Luxury Cars of Gabon's President," December 23, 2014, http://observers.france24.com/en/20141223-luxury-cars-gabon-presidency-bongo-ali.

35. Joseph Kraus, "Champagne, Disposable Shirts and Corruption in the Republic of Congo," December 20, 2013, http://www.one.org/us/2013/12/20/champagne-disposable-shirts-and-corruption-in-the-republic-of-congo/; see also Global Witness, *Undue Diligence,* 50–51, 54–55.

36. His credit card statements are available at https://www.globalwitness.org/sites/default/files/pdfs/denis_christel_sassou_nguesso_credit_card_bill.pdf.

37. "Wolfowitz Corruption Push Clashes with Debt Relief," April 12, 2007, http://www.npr.org/templates/story/story.php?storyId=9525865.

38. Levi and Reuter, "Money Laundering"; StAR, *Politically Exposed Persons: A Policy Paper on Strengthening Preventive Measures* (Washington, D.C., 2009).

39. StAR, *Few and Far.*

40. For example, John Kerry, *The New War: The Web of Crime That Threatens America's Security* (New York: Simon and Schuster, 1997); William Wechsler, "Follow the Money," *Foreign Affairs* 80 (2001): 40–57.

41. Radha Ivory, *Corruption, Asset Recovery, and the Protection of Property in Public International Law: The Human Rights of Bad Guys* (Cambridge: Cambridge University Press, 2014).

1. The Rise of the Anti-Kleptocracy Regime

1. Paul Heywood, "Political Corruption: Problems and Perspectives," *Political Studies* 45 (1997): 417–435; Staffan Kumlin and Peter Esaiasson, "Scandal Fatigue? Scandal, Elections and Satisfaction with Democracy in Western Europe, 1977–2007," *British Journal of Political Science* 42 (2012): 263–282.

2. John R. Heilbrunn, "Oil and Water? Elite Politicians and Corruption in France," *Comparative Politics* 37 (2005): 277–296; Jennifer Thompson, "Chirac Found Guilty of Corruption," *Financial Times,* December 15, 2011.

3. Dirk Tänzler, Konstantinos Maras, and Angelos Giannakopoulos, "The German Myth of a Corruption-Free Modern Country," in *The Social Construction of Corruption in Europe,* edited by Dirk Tänzler, Konstantinos Maras, and Angelos Giannakopoulos (Farnham, UK: Ashgate, 2012), 87–106.

4. Donatella Della Porta and Alberto Vannucci, "Corruption and Anti-Corruption: The Political Defeat of 'Clean Hands' in Italy," *West European Politics* 30 (2007): 830–853.

5. Carlo Guanieri, "Courts Enforcing Political Accountability: The Role of Criminal Justice in Italy," in *Consequential Courts: Judicial Roles in Global Perspective,* edited by Diana Kapiszewski, Gordon Silverstein, and Robert A. Kagan (Cambridge: Cambridge University Press, 2013), 163–180; Donatella della Porta, Salvatore Sberna, and Alberto Vannucci, "Centripetal and Centrifugal Corruption in Post-Democratic Italy," *Italian Politics* 30 (2015): 198–217.

6. J. C. Sharman, *The Money Laundry: Regulating Criminal Finance in the Global Economy* (Ithaca: Cornell University Press, 2011), 16.

7. William Kaplan, *A Secret Trial: Brian Mulroney, Stevie Cameron, and the Public Trust* (Montreal: McGill-Queens University Press, 2004).

8. Benjamin Nyblade and Steven R. Reed, "Who Cheats? Who Loots? Political Competition and Corruption in Japan, 1947–1993," *American Journal of Political Science* 52 (2008): 926–941; David C. Kang, "Bad Loans to Good Friends: Money Politics and the Developmental State in South Korea," *International Organization* 56 (2002): 177–207.

9. Quoted in Karen Dawisha, *Putin's Kleptocracy: Who Owns Russia?* (New York: Simon and Schuster, 2014), 17.

10. William Reno, "Ironies of Post–Cold War Structural Adjustment in Africa," *Review of African Political Economy* 23 (1996): 7–18; William Reno, *Warlord Politics and African States* (Boulder, CO: Lynne Rienner, 1998); William Reno, "Congo: From State Collapse to 'Absolutism,' to State Failure," *Third World Quarterly* 27 (2006): 43–56.

11. Quoted in Leonce Ndikumana and James Boyce, "Congo's Odious Debt: External Borrowing and Capital Flight in Zaire," *Development and Change* 29 (1998): 208.

12. Steve Askin and Carole Collins, "External Collusion with Kleptocracy: Can Zaire Recapture Its Stolen Wealth?" *Review of African Political Economy* 57 (1993): 72–85; Ndikumana and Boyce, "Congo's Odious Debt"; Michela Wrong, *In the Footsteps of Mr Kurtz* (London: Fourth Estate, 2000); Reno, "Congo."

13. Jennifer M. Hartman, "Government by Thieves: Revealing the Monsters behind the Kleptocratic Masks," *Syracuse Journal of International Law and Commerce* 24 (1997): 159.

14. Askin and Collins, "External Collusion with Kleptocracy," 75.

15. Michael G. Schatzberg, *Mobutu or Chaos? The United States in Zaire, 1960–1990* (Lanham, MD: University Press of America, 1991); Sean Kelly, *America's Tyrant: The CIA and Mobutu of Zaire* (Lanham, MD: University Press of America, 1993).

16. Schatzberg, *Mobutu or Chaos?*; Kelly, *America's Tyrant*.

17. Askin and Collins, "External Collusion with Kleptocracy," 84.

18. Ndikumana and Boyce, "Congo's Odious Debt," 205.

19. StAR, *Few and Far: The Hard Facts about Asset Recovery* (Washington, D.C., 2014), 18; Frank Vogl, *Waging War on Corruption: Inside the Movement Fighting the Abuse of Power* (Lanham, MD: Rowman and Littlefield, 2012), 91; Nuhu Ribadu, *Show Me the Money: Leveraging Anti–Money Laundering Tools to Fight Corruption in Nigeria* (Washington, D.C.: Center for Global Development, 2010), 32.

20. Wrong, *In the Footsteps of Mr Kurtz*, 288.

21. David Chaikin, "Policy and Legal Obstacles in Recovering Dictators' Plunder," *Bond Law Review* 17 (2005): 38.

22. Wrong, *In the Footsteps of Mr Kurtz*, 292.

23. Filip Reyntjens, *The Great African War: Congo and Regional Geopolitics, 1996–2002* (Cambridge: Cambridge University Press, 2009).

24 Max Mader, "Civil Society Facilitators of Asset Recovery: The Two Swiss Cases Mobutu and Abacha," in *Non-State Actors and Asset Recovery*, edited by Daniel Thelesklaf and Pedro Gomes Pereira (Bern: Peter Lang, 2011), 116.

25 Mader, "Civil Society Facilitators," 111.

26. Schatzberg, *Mobutu or Chaos?*; Kelly, *America's Tyrant*.

27. StAR, *The Puppet Masters: How the Corrupt Use Legal Structures to Hide Their Stolen Assets and What to Do about It* (Washington, D.C.: World Bank, 2011); Michael G. Findley, Daniel L. Nielson, and J. C. Sharman, *Global Shell Games: Experiments in Transnational Relations, Crime and Terrorism* (Cambridge: Cambridge University Press, 2014).

28. Askin and Collins, "External Collusion with Kleptocracy," 73–74.

29. Peter Andreas and Kelly M. Greenhill (eds.), *Sex, Drugs, and Body Counts: The Politics of Numbers in Global Crime and Conflict* (Ithaca: Cornell University Press, 2010).

30. Wrong, *In the Footsteps of Mr Kurtz*, 295.

31. For example, see Mary Braid, "Mobutu Takes the Money and Runs to a Safe Haven," *The Independent*, May 17, 1997, http://www.independent.co.uk/news/world/mobutu-takes-the-money-and-runs-to-a-safe-haven-1261945.html; UN Ad Hoc Committee for Negotiation of Convention Against Corruption, Fourth Session, Vienna, January 13–24, 2003, 3.

32. Ndikumana and Boyce, "Congo's Odious Debt," 195.

33. Wrong, *In the Footsteps of Mr Kurtz*, 297 (quotation); Reno, "Congo," 49–52.

34. Askin and Collins, "External Collusion with Kleptocracy," 76.

35. "The Mobutu Assets in Switzerland: A Statement of the Swiss Ambassador to the Democratic Republic of the Congo, Kinshasa," July 21, 2009.

36. Reno, *Warlord Politics*.

37. Author's interview, former head of Philippine Center for Investigative Journalism, New York City, October 29, 2014.

38. Leslie Holmes, *The End of Communist Power: Anti-Corruption Campaigns and Legitimation Crisis* (Oxford: Oxford University Press, 1993); Leslie Holmes, *Rotten States? Communism, Post-Communism and Neo-Liberalism* (Raleigh, NC: Duke University Press, 2006).

39. John Brademas and Fritz Heimann, "Tackling International Corruption: No Longer Taboo," *Foreign Affairs* 77 (1998): 18.

40. Miriam A. Golden and Eric C. C. Chang, "Competitive Corruption: Factional Conflict and Political Malfeasance in Postwar Italian Christian Democracy," *World Politics* 53 (2001): 588–622.

41. Moisés Naím, "The Corruption Eruption," *Brown Journal of World Affairs* 2 (1995): 245.

42 Kenneth W. Abbott and Duncan Snidal, "Values and Interests: International Legalization in the Fight against Corruption," *Journal of Legal Studies* 31 (2002): 164.

43. Catherine Weaver, *Hypocrisy Trap: The World Bank and the Poverty of Reform* (Princeton: Princeton University Press, 2008).

44. William Easterly, "What Did Structural Adjustment Adjust? The Association of Policies and Growth with Repeated IMF and World Bank Adjustment Loans," *Journal of Development Economics* 76 (2006): 1–22.

45. Vito Tanzi, "Corruption, Governmental Activities, and Markets," IMF Working Paper 94/99 (Washington, D.C., 1994); Vito Tanzi and Hamid Davoodi, "Roads to Nowhere: How Corruption in Public Investment Hurts Growth," Economic Issues Series #12 (Washington, D.C.: IMF, 1998); Michael Camdessus, "The IMF and Good Governance," Address by the Managing Director of the IMF at Transparency International, Paris, France, January 21, 1998, www.imf.org/external/np/speeches/1998/012198.HTM; Paolo Mauro, "The Persistence of Corruption and Slow Economic Growth," *IMF Staff Papers* 51 (2004): 1–18.

46. Maxim Boycko, Andrei Shleifer, and Robert Vishny, *Privatizing Russia* (Cambridge, MA: MIT Press, 1995); Jeffrey Sachs and Katharina Pistor, *The Rule of Law and Economic Reform in Russia* (Boulder, CO: Westview Press, 1997).

47. Douglass C. North, *Institutions, Institutional Change, and Economic Performance* (Cambridge: Cambridge University Press, 1990).

48. Mlada Bukovansky, "The Hollowness of Anti-Corruption Discourse," *Review of International Political Economy* 13 (2006): 183; Weaver, *Hypocrisy Trap*; Vogl, *Waging War on Corruption*, 262.

49. Nathaniel Leff, "Economic Development through Bureaucratic Corruption," *American Behavioral Scientist* 8 (1964): 8–14; Joseph S. Nye, "Corruption and Political Development," *American Political Science Review* 61 (1967): 417–427; Samuel Huntington, *Political Order in Changing Societies* (New Haven: Yale University Press, 1968).

50. Susan Rose-Ackerman, *Corruption: A Study in Political Economy* (New York: Academic Press, 1978); Anne O. Krueger, "The Political Economy of the Rent-Seeking Society," *American Economic Review* 64 (1974): 291–303.

51. E.g., Kevin M. Murphy, Andrei Vishny, and Robert W. Shleifer, "The Allocation of Talent," *Quarterly Journal of Economics* 106 (1991): 503–530; Andrei Shleifer and Robert W. Vishny, "Corruption," *Quarterly Journal of Economics* 109 (1993): 599–617.

52. Paolo Mauro, "Corruption and Growth," *Quarterly Journal of Economics* 110 (1995): 681–712; see also Daniel Kaufmann, "Corruption: The Facts," *Foreign Policy* 107 (1997): 114–131.

53. For reviews of work in this period, see Johann Graf Lambsdorff, "Consequences and Causes of Corruption: What Do We Know from a Cross-Section of Countries?" Working Paper (University of Passau, 2005); Johann Graf Lambsdorff, *The New Institutional Economics of Corruption and Reform: Theory, Policy and Evidence* (Cambridge: Cambridge University Press, 2007); Daniel Treisman, "What Have We Learned about Corruption from Ten Years of Cross-National Research?," *Annual Review of Political Science* 10 (2007): 211–244; Nauro F. Campos, Ralitza Dimova, and Ahmad Saleh, "Whither Corruption? A Quantitative Survey of the Literature on Corruption and Growth," IZA Discussion Paper No. 5334, 2010.

54. E.g., Andrew Wedeman, *Double Paradox: Rapid Growth and Rising Corruption in China* (Ithaca: Cornell University Press, 2012).

55. Susan Rose-Ackerman, *Corruption and Government: Causes, Consequences, and Reform* (Cambridge: Cambridge University Press, 1999), 196; Abbott and Snidal, "Values and Interests," 159; Michael C. Johnston, *Syndromes of Corruption: Wealth, Power, and Democracy* (Cambridge: Cambridge University Press, 2005), 18; Bukovansky, "Hollowness of Anti-Corruption Discourse," 182; Janine R. Wedel, "Rethinking Corruption in an Age of Ambiguity," *Annual Review of Law and Social Science* 8 (2012): 464; author's interviews: Transparency International, Berlin, September 5–6, 2011; World Bank, Washington, D.C., September 7, 2004; and IMF, Washington, D.C., February 24, 2010; author's observation, Asian Development Bank/OECD Anti-Corruption Initiative for the Asia-Pacific, Regional Anti-Corruption Summit, Hanoi, Vietnam, October 23–24, 2010.

56. Quoted in Ellen Gutterman, "The Legitimacy of Transnational NGOs: Lessons from the Experience of Transparency International in Germany and France," *Review of International Studies* 40 (2014): 401.

57. United Nations Convention Against Corruption, 2003, iv. Foreword to the treaty document, https://www.unodc.org/documents/brussels/UN_Convention_Against_Corruption.pdf.

58. World Bank, "Sub-Saharan Africa: From Crisis to Sustainable Growth; A Long-Term Perspective Study" (Washington, D.C., 1989), xii.

59. World Bank, "Sub-Saharan Africa," 3.

60. World Bank, "Sub-Saharan Africa," 6.

61. Weaver, *Hypocrisy Trap*, 103–104.

62. James D. Wolfensohn, *A Global Life: My Journey among Rich and Poor, from Sydney to Wall Street to the World Bank* (New York: Public Affairs, 2010).

63. World Bank, "Helping Countries Combat Corruption: The Role of the World Bank" (Washington, D.C., 1997), 5.

64. World Bank, "Helping Countries Combat Corruption," 65.

65. World Bank, "Helping Countries Combat Corruption," 9.

66. Brademas and Heimann, "Tackling International Corruption," 17; International Monetary Fund, "The OECD Convention on Combating the Bribery of Foreign Officials in International Business Transactions" (Washington, D.C., 2001), 3; Jennifer McCoy and Heather Heckel, "The Emergence of a Global Anti-Corruption Norm," *International Politics* 38 (2001): 71; Bukovansky, "Hollowness of Anti-Corruption Discourse," 186.

67. Author's interview, Jack Blum, Washington, D.C., December 10, 2014.

68. Kevin E. Davis, "Why Does the U.S. Regulate Foreign Bribery: Moralism, Self-Interest or Altruism?" *New York University Annual Survey of American Law* 67 (2012): 497–512.

69. "OECD Will Issue Guidelines and Begin an Initiative to Curb Bribery in International Transactions," *International Enforcement Law Reporter* 9 (1993): 207–208.

70. Abbott and Snidal, "Values and Interests."

71. "OAS Initiates Project against Foreign Aspects of Corruption," *International Enforcement Law Reporter* 10 (1994): 223.

72. "Caldera Tries to Give Regional Anti-Corruption Effort a Push," *International Enforcement Law Reporter* 10 (1994): 404.

73. See http://eur-lex.europa.eu/legal-content/EN/TXT/?uri=URISERV%3Al33027.

74. Bukovansky, "Hollowness of Anti-Corruption Discourse," 189.

75. Wayne Sandholtz and Mark M. Gray, "International Integration and National Corruption," *International Organization* 57 (2003): 771.

76. "Council of Europe Acts against Foreign Corruption," *International Enforcement Law Reporter* 10 (1994): 265.

77. Naím, "Corruption Eruption," 256.

78. "International Chamber of Commerce Rules to Combat Extortion and Bribery in International Business Transactions" (Paris, 1996), http://www.iccwbo.org/Advocacy-Codes-and-Rules/Document-centre/1996/ICC-Rules-of-Conduct-to-Combat-Extortion-and-Bribery-in-International-Business-Transactions-%281996-Edition%29/.

79. Carolyn Hotchkiss, "The Sleeping Dog Stirs: New Signs of Life in Efforts to End Corruption in International Business," *Journal of Public Policy and Marketing* 17 (1998): 112; Sandholtz and Gray, "International Integration," 773.

80. Hongying Wang and James N. Rosenau, "Transparency International and Corruption as an Issue of Global Governance," *Global Governance* 7 (2001): 37; Bukovansky, "Hollowness of Anti-Corruption Discourse," 190; Vogl, *Waging War on Corruption*, 176; Peter Eigen, "International Corruption: Organized Civil Society for Better Global Governance," *Social Research* 80 (2013): 1294; Gutterman, "Legitimacy of Transnational NGOs," 401.

81. Peter Eigen, "Combatting Corruption around the World," *Journal of Democracy* 7 (1996): 158; Vogl, *Waging War on Corruption*, 71.

82. "Draft Standards on Transparency and Accountability in International Business Transactions Are Announced," *International Enforcement Law Reporter* 8 (1992): 315–318.

83. Eigen, "Combatting Corruption," 158–159.

84. Eigen, "Combatting Corruption," 163.

85. Eigen, "International Corruption," 1297.

86. Vogl, *Waging War on Corruption*, 66.

87. Author's interview, Transparency International, Berlin, September 5, 2011.

88. Author's interview, Transparency International, Berlin, September 6, 2011.

89. Eigen, "International Corruption," 1301.

90. Vogl, *Waging War on Corruption*, 68; Eigen, "International Corruption," 1302.

91. Global Witness, *Forests, Famine and War—The Key to Cambodia's Future* (London, 1996).

92. See www.globalwitness.org.

93. Eigen, "International Corruption"; Mabel van Oranje and Henry Parham, "Publishing What We Learned: An Assessment of the Publish What You Pay Coalition," 2009, https://eiti.org/files/Publishing%20What%20We%20Learned.pdf.

94. See http://www.financialtransparency.org/where-are-our-allies//.

95. Author's interviews: StAR, Washington, D.C., March 21, 2011: Metropolitan Police, London, September 8, 2011; Department of Justice, Washington, D.C., April 27, 2012; IMF, Washington, D.C., February 9, 2015; US Treasury, Washington, D.C., February 12, 2015; UK Department for International Development, London, September 17, 2015; Swiss Department of Foreign Affairs, Bern, Switzerland, October 12, 2015.

96. Anne Lugon-Moulin, "The Role of Donors in Supporting NSAs," in *Non-State Actors in Asset Recovery*, edited by Daniel Thelesklaf and Pedro Gomes Pereira (Bern: Peter Lang, 2011), 151.

97. E.g., Brademas and Heimann, "Tackling International Corruption"; Wang and Rosenau, "Transparency International and Corruption"; McCoy and Heckel, "Emergence of a Global Anti-Corruption Norm"; Johnston, *Syndromes of Corruption*.

98. Naím, "Corruption Eruption," 258.

99. Hotchkiss, "Sleeping Dog Stirs," 108.

100. Abbott and Snidal, "Values and Interests," 160.

101. Gutterman, "Legitimacy of Transnational NGOs," 400.

102. Martha Finnemore and Kathryn Sikkink, "International Norm Dynamics and Political Change," *International Organization* 52 (1998): 887–917.

103. Finnemore and Sikkink, "International Norm Dynamics."

104. Susan Park, *World Bank Group Interactions with Environmentalists: Changing International Organisation Identities* (Manchester, UK: Manchester University Press, 2010).

105. Kathryn Sikkink, *The Justice Cascade: How Human Rights Prosecutions Are Changing World Politics* (New York: W. W. Norton, 2013).

106. Richard Price, "Reversing the Gun Sights: Transnational Civil Society Targets Landmines," *International Organization* 52 (1998): 613–644.

107. Abbott and Snidal, "Values and Interests," 154, 163; Sandholtz and Gray, "International Integration," 772; Vogl, *Waging War on Corruption*, 180, 185.

108. E.g., W. Michael Reisman, "Harnessing International Law to Restrain and Recapture Indigenous Spoliations," *American Journal of International Law* 83 (1989): 56–59; Ndiva Kofele-Kale, "Patrimonicide: The International Economic Crime of Indigenous Spoliation," *Vanderbilt Journal of Transnational Law* 28 (1995): 45–117; Susan Rose-Ackerman, "Democracy and 'Grand' Corruption," *International Social Science Journal* 48 (1996): 365–380.

109. See Reisman, "Indigenous Spoliations."

110. See http://www.pambazuka.org/en/category/wgender/208.

111. Transparency International, *Global Corruption Report* (Berlin 2004), 13.

112. Author's interviews: Transparency International, Berlin, September 5, 2011, and US Department of Justice, Washington, D.C., April 28, 2012.

113. Daniel Scher, "Asset Recovery: Repatriating Africa's Looted Billions," *African Security Review* 14 (2005): 20.

114. See http://www.un.org/News/Press/docs/2002/gaef3002.doc.htm.

115. Leonardo S. Borlini and Giulio Nessi, "International Asset Recovery: Origins, Evolution and Current Challenges," Baffi Center Research Paper, February 6, 2014, 8.

116. United Nations General Assembly Resolution 55/61, December 4, 2000.

117. United Nations General Assembly Resolution 55/188, December 20, 2000.

118. United Nations Office on Drugs and Crime, "Global Study on the Transfer of Funds of Illicit Origin, Especially Funds Derived from Acts of Corruption," 2002, 3, https://www.unodc.org/pdf/crime/convention_corruption/session_4/12e.pdf.

119. Author's interviews: Australian G20 Anti-Corruption Working Group delegate, Canberra, Australia, May 27, 2011; UK G20 Anti-Corruption Working Group delegate, London, September 8, 2011; US State Department, Washington, D.C., April 12, 2013; UK G20 Anti-Corruption Working Group delegate, London, June 17, 2013; Department of Justice, Washington, D.C., December 9, 2014; and US Treasury, Washington, D.C., February 12, 2015; author's observation, G20 Anti-Corruption Working Group meeting, Sydney, Australia, February 28, 2014.

120. People's Bank of China, "A Study on Methods of Transferring Assets outside China by Chinese Corruptors and Monitoring Methods for This Problem" (Beijing, 2008).

121. Carlyle K. Rogers, "Vladimir Putin and 'De-Offshorization': Is This the End of Russia as a Source of Business for International Financial Centers?" *Cayman Financial Review*, January 30, 2015, http://www.compasscayman.com/cfr/2015/01/30/Vladimir-Putin-and-%E2%80%98de-offshorization%E2%80%99-/.

122. Author's interview, Department of Justice, Washington, D.C., December 9, 2014.

123. Author's interview, Department of Justice, Washington, D.C., December 9, 2014.

124. "UN General Assembly Approves UN Convention against Corruption," *International Enforcement Law Reporter* 20 (2004): 27.

125. "100 Countries Sign the UN Convention against Corruption," *International Enforcement Law Reporter* 20 (2004): 73.

126. StAR, *Good Practices Guide for Non-Conviction Based Forfeiture* (Washington, D.C., 2009); StAR, *Public Wrongs, Private Actions: Civil Lawsuits to Recover Stolen Assets* (Washington, D.C., 2014); Asian Development Bank/OECD Anti-Corruption Initiative for the Asia-Pacific, *Mutual Legal Assistance, Extradition and Recovery of Proceeds of Corruption in Asia and the Pacific* (Manila, 2007).

127. Guillermo Jorge, "The Peruvian Efforts to Recover Proceeds from Montesinos's Criminal Network of Corruption," in Asian Development Bank/OECD Anti-Corruption Initiative for the Asia-Pacific, *Asset Recovery and Mutual Legal Assistance in Asia and the Pacific* (Manila, 2008), 189–223; Tim Daniel, "Repatriation of Looted State Assets: Selected Case Studies and the UN Convention Against Corruption," in Transparency International, *Global Corruption Report* (Berlin, 2004), 100–102; StAR, *Barriers to Asset Recovery: An Analysis of Key Barriers and Recommendations for Action* (Washington, D.C., 2011); Kenneth Oliver, "'Excellent!' I Cried. 'Elementary!' said He. Mutual Legal Assistance and the Present Challenges Faced by the Legal Community in the Never-Ending Quest for the Recovery of Stolen Assets," in *Non-State Actors and Asset Recovery*, edited by Daniel Thelesklaf and Pedro Gomes Pereira (Bern: Peter Lang, 2011), 160–182.

128. Author's interviews: StAR, Washington, D.C., April 25, 2012, and February 12, 2015.

129. StAR, "World Bank and United Nations Office on Drugs and Crime: Work Plan" (Washington, D.C., November 24, 2008); author's interview, StAR, Washington, D.C., February 12, 2015.

130. StAR, *Politically Exposed Persons: A Policy Paper on Strengthening Preventive Measures* (Washington, D.C., 2009); StAR, *Puppet Masters*.

131. Author's observation, G20 Anti-Corruption Working Group, Sydney, Australia, February 28, 2014.

132. StAR, "Work Plan," 1.

133. Author's interviews: StAR, Washington, D.C., March 21–22, 2011; April 25, 2012; April 10–11, 2013; December 9, 2014; and February 12, 2015.

2. The United States

1. Author's interviews: Jack Blum, Washington, D.C., December 10, 2014, and Frank Vogl, Washington, D.C., December 8, 2014; Kevin E. Davis, "Why Does the U.S. Regulate Foreign Bribery: Moralism, Self-Interest or Altruism?" *New York University Annual Survey of American Law* 67 (2012): 497–512.

2. J. C. Sharman, *The Money Laundry: Regulating Criminal Finance in the Global Economy* (Ithaca: Cornell University Press, 2011).

3. William Wechsler, "Follow the Money," *Foreign Affairs* 80 (2001): 40–57; Anja P. Jakobi, *Common Goods and Evils? The Formation of Global Crime Governance* (Oxford: Oxford University Press, 2013).

4. Author's interviews: US Senate Permanent Subcommittee on Investigations, Washington, D.C., December 11, 2014, and former Treasury Department official, Washington, D.C., December 10, 2014.

5. US Senate Permanent Subcommittee on Investigations, *Private Banking and Money Laundering: A Case Study of Opportunities and Vulnerabilities* (Washington, D.C., 1999).

6. US Senate Permanent Subcommittee on Investigations, *Private Banking and Money Laundering*, opening statement of Sen. Levin, 6.

7. Author's interviews: US Senate Permanent Subcommittee on Investigations, Washington, D.C., March 21, 2011; April 24, 2014; and December 10, 2014.

8. US Senate Permanent Subcommittee on Investigations, *Private Banking and Money Laundering*, 897/26.

9. US Senate Permanent Subcommittee on Investigations, *Private Banking and Money Laundering*, 913/42.

10. US Senate Permanent Subcommittee on Investigations, *Private Banking and Money Laundering*, 932/61.

11. US Senate Permanent Subcommittee on Investigations, *Private Banking and Money Laundering*, 913/42.

12. US Senate Permanent Subcommittee on Investigations, *Private Banking and Money Laundering*, 921/50.

13. Eva Joly, *Justice under Siege: One Woman's Battle against a European Oil Company* (London: Arcadia Books, 2007).

14. US Senate Permanent Subcommittee on Investigations, *Private Banking and Money Laundering*, 57.

15. US Senate Permanent Subcommittee on Investigations, *Private Banking and Money Laundering*, 59.

16. US Senate Permanent Subcommittee on Investigations, *Private Banking and Money Laundering*, 879/8.

17. Author's interviews: former bank compliance officer, London, May 18, 2012; international auditor, by phone, June 4, 2014; and international auditor, New York City, May 4, 2015.

18. Author's interviews: international bank, New York City, November 21, 2014, and international bank, Hong Kong, November 18, 2011.

19. Author's interview, Department of Justice, Washington, D.C., December 9, 2014.

20. Sally Bowen and Jane Holligan, *The Imperfect Spy: The Many Lives of Vladimiro Montesinos* (Lima: Peisa, 2003).

21. "Guidance on Enhanced Scrutiny for Transactions That May Involve the Proceeds of Foreign Official Corruption," US Department of Treasury, January 17, 2001; see "U.S. Issues Guidance on Transactions Involving Proceeds of Foreign Official Corruption," *International Enforcement Law Reporter* 17 (2001): 126.

22. Author's interviews: StAR, Washington, D.C., December 9, 2014, and February 12, 2015.

23. US Senate Permanent Subcommittee on Investigations, *Money Laundering and Foreign Corruption: Enforcement and Effectiveness of the Patriot Act* (Washington, D.C., 2004).

24. US Senate Permanent Subcommittee on Investigations, *U.S. Vulnerability to Money Laundering, Drugs, and Terrorist Financing: HSBC Case History* (Washington, D.C., 2012), 319.

25. Robert E. Williams, "From Malabo to Malibu: Addressing Corruption and Human Rights Abuse in an African Petrostate," *Human Rights Quarterly* 33 (2011): 620–648.

26. Ken Silverstein, "The Crude Politics of Trading Oil," *Los Angeles Times*, December 6, 2002; Ken Silverstein, "Oil Boom Enriches African Ruler," *Los Angeles Times*, January 20, 2003; see also Peter Maass, "A Touch of Crude," *Mother Jones*, January/February 2005.

27. US Senate Permanent Subcommittee on Investigations, *Money Laundering and Foreign Corruption*, 51.

28. US Senate Permanent Subcommittee on Investigations, *Money Laundering and Foreign Corruption*, 69.

29. US Senate Permanent Subcommittee on Investigations, *Money Laundering and Foreign Corruption*, 71.

30. US Senate Permanent Subcommittee on Investigations, *Money Laundering and Foreign Corruption*, 87.

31. US Senate Permanent Subcommittee on Investigations, *Money Laundering and Foreign Corruption*, 88–89.

32. Author's interviews: US Senate Permanent Subcommittee on Investigations, Washington, D.C., December 11, 2014, and Global Witness, New York City, September 24, 2014.

33. General Accounting Office, "Anti–Money Laundering: Issues Concerning Depository Institution Regulatory Oversight" (Washington, D.C., June 3, 2004), http://www.gao.gov/assets/120/110994.html.

34. US Senate Permanent Subcommittee on Investigations, *Money Laundering and Foreign Corruption*, statement of Sen. Levin, July 15, 2004, 40.

35. US Senate Permanent Subcommittee on Investigations, *Money Laundering and Foreign Corruption*, July 15, 2004, 39–40.

36. US Senate Permanent Subcommittee on Investigations, *Money Laundering and Foreign Corruption: Hearings*, testimony of Andrew P. Swiger, Exxon Production Vice-President, July 2004, 15.

37. Ken Silverstein, *The Secret World of Oil* (New York: Verso, 2014); Peter Maass, *Crude World: The Violent Twilight of Oil* (New York: Vintage Books, 2009).

38. US Senate Permanent Subcommittee on Investigations, *Money Laundering and Foreign Corruption*, 46.

39. Author's interviews: former Treasury Department official, Washington, D.C., December 10, 2014; US Senate Permanent Subcommittee on Investigations, Washington, D.C., December 11, 2014; and Department of Justice, Washington, D.C., December 9, 2014.

40. "US Creates Multi-Agency Task Force to Investigate Laundering by Foreign Politicians," *International Enforcement Law Reporter* 19 (2003): 421.

41. See http://star.worldbank.org/corruption-cases/node/18466.

42. "U.S. Wants Foreign Leaders' Laundered Assets," *New York Times*, August 23, 2003.

43. Bowen and Holligan, *Imperfect Spy*; John McMillan and Pablo Zoido, "How to Subvert Democracy: Montesinos in Peru," *Journal of Economic Perspectives* 18 (2004): 69–92.

44. Aaron Selverston, "Busted," PBS Frontline: World, November 2, 2005, http://www.pbs.org/frontlineworld/blog/2005/11/peru_busted.html.

45. Guillermo Jorge, "The Peruvian Efforts to Recover Proceeds from Montesinos's Criminal Network of Corruption," in Asian Development Bank/OECD Anti-Corruption Initiative for the Asia-Pacific, *Asset Recovery and Mutual Legal Assistance in Asia and the Pacific* (Manila, 2008), 189–223.

46. Author's interview, US Department of Justice, Perth, Australia, July 1, 2007.

47. "U.S. Detains Former Ukrainian Prime Minister under Corruption Investigations," *International Enforcement Law Reporter* 15 (1999): 156–157.

48. FBI San Francisco Division, "Former Ukrainian Prime Minister Sentenced to 97 Months Prison Fined $9 Million for Role in Laundering $30 Million of Extortion Proceeds," November 19, 2009, http://www.fbi.gov/sanfrancisco/press-releases/2009/sf111909a.htm.

49. See https://star.worldbank.org/corruption-cases/node/18662.

50. Author's interview, FBI, Washington, D.C., May 18, 2010.

51. Jai Ramaswamy, Department of Justice, Center for the Advancement of Public Integrity conference, Columbia University, New York City, November 14, 2014.

52. Kelly Carr and Brian Grow, "A Little House of Secrets on the Great Plains," Reuters, June 28, 2011, http://uk.reuters.com/article/2011/06/28/uk-usa-shell-companies-idUKTRE75R4FT20110628.

53. Global Witness, *The Secret Life of a Shopaholic: How an African Dictator's Playboy Son Went on a Spending Spree in the United States* (London, 2009), 2.

54. "Statement by the President on Kleptocracy," August 10, 2006, http://2001-2009.state.gov/p/inl/rls/prsrl/ps/70194.htm.

55. "Fighting Corruption and Improving Transparency: A G8 Action Plan," June 3, 2003, http://www.g8.fr/evian/english/navigation/2003_g8_summit/summit_documents/fighting_corruption_and_improving_transparency_-_a_g8_action_plan.html.

56. US Senate Permanent Subcommittee on Investigations, *Keeping Foreign Corruption Out of the United States: Four Case Histories* (Washington, D.C., 2010), 14.

57. Author's interviews: international bank, Singapore, October 20, 2009; international bank, Hong Kong, October 18, 2011; international bank, Geneva, Switzerland, June 20, 2013; Liechtenstein Bankers' Association, Vaduz, Liechtenstein, June 24, 2013; international bank, Nassau, The Bahamas, May 13, 2014; international bank, New York City, October 30, 2014; international bank, New York City, November 21, 2014; international bank, Geneva, Switzerland, June 17, 2015; and international bank, London, June 23, 2015.

58. Michael G. Findley, Daniel L. Nielson, and J. C. Sharman, *Global Shell Games: Experiments in Transnational Relations, Crime and Terrorism* (Cambridge: Cambridge University Press, 2014).

59. US Senate Permanent Subcommittee on Investigations, *Keeping Foreign Corruption Out of the United States*, 278.

60. US Senate Permanent Subcommittee on Investigations, *Keeping Foreign Corruption Out of the United States: Hearings*, Volume 1 (Washington, D.C., February 4, 2010), 763.

61. US Senate Permanent Subcommittee on Investigations, *Keeping Foreign Corruption Out of the United States*, 280–281.

62. Associação Mãos Livres/Corruption Watch UK, *Deception in High Places: The Corrupt Angola-Russia Debt Deal* (London, 2013); Tom Burgis, *The Looting Machine: Warlords, Oligarchs, Corporations, Smugglers, and the Theft of Africa's Wealth* (New York: Public Affairs, 2015).

63. US Senate Permanent Subcommittee on Investigations, *Keeping Foreign Corruption Out of the United States*, 282.

64. US Senate Permanent Subcommittee on Investigations, *Keeping Foreign Corruption Out of the United States*, 282.

65. US Senate Permanent Subcommittee on Investigations, *Keeping Foreign Corruption Out of the United States*, 289.

66. US Senate Permanent Subcommittee on Investigations, *Keeping Foreign Corruption Out of the United States*, 296.

67. US Senate Permanent Subcommittee on Investigations, *Keeping Foreign Corruption Out of the United States*, 298.

68. US Senate Permanent Subcommittee on Investigations, *Keeping Foreign Corruption Out of the United States*, 298.

69. Testimony before the US Senate Permanent Subcommittee on Investigations, Weicher H. Mandemaker, Director General Compliance, HSBC USA, Washington, D.C., February 4, 2010, 8.

70. "Clinton Praises Angola, but Urges More Reform," *New York Times*, August 9, 2009, http://www.nytimes.com/2009/08/10/world/africa/10clinton.html.

71. United States District Court for the Central District of California, "United States of America vs. One Crystal-Covered 'Bad' Tour Glove," CV 2: 11–3582-GW-SS, June 11, 2012, 20.

72. "United States of America vs. One Crystal-Covered 'Bad' Tour Glove," 47; Ken Silverstein, "Keep Dictators Out of Malibu," *New York Times*, July 2, 2012; "A French Shift on Africa Strips a Dictator's Son of His Treasures," *New York Times*, August 23, 2012; author's interviews: Department of Justice, Washington, D.C., December 9, 2014; Global Witness, New York City, September 24, 2014; and Open Society Foundations, New York City, February 13, 2015.

73. Global Witness, *Secret Life of a Shopaholic*, 13.

74. US Senate Permanent Subcommittee on Investigations, *Keeping Foreign Corruption Out of the United States*, 17.

75. Global Witness, *Secret Life of a Shopaholic*, 3.

76. Global Witness, *Secret Life of a Shopaholic*, 3.

77. Global Witness, *Secret Life of a Shopaholic*, 20.

78. "US Door Stays Open in Face of Swirl of Corruption," *New York Times*, November 16, 2009.

79. Global Witness, *Secret Life of a Shopaholic*, 20–21.

80. See, for example, "United States of America vs. One Crystal-Covered 'Bad' Tour Glove," 57–60, 65–69, 71–72, 75, 77–78.

81. US Senate Permanent Subcommittee on Investigations, *Keeping Foreign Corruption Out of the United States*, 29–35; "United States of America vs. One Crystal-Covered 'Bad' Tour Glove," 75–77.

82. US Senate Permanent Subcommittee on Investigations, *Keeping Foreign Corruption Out of the United States*, 35.

83. US Senate Permanent Subcommittee on Investigations, *Keeping Foreign Corruption Out of the United States*, 54–55; "United States of America vs. One Crystal-Covered 'Bad' Tour Glove," 60–65 (see also 54–57 for a similar scheme involving Nagler and Union Bank of California).

84. US Senate Permanent Subcommittee on Investigations, *Keeping Foreign Corruption Out of the United States*, 58–59; "United States of America vs. One Crystal-Covered 'Bad' Tour Glove," 60–65.

85. "United States of America vs. One Crystal-Covered 'Bad' Tour Glove," 80–82.

86. See https://www.wikileaks.org/plusd/cables/09MALABO48_a.html, May 21, 2009.

87. US Senate Permanent Subcommittee on Investigations, *Keeping Foreign Corruption Out of the United States*, 68.

88. US Senate Permanent Subcommittee on Investigations, *Keeping Foreign Corruption Out of the United States*, 70.

89. "Most Expensive House Sales," *Forbes*, December 12, 2006.

90. US Senate Permanent Subcommittee on Investigations, *Keeping Foreign Corruption Out of the United States*, 87.

91. Global Witness, "U.S. Takes Welcome Action to Seize Dictator's Son's Haul," press release, October 14, 2011, https://www.globalwitness.org/en/archive/us-takes-welcome-action-seize-dictators-sons-haul/.

92. "Efforts against Equatorial Guinea Official Shows Challenge of US in Foreign Corruption Case," *Washington Post*, October 30, 2011.

93. Author's interviews: Department of Justice, Washington, D.C., April 27, 2012; former FBI agent, Washington, D.C., September 22, 2013; US Senate Permanent Subcommittee on Investigations, Washington, D.C., April 24, 2014; private lawyer, Washington, D.C., December 8, 2014; Department of Justice, Washington, D.C., December 9, 2014; private lawyer, Washington, D.C., February 10, 2015; Treasury Department, Washington, D.C., February 12, 2015; StAR, Washington, D.C., February 12, 2015; and Open Society Foundations, New York City, February 13, 2015.

94. "United States vs. One Crystal-Covered 'Bad' Tour Glove," 52–57, 61–63, 65, 71–72, 82.

95. "U.S. Court Deals Blow to Forfeiture Case against Obiang," *Wall Street Journal*, May 9, 2014.

96. United States District Court for the Central District of California, Stipulation and Settlement Agreement No. CV 13–9169-GW-SS.

97. "When U.S. Targets Foreign Leaders for Corruption, Recovering Loot Is a Challenge," *Wall Street Journal*, October 10, 2014.

98. Department of Justice, "Second Vice President of Equatorial Guinea Agrees to Relinquish More Than $30 Million of Assets Purchased with Corruption Proceeds," press release 14–1114,

October 10, 2014, http://www.justice.gov/opa/pr/second-vice-president-equatorial-guinea-agrees-relinquish-more-30-million-assets-purchased.

99. William Sands, "Equatorial Guinea: Legitimizing Obiang," Pulitzer Center, April 24, 2012, http://pulitzercenter.org/reporting/equatorial-guinea-president-teodoro-obiang-legitimization-corruption-oil-unesco-eiti-dodd-frank.

100. "When U.S. Targets Foreign Leaders for Corruption"; author's interviews: private lawyer, Washington, D.C., December 8, 2014; Department of Justice, Washington, D.C., December 9, 2014; private lawyer, Washington, D.C., February 10, 2015; Treasury Department, Washington, D.C., February 12, 2015; StAR, Washington, D.C., February 12, 2015; Open Society Foundations, New York City, February 13, 2015; and International Centre for Asset Recovery, Basel, Switzerland, October 14, 2015.

101. United States Southern District Court Southern District of Manhattan 1:09-cr-01142-RPP, May 10, 2010, http://star.worldbank.org/corruption-cases/node/18457; see also "U.S. Charges Former Guatemalan President with Money Laundering," *International Enforcement Law Reporter* 26 (2010).

102. "Impunity in Guatemala: Two Steps Forward, One Step Back," *Economist*, June 8, 2011.

103. "Guatemalan President Authorizes Extradition of Former President to the US on Money Laundering Charges," *International Enforcement Law Reporter* 28 (2012).

104. "Ex-Guatemalan President Extradited to U.S. in Corruption Case," *New York Times*, May 24, 2013.

105. US Court record 1:09-cr-01142-RPP, http://star.worldbank.org/corruption-cases/node/18457.

106. "U.S. Charges Former Guatemalan President with Money Laundering," *International Enforcement Law Reporter* 26 (2010), n.p.

107. Department of Justice, press release, "U.S. Forfeits over $480 Million Stolen by Former Nigerian Dictator in Largest Forfeiture Ever Obtained through a Kleptocracy Action," August 7, 2014, http://www.justice.gov/opa/pr/us-forfeits-over-480-million-stolen-former-nigerian-dictator-largest-forfeiture-ever-obtained; US District Court for the District of Columbia Case: 1:13-cv-01832JDB, filed November 18, 2013; http://star.worldbank.org/corruption-cases/node/20317.

108. "When U.S. Targets Foreign Leaders."

109. Author's interviews: Department of Justice, Washington, D.C., December 9, 2014, and Treasury Department, Washington, D.C., February 12, 2015.

110. Ken Silverstein, "Miami: Where Luxury Real Estate Meets Dirty Money," *Nation*, October 2, 2013, http://www.thenation.com/article/miami-where-luxury-real-estate-meets-dirty-money/.

111. StAR, *The Puppet Masters: How the Corrupt Use Legal Structures to Hide Their Stolen Assets and What to Do about It* (Washington, D.C., 2011); Findley et al., *Global Shell Games*.

112. Author's interviews: Global Witness, New York City, September 24, 2014; private lawyer, Washington, D.C., December 8, 2014; US Senate Permanent Subcommittee on Investigations, Washington, D.C., December 14, 2014; private lawyer, Washington, D.C., February 10, 2015; and Treasury Department, Washington, D.C., February 12, 2015.

113. Andrew Rice and Michael Hudson, "Stash Pad," *New York Magazine*, June 29, 2014.

114. Author's interview, journalist, New York City, December 5, 2014.

115. Rice and Hudson, "Stash Pad."

116. Rice and Hudson, "Stash Pad."

117. "A Summary: The Hidden Money Buying Condos at Time Warner," *New York Times*, February 7, 2015; see also "A Mansion, a Shell Company, and Resentment in Bel Air," *New York Times*, December 14, 2015.

118. Global Witness, *Lowering the Bar: How American Lawyers Told Us How to Funnel Suspect Funds into the United States* (Washington, D.C., 2016); see also https://www.globalwitness.org/shadyinc/?gclid=CMmHzvzqkcsCFYKYvAodG6sFZA.

119. "United States vs. One Crystal-Covered 'Bad' Tour Glove," 52–57, 61–63, 65, 71–72, 82.

120. Author's interviews: journalist, New York City, December 5, 2014; former Treasury Department official, Washington, D.C., December 10, 2014; former FBI agent, Washington, D.C., February 9, 2015; private lawyer, Washington, D.C., February 10, 2015; and Treasury Department, Washington, D.C., February 12, 2015.

121. Robert Tie, "C-Suite Fraud Options: How CFEs Can Help Keep Execs on the Straight and Narrow: Part 2," *Fraud Magazine*, November/December 2014.

3. Switzerland

1. StAR, *Few and Far: The Hard Facts on Asset Recovery* (Washington, D.C., 2014), 19–20.

2. Bernard Bertossa, "What Makes Asset Recovery So Difficult in Practice? A Practitioner's Perspective," in *Recovering Stolen Assets*, edited by Mark Pieth (Bern: Peter Lang, 2008), 20; David Chaikin, "Policy and Legal Obstacles in Recovering Dictators' Plunder," *Bond Law Review* 17 (2005): 28.

3. Author's interviews: international bankers and lawyers, Geneva, Switzerland, June 20–22, 2013; former Swiss prosecutor, Providence, Rhode Island, May 6, 2015; international bankers and lawyers, Geneva, Switzerland, June 16–18, 2015; Federal Department of Foreign Affairs, Bern, Switzerland, October 12, 2015; Swiss Financial Intelligence Unit, Bern, Switzerland, October 13, 2015; former Swiss Financial Intelligence Unit official, Zurich, Switzerland, October 13, 2015; International Centre for Asset Recovery, Basel, Switzerland, October 14–15, 2015; and Berne Declaration, Lausanne, Switzerland, October 16, 2015.

4. J. C. Sharman, "Regional Deals and the Global Imperative: The External Dimension of the European Union Savings Tax Directive," *Journal of Common Market Studies* 46 (2008): 1049–1069; Thomas Rixen and Peter Schwarz, "The Effectiveness of the EU Savings Tax Directive—Evidence from Four Countries," *Journal of Common Market Studies* 50 (2012): 151–168; Niels Johannesen, "Tax Evasion and Swiss Bank Deposits," *Journal of Public Economics* 111 (2014): 46–62; Niels Johannesen and Gabriel Zucman, "The End of Bank Secrecy? An Evaluation of the G20 Tax Crack-Down," *American Economic Journal: Economic Policy* 6 (2014): 65–91; Gabriel Zucman, *The Hidden Wealth of Nations: The Scourge of Tax Havens* (Chicago: University of Chicago Press, 2015).

5. See http://www.swissbanking.org/en/home/finanzplatz-link/facts_figures.htm.

6. Ronen Palan, Richard Murphy, and Christian Chavagneux, *Tax Havens: How Globalization Really Works* (Ithaca: Cornell University Press, 2010), 111–112, 115–116, 119–122.

7. Ronen Palan, *The Offshore World: Sovereign Markets, Virtual Places, and Nomad Millionaires* (Ithaca: Cornell University Press, 2003), 103–104.

8. Palan et al., *Tax Havens*, 120–122.

9. Author's interviews: Liechtenstein Bankers' Association, Vaduz, Liechtenstein, January 29, 2004, and June 24, 2013; and Liechtenstein Financial Markets Authority, Vaduz, Liechtenstein, June 24, 2013; David Beattie, *Liechtenstein: A Modern History* (London: I. B. Tauris, 2004).

10. Rebecca G. Peters, "Money Laundering in Switzerland," *Northwestern Journal of International Law and Business* 11 (1990): 117–119.

11. Philippe Braillard, *Switzerland as a Financial Centre: Structures and Policies* (Berlin: Springer, 1988); Henri B. Meier, John E. Marthinsen, and Pascal A. Gantebein, *Swiss Finance: Capital Markets, Banking, and the Swiss Value Chain* (Hoboken, NJ: Wiley, 2012).

12. Peters, "Money Laundering in Switzerland," 111–112.

13. Author's interview, former Swiss prosecutor, Basel, Switzerland, October 14, 2015.

14. US Department of Commerce, *U.S. and Allied Efforts to Recover and Restore Gold and Other Assets Stolen or Hidden by Germany during World War II* (Washington, D.C., 1997).

15. Chaikin, "Recovering Dictators' Plunder"; Paul Gully-Hart, "International Asset Recovery of Corruption-Related Assets: Switzerland," in *Recovering Stolen Assets*, edited by Mark Pieth (Bern: Peter Lang, 2008), 165–185.

16. Peters, "Money Laundering in Switzerland."

17. Associação Mãos Livres/Corruption Watch UK, *Deception in High Places: The Corrupt Angola-Russia Debt Deal* (London, 2013), 37.

18. Swiss Federal Banking Commission, "Abacha Funds at Swiss Banks" (Bern, August 30, 2000), 3.

19. Gully-Hart, "International Asset Recovery," 169.

20. Andrew Wedeman, "Looters, Rent-Scrapers, and Dividend Collectors: Corruption and Growth in Zaire, South Korea, and the Philippines," *Journal of Developing Areas* 31 (1997): 472; Sergio Salvioni, "Recovering the Proceeds of Corruption: Ferdinand Marcos of the Philippines," in *Recovering Stolen Assets*, edited by Mark Pieth (Bern: Peter Lang, 2008), 80.

21. David Chaikin and J. C. Sharman, *Corruption and Money Laundering: A Symbiotic Relationship* (New York: Palgrave, 2009), 170–171.

22. Salvioni, "Ferdinand Marcos," 80.

23. Chaikin and Sharman, *Corruption and Money Laundering*, 173.

24. Simeon V. Marcelo, "The Long Road from Zurich to Manila: The Recovery of the Marcos Swiss Dollar Deposits," in *Recovering Stolen Assets*, edited by Mark Pieth (Bern: Peter Lang, 2008), 92.

25. Pierre-Yves Morier, "Is Autonomous Confiscation the Acme of Asset Recovery?" in *Recovering Stolen Assets*, edited by Mark Pieth (Bern: Peter Lang, 2008), 270.

26. Chaikin, "Recovering Dictators' Plunder," 31.

27. Tim Daniel, "Repatriation of Looted State Assets: Selected Case Studies and the UN Convention Against Corruption," in Transparency International, *Global Corruption Report* (Berlin, 2004), 101.

28. Quoted in Chaikin and Sharman, *Corruption and Money Laundering*, 177.

29. Salvioni, "Ferdinand Marcos," 86.

30. Marcelo, "From Zurich to Manila," 93.

31. Marcelo, "From Zurich to Manila," 109.

32. Enrico Monfrini, "The Abacha Case," in *Recovering Stolen Assets*, edited by Mark Pieth (Bern: Peter Lang, 2008), 50.

33. Daniel Scher, "Asset Recovery: Repatriating Africa's Looted Billions," *African Security Review* 14 (2005): 20.

34. Andrea Clementi, "Swiss Hunter of Embezzled Funds Comes Clean," Swissinfo.ch, March 30, 2011, http://www.swissinfo.ch/eng/swiss-hunter-of-embezzled-funds-comes-clean/29877404.

35. Tim Daniel and James Maton, "Civil Proceedings to Recover Corruptly Acquired Assets of Public Officials," in *Recovering Stolen Assets*, edited by Mark Pieth (Bern: Peter Lang, 2008), 248.

36. Scher, "Africa's Looted Billions," 18.

37. Swiss Federal Banking Commission, "Abacha Funds at Swiss Banks," 8.

38. Monfrini, "Abacha Case," 50, 55.

39. US Department of Justice vs. Muhammed Sani, US District Court for the District of Columbia, case 1:13-cv-01832-JDB, filed November 18, 2013, 5–6.

40. Swiss Federal Banking Commission, "Abacha Funds at Swiss Banks," 6.

41. Swiss Federal Banking Commission, "Abacha Funds at Swiss Banks," 6.

42. Swiss Federal Banking Commission, "Abacha Funds at Swiss Banks," 7.

43. Author's interview, international bankers, Geneva, Switzerland, June 18, 2015.

44. Swiss Federal Banking Commission, "Abacha Funds at Swiss Banks," 9.

45. Swiss Federal Banking Commission, "Abacha Funds at Swiss Banks," 9–10.

46. Swiss Federal Banking Commission, "Abacha Funds at Swiss Banks," 16.

47. Swiss Federal Banking Commission, "Abacha Funds at Swiss Banks," 15.

48. Scher, "Africa's Looted Billions," 20.

49. "Nigerian Government Defends Honoring Sani Abacha," Pulse.ng, March 8, 2014, http://pulse.ng/gist/the-centenary-award-was-not-a-test-of-sainthood-nigerian-government-defends-honoring-sani-abacha-id2722877.html.

50. Daniel and Maton, "Nation's Thief"; US Department of Justice vs. Muhammed Sani.

51. Monfrini, "Abacha Case," 57–58.

52. Author's interview, former Swiss prosecutor, Basel, Switzerland, October 14, 2015.

53. Max Mader, "Civil Society Facilitators of Asset Recovery: Two Swiss Cases; Mobutu and Abacha," in *Non-State Actors and Asset Recovery*, edited by Daniel Thelesklaf and Pedro Gomes Pereira (Bern: Peter Lang, 2011), 109–130.

54. Dimitri Vlassis and Dorothee Gottwald, "Implementing the Asset Recovery Provisions of UNCAC," in *Recovering Stolen Assets*, edited by Mark Pieth (Bern: Peter Lang, 2008), 366–367.

55. Author's interview, Federal Department of Foreign Affairs, Bern, Switzerland, October 12, 2015.

56. For the full text of the deal, see http://media.premiumtimesng.com/wp-content/files/2015/05/20140714_Abacha_Repatriation-Agreement.pdf.

57. The text of the agreement specifies only the balance held in two Liechtenstein accounts, $10,380,011.11 and $232,198,530.61, from which Liechtenstein withheld costs of $6,064,463.60 (see http://media.premiumtimesng.com/wp-content/files/2015/05/20140714_Abacha_Repatriation-Agreement.pdf). The US Department of Justice in rem action specifies $445.6 million, €95,910,223 and £21.7 million, plus unspecified assets owned by a range of named companies, trusts, foundations, and establishments. Finally, various news sources report Swiss ambassador to Nigeria Hans Rudolf Hodel announcing the news of the discovery of $370 million in Luxembourg ("Swiss Govt to Help Nigeria Reclaim Abacha's $370 million Loot in Luxembourg—Ambassador," *Vanguard*, April 28, 2015, http://www.vanguardngr.com/2015/04/swiss-govt-to-help-nigeria-reclaim-abacha-370m-in-luxembourg-ambassador/).

58. "Abacha Funds: Catastrophic Repatriation by Swiss Authorities," Berne Declaration press release, May 18, 2015, https://www.bernedeclaration.ch/media/press-release/abacha_funds_catastrophic_repatriation_by_swiss_authorities/.

59. "Abacha Loot: Inside the Secret Deal Jonathan Authorized to Shield Ex-Dictator's Family from Prosecution," *Premium Times*, May 15, 2015; "Civil Society Groups Write to UK Prime Minister, Demand Rejection of Abacha Loot Agreement," *Premium Times*, June 6, 2015.

60. Author's interview, private lawyer, London, December 9, 2015.

61. Author's interview, private lawyer, London, December 9, 2015.

62. Chaikin, "Recovering Dictators' Plunder," 39; Nuhu Ribadu, *Show Me the Money: Leveraging Anti–Money Laundering Tools to Fight Corruption in Nigeria* (Washington, D.C.: Center for Global Development, 2010), 32.

63. Sally Bowen and Jane Holligan, *The Imperfect Spy: The Many Lives of Vladimiro Montesinos* (Lima: Peisa, 2003).

64. Guillermo Jorge, "The Peruvian Efforts to Recover Proceeds from Montesinos's Criminal Network of Corruption," in Asian Development Bank/OECD Anti-Corruption Initiative for the Asia-Pacific, *Asset Recovery and Mutual Legal Assistance in Asia and the Pacific* (Manila, 2008), 201–202.

65. StAR Database, Vladimiro Montesinos (Switzerland), http://star.worldbank.org/corruption-cases/node/18595.

66. Jorge, "Montesinos's Criminal Network of Corruption," 213.

67. Swiss Federal Office of Justice, "Montesinos Case: Switzerland Transfers 77 million US Dollars to Peru," press release, August 20, 2002, http://star.worldbank.org/corruption-cases/

sites/corruption-cases/files/documents/arw/Montesinos_Switzerland_EJPD_Press_Release_
Aug_20_2002.pdf.

68. Jorge, "Montesinos's Criminal Network of Corruption," 213.

69. Morier, "Acme of Asset Recovery?" 272.

70. Luis Largas Valdivia, "Corruption and Criminal Organization: Peru's Experience," in
Asian Development Bank/OECD, *Asset Recovery and Mutual Legal Assistance in Asia and the Pacific*
(Manila, 2008), 225–228.

71. Financial Action Task Force, *Laundering the Proceeds of Corruption* (Paris, 2011), 32.

72. For example, Antenor Madruga, "Expectations of Developing Economies: A View from
the Americas," in *Recovering Stolen Assets*, edited by Mark Pieth (Bern: Peter Lang, 2008), 374–375;
StAR, *Politically Exposed Persons: A Policy Paper on Strengthening Preventive Measures* (Washington,
D.C., 2009).

73. United Nations Office on Drugs and Crime, "Estimating Illicit Financial Flows Resulting from Drug Trafficking and Other Transnational Organized Crimes" (Vienna, 2011); StAR,
Few and Far.

74. Radha Ivory, *Corruption, Asset Recovery, and the Protection of Property in Public International Law: The Human Rights of Bad Guys* (Cambridge: Cambridge University Press, 2014), 43–46.

75. Elizabeth Abbott, *Haiti: The Duvaliers and Their Legacy* (New York: McGraw-Hill, 1988).

76. "Republic of Haiti and Others v Duvalier and Others," All England Law Reports, All
ER 1989 Volume 1, July 1988, http://www.uniset.ca/other/cs2/19891AER456.html; http://star.
worldbank.org/corruption-cases/node/18515.

77. Quoted in Mark V. Vlasic and Gregory Cooper, "Beyond the Duvalier Legacy: What the
New 'Arab Spring' Governments Can Learn from Haiti and the Benefits of Stolen Asset Recovery," *Northwestern Journal of International Human Rights* 10 (2011): 23.

78. Transparency International, *Global Corruption Report* (Berlin, 2004), 13.

79. "'Baby Doc' Duvalier's Family Can Reclaim £2.9 million in Swiss Bank, Court Rules,"
Guardian, February 3, 2010.

80. Author's interview, Federal Department of Foreign Affairs, Bern, Switzerland,
October 12, 2015.

81. "Some See Cash Motive in Duvalier's Return," *New York Times*, January 20, 2011.

82. "Baby Doc Duvalier: Like Father, Like Son," *Economist*, October 11, 2014.

83. Rita Adam and Valentin Zellweger, "The Proposed Swiss Comprehensive Act on Asset
Recovery," in *Emerging Trends in Asset Recovery*, edited by Gretta Fenner Zinkernagel, Charles
Monteith, and Pedro Gomez Pereira (Bern: Peter Lang, 2013), 173–181; Vlasic and Cooper,
"Beyond the Duvalier Legacy," 24–25; Ivory, *Human Rights of Bad Guys*, 44–45.

84. Author's interviews: private lawyer, London, June 17, 2013; Department of Justice, Washington, D.C., December 9, 2014; StAR, Washington, D.C., December 9, 2014; and private lawyer,
London, December 9, 2015.

85. Vlasic and Cooper, "Beyond the Duvalier Legacy," 25.

86. Bola Ige, "Abacha and the Bankers: Cracking the Conspiracy," *Forum on Crime and Society* 2
(2002): 113.

87. For example, author's interviews: prosecutor, Sofia, Bulgaria, September 29, 2010, and
StAR, Washington, D.C., March 21, 2011.

88. Co-ordinating Group on Combating Money Laundering and the Financing of Terrorism,
"Report on the National Evaluation of the Risks of Money Laundering and Terrorist Financing
in Switzerland" (Bern, 2016), 20.

89. Author's interviews: Federal Department of Foreign Affairs, Bern, Switzerland, October 12,
2015; International Centre for Asset Recovery, Basel, Switzerland, October 14, 2015; and Berne
Declaration, Lausanne, Switzerland, October 16, 2015.

90. US Senate Permanent Subcommittee on Investigations, *Private Banking and Money Laundering: A Case Study of Opportunities and Vulnerabilities* (Washington, D.C., 1999); StAR Database: Ali Asif Zardari/Benazir Bhutto, https://star.worldbank.org/corruption-cases/node/18731; Jeremy Carver, "The Hunt for Looted State Assets: The Case of Benazir Bhutto," in Transparency International, *Global Corruption Report* (Berlin, 2004), 102–104.

91. Raymond Baker, *Capitalism's Achilles Heel: Dirty Money and How to Renew the Free-Market System* (Hoboken, NJ: Wiley, 2005), 82–85.

92. "House of Graft: Tracing the Bhutto Millions," *New York Times*, January 9, 1998.

93. US Senate Permanent Subcommittee on Investigations, *Private Banking and Money Laundering*, 32/903.

94. "House of Graft."

95. US Senate Permanent Subcommittee on Investigations, *Private Banking and Money Laundering*, 36/907.

96. "Pakistan: Dropped Corruption Case May Free up Mansion Cash," *Guardian*, September 22, 2008.

97. Author's interview, private lawyer, London, June 17, 2013.

98. Carver, "Case of Benazir Bhutto," 102; StAR Database: Ali Asif Zardari/Benazir Bhutto.

99. Carver, "Case of Benazir Bhutto," 104.

100. Quoted in Olivier Longchamp and Mark Herkenrath, "Money Laundering, Liability and Sanctions for Financial Intermediaries—The Issue of Having the Assets of Politically Exposed Persons in Switzerland," in *Emerging Trends in Asset Recovery*, edited by Gretta Fenner Zinkernagel, Charles Monteith, and Pedro Gomez Pereira (Bern: Peter Lang, 2013), 128.

101. StAR, *Few and Far*, 24.

102. StAR, *Few and Far*, 48; author's interview, Federal Department of Foreign Affairs, Bern, Switzerland, October 12, 2015; Co-ordinating Group on Combating Money Laundering and the Financing of Terrorism, "Report on the National Evaluation."

103. Longchamp and Herkenrath, "Money Laundering," 131.

104. M. Cherif Bassiouni, "Corruption Cases against Officials of the Mubarak Regime," paper published by the Egyptian-American Rule of Law Association, March 23, 2012.

105. Author's interview, International Centre for Asset Recovery, Basel, Switzerland, October 13, 2015.

106. Bassiouni, "Corruption Cases against the Mubarak Regime"; Sarah Chayes, *Thieves of State: Why Corruption Threatens Global Security* (New York: W. W. Norton, 2015); author's interviews: UK Department for International Development, London, May 17, 2012; private lawyer, Washington, D.C., April 10, 2013; StAR, Washington, D.C., April 11, 2013; and former Swiss Financial Intelligence Unit official, Zurich, Switzerland, October 13, 2015.

107. Bassiouni, "Corruption Cases against the Mubarak Regime," 15–16.

108. Author's interviews: StAR, Washington, D.C., April 11, 2013, and February 12, 2015; United Nations Office on Drugs and Crime, Washington, D.C., April 13, 2013; US Department of Justice, December 9, 2014; International Monetary Fund, Washington, D.C., February 9, 2015; Department of the Treasury, Washington, D.C., February 12, 2015; and Swiss Financial Intelligence Unit, October 13, 2015.

109. Ahmed Saad, Urs Feller, Marcel Frey, Kamal Shah, and Charlotte Welsh, "Recovering Stolen Assets: The Egyptian Experience," in *Emerging Trends in Asset Recovery*, edited by Gretta Fenner Zinkernagel, Charles Monteith, and Pedro Gomez Pereira (Bern: Peter Lang 2013), 23. However, the same source stretches credulity in claiming that "the independence of the judiciary remains a cornerstone in Egyptian society" (18).

110. Adam and Zellweger, "Comprehensive Act on Asset Recovery"; Ivory, *Human Rights of Bad Guys*, 47–54.

111. Author's interviews: Federal Department for Foreign Affairs, Bern, Switzerland, October 12, 2015; International Centre for Asset Recovery, Basel, Switzerland, October 13, 2015; former Swiss Financial Intelligence Unit official, Zurich, October 13, 2015; and Berne Declaration, Lausanne, Switzerland, October 16, 2015.

112. *FINMA Annual Report, 2012* (Bern: Swiss Financial Market Supervisory Authority), 70.

113. "Banks Probed over Dictator Asset Rules," Swissinfo.ch, November 10, 2011, http://www.swissinfo.ch/eng/banks-probed-over-dictator-asset-rules/31537562.

114. US Senate Permanent Subcommittee on Investigations, *Offshore Tax Evasion: Efforts to Collect Unpaid Taxes on Billions in Offshore Accounts* (Washington, D.C., 2014).

115. Organized Crime and Corruption Reporting Project, "Following Gulnara's Money," March 21, 2015, https://www.occrp.org/corruptistan/uzbekistan/gulnara_karimova/the-prodigal-daughter/following-gulnaras-money.php.

116. "Uzbek Corruption Probe Widens to Include VimpelCom," *Financial Times*, March 12, 2014; "Swiss Investigate Uzbek President's Daughter," Swissinfo.ch, March 12, 2014, http://www.swissinfo.ch/eng/money-laundering_swiss-investigate-uzbek-president-s-daughter/38142038.

117. Organized Crime and Corruption Reporting Project, "Following Gulnara's Money."

118. "U.S. Brings Civil Forfeiture Case against Kickbacks of Uzbek Ruling Family," *International Enforcement Law Reporter*, 31 (2015), 310–11.

119. "No End to Scrutiny over Millions Sent to Malaysian Leader's Accounts," *New York Times*, February 5, 2016; "Malaysia: The 1MDB Money Trail," *Financial Times*, February 15, 2016.

120. "Malaysia Accuses Switzerland of 'Misinformation' over Stolen 1MDB Billions," *Guardian*, February 2, 2016. The Swiss attorney-general's office later clarified that it was not investigating Najib personally.

121. Author's interviews: international banks and lawyers, Geneva, Switzerland, June 20–22, 2013; former Swiss prosecutor, Providence, Rhode Island, May 6, 2015; international bankers and lawyers, Geneva, Switzerland, June 16–18, 2015; Federal Department of Foreign Affairs, Bern, Switzerland, October 12, 2015; Swiss Financial Intelligence Unit, Bern, Switzerland, October 13, 2015; former Swiss Financial Intelligence Unit official, Zurich, Switzerland, October 13, 2015; International Centre for Asset Recovery, Basel, Switzerland, October 14–15, 2015; and Berne Declaration, Lausanne, Switzerland, October 16, 2015.

122. John Kerry, *The New War: The Web of Crime That Threatens America's Security* (New York: Simon and Schuster, 1997); William Wechsler, "Follow the Money," *Foreign Affairs* 80 (2001): 40–57.

123. Scher, "Africa's Looted Billions," 20.

124. Author's interview, Department of Justice, Washington, D.C., December 9, 2014.

125. Author's interview, Swiss Financial Intelligence Unit, Bern, October 13, 2015.

126. Author's observations, wealth planning conferences: Geneva, Switzerland, June 18–20, 2013; Nassau, The Bahamas, May 12–14, 2014; and Geneva, Switzerland, June 16–18, 2015.

127. J. C. Sharman, *Havens in a Storm: The Struggle for Global Tax Regulation* (Ithaca: Cornell University Press, 2006); Richard Eccleston, *The Dynamics of Global Economic Governance: The Financial Crisis, the OECD and the Politics of International Tax Co-operation* (Cheltenham, UK: Edward Elgar, 2014); Niels Johannesen, "Tax Evasion and Swiss Bank Deposits," *Journal of Public Economics* 111 (2014): 46–62; Gabriel Zucman, *The Hidden Wealth of Nations: The Scourge of Tax Havens* (Chicago: University of Chicago Press, 2015).

128. The contribution of the finance center as a whole is considerably larger thanks to the insurance sector; see Swiss Bankers Association, http://www.swissbanking.org/en/home/finanzplatz-link/facts_figures.htm.

129. Author's interview, private lawyer, Geneva, Switzerland, May 14, 2013.

130. Author's interviews: international bankers, Zurich, Switzerland, September 16–17, 2010; international bankers, Geneva, Switzerland, June 18–20, 2013, and June 16–18, 2015; Liechtenstein

Bankers' Association, Vaduz, Liechtenstein, June 24, 2013; and Swiss Financial Intelligence Unit, October 13, 2015.

131. StAR, *Barriers to Asset Recovery: An Analysis of Key Barriers and Recommendations for Action* (Washington, D.C., 2011), 15–17.

132. Author's interview, Kenyan Ethics and Anti-Corruption Commission, London, November 17, 2015.

133. Author's interviews: international bankers, Geneva, Switzerland, June 18–20, 2013, and June 16–18, 2015.

134. Chaikin, "Recovering Dictators' Plunder," 39–40.

135. Longchamp and Herkenrath, "Money Laundering," 128.

136. E.g., Salvioni, "Ferdinand Marcos"; Monfrini, "Abacha Case."

137. Author's interview, Swiss banker, Providence, Rhode Island, May 6, 2015.

138. Author's observations, wealth planning conference, Geneva, Switzerland, June 16–18, 2015.

139. StAR, *Politically Exposed Persons*; author's observations, wealth planning conferences: Hong Kong, November 9–10, 2010; Geneva, Switzerland, June 18–20, 2013; Nassau, The Bahamas, May 12–14, 2014; New York City, October 30, 2014; Geneva, Switzerland, June 16–18, 2015; London, December 2, 2015.

140. Author's interviews, international banks: Hong Kong, October 18, 2011; New York, November 21, 2014; Providence, Rhode Island, May 6, 2015; Geneva, June 18, 2015; and London, June 23, 2015.

4. The United Kingdom

1. "The Ukrainian Oligarchs Living It Large in London," *Daily Telegraph*, February 23, 2014.

2. For examples, see Andrew Wilson, *Ukraine's Orange Revolution* (New Haven: Yale University Press, 2006); Margarita M. Balmaceda, *Energy Dependency, Politics and Corruption in the Former Soviet Union: Russia's Power, Oligarchs' Corruption and Ukraine's Missing Energy Policy, 1995–2006* (London: Routledge, 2008); Heiko Pleines, "Manipulating Politics: Domestic Investors in Ukrainian Privatisation Auctions, 2000–2004," *Europe Asia Studies* 60 (2008): 1177–1197.

3. "Tackling Corruption: PM Speech in Singapore," July 28, 2015, https://www.gov.uk/government/speeches/tackling-corruption-pm-speech-in-singapore.

4. Christie's International Real Estate, "Luxury Defined: An Insight into the Luxury Residential Property Market" (2015), 47.

5. Oliver Morrissey, "British Aid Policy in the 'Short-Blair' Years,'" in *Perspectives on European Development Co-operation: Policy and Performance of Individual Donor Countries in the EU*, edited by Paul Hoebink and Olav Stokke (London: Routledge, 2005), 161.

6. Transparency International UK, *Combating Money Laundering and Recovering Looted Gains: Raising the UK's Game* (London, 2009), 51; author's interviews: Department for International Development, London, May 17, 2012; June 17, 2013; and September 17, 2015; Transparency International, Berlin, September 14, 2015; Global Witness, London, December 15, 2015; Transparency International UK, London, December 10, 2015; and National Crime Agency, London, October 28, 2015.

7. StAR, *The Puppet Masters: How the Corrupt Use Legal Structures to Hide Their Stolen Assets and What to Do about It* (Washington, D.C., 2011); Michael G. Findley, Daniel L. Nielson, and J. C. Sharman, *Global Shell Games: Experiments in Transnational Relations, Crime and Terrorism* (Cambridge: Cambridge University Press, 2014).

8. Author's interview, Department for International Development, London, June 17, 2013; "Tackling Corruption: PM Speech in Singapore"; David Collier presentation, London, December 4, 2015.

9. Author's interviews: Department for International Development, London, September 17, 2015; Transparency International, Berlin, September 14, 2015; Global Witness, London, December 15, 2015; Transparency International UK, London, December 10, 2015; and National Crime Agency, London, October 28, 2015.

10. Nuhu Ribadu, *Show Me the Money: Leveraging Anti–Money Laundering Tools to Fight Corruption in Nigeria* (Washington, D.C.: Center for Global Development, 2010).

11. "Nigerian Police Recover Part of Sani Abacha's $4.3bn Hoard from Robbers," *Guardian*, October 5, 2012.

12. Tim Daniel and James Maton, "Recovering the Proceeds of Corruption: General Sani Abacha—A Nation's Thief," in *Recovering Stolen Assets*, edited by Mark Pieth (Bern: Peter Lang, 2008), 67; Enrico Monfrini, "The Abacha Case," in *Recovering Stolen Assets*, edited by Mark Pieth (Bern: Peter Lang, 2008), 44.

13. Daniel and Maton, "Nation's Thief," 63.

14. Bola Ige, "Abacha and the Bankers: Cracking the Conspiracy," *Forum on Crime and Society* 2 (2002): 111.

15. Ige, "Abacha and the Bankers," 112.

16. Monfrini, "Abacha Case"; Transparency International UK, *Recovering Looted Gains*, 60.

17. US Senate Permanent Subcommittee on Investigations, *Private Banking and Money Laundering: A Case Study of Opportunities and Vulnerabilities* (Washington, D.C., 1999), 15.

18. "FSA Publishes the Results of Money Laundering Investigation," FSA/PN/029/2001, March 8, 2001, http://www.fsa.gov.uk/pages/Library/Communication/PR/2001/029.shtml.

19. Global Witness, *International Thief Thief: How British Banks Are Complicit in Nigerian Corruption* (London, 2010), 5.

20. US Senate Permanent Subcommittee on Investigations, *Private Banking and Money Laundering*; Swiss Federal Banking Commission, "Abacha Funds at Swiss Banks" (Bern, August 30, 2000).

21. Author's interviews: former bank compliance officer, London, May 18, 2012; StAR, Washington, D.C., December 9, 2014, and February 12, 2015; US Senate Permanent Subcommittee on Investigations, Washington, D.C., December 11, 2014; and private lawyer, London, December 9, 2015.

22. US Senate Permanent Subcommittee on Investigations, *Private Banking and Money Laundering: A Case Study of Opportunities and Vulnerabilities: Hearings* (Washington, D.C., November 9–10, 1999), 16.

23. "Britons Hired by the Abachas," *Guardian*, October 4, 2001.

24. Alan Bacarese, "Asset Recovery in a Common Law System: The United Kingdom," in *Recovering Stolen Assets*, edited by Mark Pieth (Bern: Peter Lang, 2008), 147–163.

25. Financial Action Task Force, *Third Mutual Evaluation Report: Anti–Money Laundering and Combating the Financing of Terrorism; United Kingdom* (Paris, 2007), 115.

26. "FSA Publishes the Results of Money Laundering Investigation"; US Senate Permanent Subcommittee on Investigations, *Private Banking and Money Laundering*, 57/928–58/929.

27. Bacarese, "Asset Recovery in a Common Law System," 147–149; Transparency International UK, *Recovering Looted Gains*, 34.

28. Financial Action Task Force, *Evaluation Report: United Kingdom*; Transparency International UK, *Recovering Looted Gains*, 27; Global Witness, *International Thief Thief*.

29. Author's interview, National Crime Agency, London, October 28, 2015.

30. "Britons Hired by the Abachas."

31. Author's interview, private lawyer, London, December 9, 2015.

32. Daniel and Maton, "Nation's Thief," 75–76.

33. Monfrini, "Abacha Case," 54.

34. Author's interview, private lawyer, London, December 9, 2015.

35. Daniel and Maton, "Nation's Thief," 77.

36. "Jersey Court Jails Former Nigerian Dictator's Business Associate," *Guardian*, June 27, 2010.

37. "Man in Money Launder Scam with Dictator to Repay £26.5m," BBC Jersey, June 8, 2011.

38. "US Freezes $458 Million Hidden by Former Nigerian Leader Sani Abacha," *Telegraph*, March 5, 2015.

39. "Centenary Award to Abacha Not Unlawful—Presidency," *Punch*, March 8, 2014; Repatriation Agreement between the Federal Republic of Nigeria and Mohammed Sani and Abba Abacha, July 14, 2014, http://media.premiumtimesng.com/wp-content/files/2015/05/20140714_ Abacha_Repatriation-Agreement.pdf.

40. Commission for Africa, *Our Common Interest* (London, 2005), 105, 223, 151.

41. Commission for Africa, *Our Common Interest*, 151.

42. Author's interview, Department for International Development, London, September 8, 2011; U4, "Making Development Assistance Work at Home: DfID's Approach to Clamping Down on International Bribery and Money Laundering in the UK," Practice Insight (Bergen, Norway: CMI, 2011).

43. Anne Lugon-Moulin, "The Role of Donors in Supporting NSAs," in *Non-State Actors and Asset Recovery*, edited by Daniel Thelesklaf and Pedro Gomes Pereira (Bern: Peter Lang, 2011), 154.

44. Author's interviews: Metropolitan Police, London, September 8, 2011, and National Crime Agency, London, December 14, 2015.

45. U4, "Making Development Assistance Work at Home," 3–4; Phil Mason, "Being Janus: A Donor Agency's Approach to Asset Recovery," in *Emerging Trends in Asset Recovery*, edited by Gretta Fenner Zinkernagel, Charles Monteith, and Pedro Gomez Pereira (Bern: Peter Lang, 2013), 197–204.

46. Author's interview, National Crime Agency, London, December 14, 2015.

47. Author's interview, Metropolitan Police, London, September 8, 2011; Jesse Mwangi Wachanga, "Hurdles in Asset Recovery and Fighting Corruption by Developing Countries: The Kenya Experience," in *Emerging Trends in Asset Recovery*, edited by Gretta Fenner Zinkernagel, Charles Monteith, and Pedro Gomez Pereira (Bern: Peter Lang, 2013), 147–158; Michela Wrong, *It's Our Turn to Eat: The Story of a Kenyan Whistle-Blower* (London: Fourth Estate, 2009); author's interview, Kenyan Ethics and Anti-Corruption Commission, London, November 16, 2015.

48. Author's interviews: United Nations Office on Drugs and Crime, Washington, D.C., April 13, 2013; former World Bank official, Washington, D.C., February 10, 2015; and private lawyer, London, December 9, 2015.

49. Ribadu, *Show Me the Money*.

50. "UK Police Given £8.5 Million to Probe Overseas Corruption," BBC News, February 1, 2013.

51. Author's interviews: Department for International Development, London, September 8, 2011, and June 17, 2013.

52. U4, "Making Development Assistance Work at Home," 7.

53. Ribadu, *Show Me the Money*, 31.

54. Transparency International UK, *Recovering Looted Gains*, 63.

55. U4, "Making Development Assistance Work at Home," 3.

56. Ribadu, *Show Me the Money*, 29; "Corruption: Landmark Cases Flounder as Crime Team Purged," *Financial Times*, July 20, 2009.

57. Transparency International UK, *Recovering Looted Gains*, 62–63.

58. Global Witness, *International Thief Thief*, 8–23.

59. Transparency International UK, *Recovering Looted Gains*, 29–30.

60. Ribadu, *Show Me the Money*, 29–31; "Crime Team Purged."

61. Global Witness, *International Thief Thief*, 14.

62. Transparency International UK, *Empowering the UK to Recover Corrupt Assets: Unexplained Wealth Orders and Other New Approaches to Illicit Enrichment and Asset Recovery* (London, 2015), 9.

63. Transparency International UK, *Recovering Looted Gains*, 61.

64. Transparency International UK, *Recovering Looted Gains*, 61–62; StAR, *Puppet Masters*, 179–183; author's interview, private lawyer, London, December 9, 2015.

65. Global Witness, *International Thief Thief*, 10.

66. Ribadu, *Show Me the Money*, 50.

67. Ribadu, *Show Me the Money*, 49.

68. "How Bhadresh Gohil, a UK Lawyer, Collaborated with James Ibori in Looting Delta State Treasury," Sahara Reporters, September 24, 2008, http://saharareporters.com/2008/09/24/how-bhadresh-gohil-uk-lawyer-collaborated-james-ibori-looting-delta-state-treasury.

69. "Former Wickes Cashier Who Became a Nigerian State Governor and Defrauded Some of the World's Poorest People out of £157 Million May Not Have to Pay Back a Penny," *Daily Mail*, April 10, 2014.

70. "How Bhadresh Gohil."

71. See Transparency International UK, *Empowering the UK to Recover Corrupt Assets*, 19.

72. "UK Money Laundering Trial: James Ibori Suffers Various Reverses," Sahara Reporters, September 15, 2011, http://saharareporters.com/2011/12/15/uk-money-laundering-trial-james-ibori-suffers-various-reverses.

73. Author's interviews: private lawyer, London, June 17, 2013; UK Department for International Development, London, May 17, 2012; and Global Witness, London, May 18, 2012.

74. Author's interviews: National Crime Agency, London, October 28, 2015, and December 14, 2015.

75. "Court to Restart $145-Million Nigeria Asset-Confiscation Case," Reuters, October 7, 2013, http://uk.reuters.com/article/2013/10/07/uk-britain-nigeria-ibori-idUKBRE9960KK20131007.

76. "Ibori's Release Dims as Court Adjourns Hearing until June Next Year," The Learned Friends, April 14, 2015, http://thelearnedfriends.com/news/iboris-release-dims-as-court-adjourns-hearing-till-june-next-year/.

77. Financial Action Task Force, *Evaluation Report: United Kingdom*, 123.

78. Transparency International UK, *Recovering Looted Gains*, 14.

79. Global Witness, *International Thief Thief*, 30; author's interview, Transparency International UK, London, December 10, 2015.

80. "Nigeria's Central Bank and State Clash over Missing Billions," *Financial Times*, May 4, 2014.

81. U4, "Making Hay While the Sun Shines: Experiences with the Zambian Task Force on Corruption," Practice Insight (Bergen, Norway: CMI, 2011).

82. Transparency International UK, *Recovering Looted Gains*; author's interview, Zambian Corruption Task Force, Washington, D.C., May 18, 2010.

83. U4, "Zambian Task Force on Corruption," 5.

84. Author's interview, Zambian Corruption Task Force, Washington, D.C., May 18, 2010.

85. StAR, *Puppet Masters*, 42–43.

86. Wachanga, "Kenya Experience," 152; see also Wrong, *It's Our Turn to Eat*; Kenya National Audit Office, "Special Audit Report of the Controller and Auditor General on Financing, Procurement and Implementation of Security Related Projects" (Nairobi, Kenya, April 2006); John Githongo, letter to President Mwai Kibaki, Nairobi, Kenya, November 22, 2005.

87. Wachanga, "Kenya Experience."

88. Author's interview, Kenyan Ethics and Anti-Corruption Commission, London, November 16, 2015.

89. Author's interviews: private lawyers, London, June 17, 2013, and December 9, 2015; Publish What You Pay conference presentation, Bergen, Norway, November 20, 2012.

90. "Profile: Suharto's Playboy Son," BBC News, September 15, 2000.

91. "Suhartos Sell Boltholes in the UK for £11 Million," *Independent*, March 16, 1999.

92. FSA, *Banks' Management of High Money-Laundering Risk Situations* (London, 2011), 6.

93. FSA, *High Money-Laundering Risk Situations*, 6, 9–11.

94. FSA, *High Money-Laundering Risk Situations*, 27.

95. FSA, *High Money-Laundering Risk Situations*, 13.

96. FSA, *High Money-Laundering Risk Situations*, 27.

97. FSA, *High Money-Laundering Risk Situations*, 29.

98. FSA, *High Money-Laundering Risk Situations*, 39.

99. FSA, *High Money-Laundering Risk Situations*, 16, 33.

100. "Coutts Bank Fined for Laundering Violations," *Financial Times*, March 26, 2012.

101. FSA, "Coutts Fined £8.75 Million for Anti-Money Laundering Control Failings," press release FSA/PN/032/2012, March 26, 2012, http://webarchive.nationalarchives.gov.uk/20130301170532/http:/www.fsa.gov.uk/library/communication/pr/2012/032.shtml.

102. Author's interviews: Metropolitan Police, London, September 8, 2011; World Bank, Washington, D.C., April 24, 2012; StAR, Washington, D.C., April 25, 2012; private lawyer, Washington, D.C., April 25, 2012; Department of Justice, Washington, D.C., April 27, 2012; Department for International Development, London, June 17, 2013; private lawyer, London, June 17, 2013; Swiss Federal Department of Foreign Affairs, October 12, 2015, Bern, Switzerland; and International Centre for Asset Recovery, October 14, 2015, Basel, Switzerland.

103. Simeon V. Marcelo, "The Long Road from Zurich to Manila: The Recovery of the Marcos Swiss Dollar Deposits," in *Recovering Stolen Assets*, edited by Mark Pieth (Bern: Peter Lang, 2008), 92.

104. Andrew Dornbierer and Gretta Fenner Zinkernagel, "Introduction," in *Emerging Trends in Asset Recovery*, edited by Gretta Fenner Zinkernagel, Charles Monteith and Pedro Gomez Pereira (Bern: Peter Lang, 2013), xvii.

105. Author's interviews: Metropolitan Police, London, September 8, 2011; private lawyer, Washington, D.C., April 25, 2012; Department of Justice, Washington, D.C., April 27, 2012; Department for International Development, London, May 17, 2012; private lawyer, Washington, D.C., April 10, 2013; Department for International Development, London, June 17, 2013; private lawyer, London, June 17, 2013; Department of Justice, Washington, D.C., December 9, 2014; Department for International Development, London, September 17, 2015; and National Crime Agency, London, December 14, 2015.

106. Author's interview, private lawyer, Washington, D.C., April 10, 2013.

107. Ahmed Saad, Urs Feller, Marcel Frey, Kamal Shah, and Charlotte Welsh, "Recovering Stolen Assets: The Egyptian Experience," in *Emerging Trends in Asset Recovery*, edited by Gretta Fenner Zinkernagel, Charles Monteith and Pedro Gomez Pereira (Bern: Peter Lang, 2013), 21; author's interviews: private lawyer, Washington, D.C., April 10, 2013; StAR, Washington, D.C., April 25, 2012; Department of Justice, Washington, D.C., April 27, 2012; UK G20 Anti-Corruption Working Group delegate, London, June 17, 2013; United Nations Office on Drugs and Crime, Washington, D.C., April 13, 2013.

108. M. Cherif Bassiouni, "Corruption Cases against Officials of the Mubarak Regime," paper published by the Egyptian-American Rule of Law Association, March 23, 2012.

109. Transparency International UK, *Empowering the UK to Recover Corrupt Assets*, 23.

110. "Scandal of Mubarak Regime Millions in the UK," *Guardian*, September 2, 2012.

111. Saad et al., "Egyptian Experience," 22; Rudolf Wyss, "Proactive Co-operation within the Mutual Legal Assistance Procedure," in *Emerging Trends in Asset Recovery*, edited by Gretta Fenner Zinkernagel, Charles Monteith and Pedro Gomez Pereira (Bern: Peter Lang, 2013), 110.

112. Author's interview, private lawyer, London, June 17, 2013.

113. Saad et al., "Egyptian Experience," 20.

114. "Recovering Stolen Assets: Making a Hash of Finding the Cash," *Economist*, May 11, 2013.

115. "Egypt's Stolen Billions," BBC, http://www.bbc.com/news/world-middle-east-27765332; see also "Scandal of Mubarak Regime Millions."

116. "Scandal of Mubarak Regime Millions."

117. United Kingdom Asset Recovery Action Plan Implementation Road Map, 2013, http://star.worldbank.org/star/sites/star/files/uk_asset_recovery_action_plan_road_map-final.pdf.

118. Author's interview, Global Witness, London, May 18, 2012.

119. The State of Libya and Capitana Seas Ltd, Royal Courts of Justice, London, March 9, 2012, EWHC 602 (Com.), https://star.worldbank.org/corruption-cases/sites/corruption-cases/files/Libya_v_Capitana_Seas_UK_High_Ct_Judgment_Mar_2012.pdf.

120. Leslie Holmes, "Postcommunist Transitions and Corruption: Mapping Patterns," *Social Research* 80 (2013): 1163–1186; Karen Dawisha, *Putin's Kleptocracy: Who Owns Russia?* (New York: Simon and Schuster, 2014); Alexander Cooley and John Heathershaw, *Dictators beyond Borders* (New Haven: Yale University Press, 2016).

121. Mark Hollingsworth and Stewart Lansley, *Londongrad: From Russia with Cash; The Inside Story of the Oligarchs* (London: Fourth Estate, 2010).

122. "From Russia with Cash," Channel 4, July 12, 2015, https://www.youtube.com/watch?v=0JOFphTXHGA.

123. Anna Persson, Bo Rothstein, and Jan Teorell, "Why Anti-Corruption Reforms Fail: Systemic Corruption as a Collective Action Problem," *Governance* 26 (2013): 449–471.

124. "UK Seeking to Ensure Russia Sanctions Do Not Harm City of London," *Guardian*, March 3, 2014.

125. Boris Abramovich Berezovsky vs. Roman Arkedievich Abramovich and Boris Abramovich Berezovsky vs. Hine and Others, High Court, August 31, 2012, EWHC 2463 (Com.), https://www.judiciary.gov.uk/judgments/berezovsky-abramovich-hine-judgment-31082012/.

126. Christie's International Real Estate, "Luxury Defined," 33 and 46.

127. Transparency International UK, *Corruption on Your Doorstep: How Corrupt Capital Is Used to Buy Property in the UK* (London, 2015), 8.

128. Transparency International UK, *Corruption on Your Doorstep*, 12.

129. Transparency International UK, *Corruption on Your Doorstep*, 18.

130. Findley et al., *Global Shell Games*.

131. Nicholas Shaxon, "A Tale of Two Londons," *Vanity Fair*, April 2013, http://www.vanityfair.com/style/society/2013/04/mysterious-residents-one-hyde-park-london.

132. Transparency International UK, *Corruption on Your Doorstep*, 25–26; author's interviews: National Crime Agency, London, October 28, 2015, and December 14, 2015; and Transparency International UK, London, December 10, 2015.

133. Transparency International UK, *Corruption on Your Doorstep*, 27.

134. Karin Svedberg Helgesson and Ulrika Mörth, "Involuntary Public Policy-Making by For-Profit Professionals: European Lawyers on Anti–Money Laundering and Terrorism Financing," *Journal of Common Market Studies* 54 (2016): 1216–1232.

135. Transparency International UK, *Corruption on Your Doorstep*, 29.

136. Author's interviews: Global Witness, London, May 18, 2012, and December 15, 2015; and Transparency International UK, London, December 10, 2015; Graham Stack and Guntars Veidemanis, "Latvia Banks Fuel Scotland's Shell Company 'Factory' Linked to Moldova Fraud," *Business New Europe*, July 3, 2015, http://www.intellinews.com/latvia-banks-fuel-scotland-s-shell-company-factory-linked-to-moldova-fraud-500446872/?source=baltic-states&archive=bne;

Organized Crime and Corruption Reporting Project, "The Russian Laundromat," https://www.reportingproject.net/therussianlaundromat/.

137. Transparency International UK, *Empowering the UK to Recover Corrupt Assets*.

5. Australia

1. United Nations Office on Drugs and Crime, "Estimating Illicit Financial Flows Resulting from Drug Trafficking and Other Transnational Organized Crimes" (Vienna, 2011); StAR, *Few and Far: The Hard Facts on Stolen Asset Recovery* (Washington, D.C., 2014); Transparency International UK, *Empowering the UK to Recover Corrupt Assets: Unexplained Wealth Orders and Other New Approaches to Illicit Enrichment and Asset Recovery* (London, 2015).

2. Sam Koim speech to AUSTRAC major reporters, Sydney, Australia, October 4, 2012, http://www.abc.net.au/4corners/documents/PNG2013/Speech_SamKoim.pdf; author's interviews: StAR, Washington, D.C., March 21, 2011; Australian Federal Police, Brisbane, Australia, April 20, 2011; Asia-Pacific Group on Money Laundering, Sydney, Australia, May 26, 2011; Australian Attorney-General's Department, Canberra, Australia, May 27, 2011; Papua New Guinea Ombudsman's Commission, Brisbane, Australia, October 2, 2012; and Papua New Guinea Financial Intelligence Unit, Brisbane, Australia, October 2, 2012.

3. Financial Action Task Force, *Anti–Money Laundering and Counter-Terrorist Financing Measures Mutual Evaluation Report: Australia* (Paris, 2015), 7.

4. Financial Action Task Force, *Mutual Evaluation Report: Australia*, 57, 116.

5. Author's interview, Australian Attorney-General's Department, Canberra, Australia, March 5, 2013.

6. Author's interviews: StAR, Washington, D.C., April 25, 2012, and C4ADS, by phone, May 28, 2015.

7. OECD, *Measuring Responses to Illicit Financial Flows from Developing Countries* (Paris, 2013).

8. "Rich Smell," *Economist*, December 21, 2013.

9. StAR, *Few and Far*, 18.

10. Jai Ramaswamy, Department of Justice, Center for the Advancement of Public Integrity conference, Columbia University, New York City, November 14, 2014; *UK National Risk Assessment of Money Laundering and Terrorist Financing* (London: Home Office and Her Majesty's Treasury, 2015).

11. Author's interviews: Australia Attorney-General's Department, Canberra, Australia, May 27, 2011, and AUSTRAC, Sydney, Australia, July 21, 2011; "Joint Statement from the Attorney-General and Minister for Justice and Home Affairs," press release, August 27, 2013; "Julie Bishop Vows to Get Tough on Papua New Guinea Money Laundering," *Sydney Morning Herald*, July 1, 2015.

12. Author's interviews: Australian Attorney-General's Department, Canberra, Australia, March 5, 2013; Australian Federal Police, Brisbane, Australia, June 18, 2014; PNG Task Force Sweep, Brisbane, Australia, August 2, 2014; StAR, Washington, D.C., February 12, 2015; and Australian Federal Police, Brisbane, Australia, May 27, 2015.

13. Peter Larmour, "Administrative Theory, Interpersonal Relations and Anti-Corruption Practice in Papua New Guinea," Policy and Governance Discussion Paper 07–02 (Canberra: Crawford School of Economics and Government, 2007); Grant Walton, "Defining Corruption Where the State Is Weak: The Case of Papua New Guinea," *Journal of Development Studies* 51 (2015): 15–31.

14. "PNG LNG Impact Study," prepared for ExxonMobil, April 2009, http://pnglng.com/downloads/acil_tasman_impact_study_revision_01.pdf.

15. Michael L. Ross, "The Political Economy of the Resource Curse," *World Politics* 51 (1999): 297–322; Naazneen H. Barma, "The Rentier State at Work: Comparative Experiences of the Resource Curse in East Asia and the Pacific," *Asia and the Pacific Policy Studies* 2 (2014): 257–272.

16. Papua New Guinea Parliamentary Public Accounts Committee, "Inquiry into the Public Accounts of the Government of Papua New Guinea for Financial Year 2006" (Port Moresby, 2009), 1.

17. Papua New Guinea Government, *Commission of Inquiry Generally into the Department of Finance: Final Report* (Port Moresby, 2009).

18. Papua New Guinea Financial Intelligence Unit, "Due Diligence in Relation to Government Cheques and Payments" (Port Moresby, 2010), 1.

19. "Billions Lost to Fraud, Says Yakasa," *National,* February 16, 2011; Koim, speech to AUSTRAC.

20. Jeffrey Elapa, "Australia Happy to Suck Up the Proceeds of Crime from PNG," PNG Exposed blog, December 6, 2011, https://pngexposed.wordpress.com/2011/12/06/australia-happy-to-suck-up-the-proceeds-of-crime-from-png/.

21. Koim, speech to AUSTRAC.

22. AUSTRAC submission to the Australian Senate Committee on Foreign Affairs, Defence and Trade Inquiry into the Economic and Security Challenges facing Papua New Guinea and the Island States of the Southwest Pacific, October 2008, 3, emphasis added.

23. "PNG 'Dirty Money' Trail Leads to Australia," *Sydney Morning Herald,* June 19, 2013.

24. Author's interviews: Task Force Sweep, Brisbane, Australia, August 2, 2013, and Australian Federal Police, Brisbane, Australia, June 18, 2014.

25. Author's interviews: Australian Attorney-General's Department, Canberra, Australia, May 27, 2011, and AUSTRAC, Sydney, Australia, July 21, 2011; "Joint Statement from the Attorney-General and Minister for Justice and Home Affairs"; "Julie Bishop Vows to Get Tough."

26. Joint statement of AUSTRAC, Australian Federal Police, and Attorney-General's Department, 2013, www.abc.net.au/4corners/documents/PNG2013/AUSTRAC_statement.pdf.

27. Author's interview, former FATF reviewer, Washington, D.C., February 9, 2015.

28. Author's interviews: Task Force Sweep, Brisbane, Australia, August 2, 2013; October 26, 2013; January 2, 2014; June 25, 2014; and April 9, 2015; "PNG 'Dirty Money' Trail"; "Alleged PNG Crime Boss on 457 Visa Wanted over Theft of $30m," *The Age,* May 10, 2013.

29. "Alleged PNG Crime Boss."

30. District Court of Queensland, Commissioner of the Australian Federal Police vs. Eremas Wartoto, Asset Restraint BD1440/2013, April 26, 2013.

31. Author's interviews: Australian Federal Police, Brisbane, Australia, July 7, 2013, and Task Force Sweep, Brisbane, Australia, August 2, 2014.

32. See in particular Papua New Guinea Government, *Commission of Inquiry.*

33. "Alleged PNG Crime Boss"; "PNG 'Dirty Money' Trail."

34. Author's interviews: Task Force Sweep, Brisbane, June 25, 2014, and June 10, 2015; former Australian Federal Police officer, Brisbane, August 27, 2014; and Attorney-General's Department, Brisbane, Australia, February 27, 2015.

35. Xiaobo Lü, *Cadres and Corruption: The Organizational Involution of the Chinese Communist Party* (Palo Alto, CA: Stanford University Press, 2000); Yasheng Huang, *Capitalism with Chinese Characteristics: Entrepreneurship and the State* (Cambridge: Cambridge University Press, 2008); Andrew Wedeman, *Double Paradox: Rapid Growth and Rising Corruption in China* (Ithaca: Cornell University Press, 2012).

36. Financial Action Task Force, *Mutual Evaluation Report: Australia,* 30.

37. "'Princelings' in China Use Family Ties to Gain Wealth," *New York Times,* May 17, 2012.

38. "Xi Jinping Relations Reveal Fortunes of the Elite," *Bloomberg,* June 29, 2012.

39. "Mistakenly Released Report Reveals the Embarrassing Extent of Chinese Corruption," *The Times*, June 17, 2011.

40. People's Bank of China, "A Study on Methods of Transferring Assets outside China by Chinese Corruptors and Monitoring Methods for This Problem" (Beijing, 2008), 14.

41. People's Bank of China, "Methods of Transferring Assets outside China," 15.

42. People's Bank of China, "Methods of Transferring Assets outside China," 33–35.

43. Author's interview, Australian Federal Police, Brisbane, Australia, July 7, 2013.

44. People's Bank of China, "Methods of Transferring Assets outside China," 35–37.

45. People's Bank of China, "Methods of Transferring Assets outside China," 37–44.

46. People's Bank of China, "Methods of Transferring Assets outside China," 45–66.

47. People's Bank of China, "Methods of Transferring Assets outside China," 50.

48. People's Bank of China, "Methods of Transferring Assets outside China," 53.

49. People's Bank of China, "Methods of Transferring Assets outside China," 53.

50. "Hunt for Corrupt Officials Fleeing Overseas Meets Legal Barriers," *Global Times*, April 9, 2014.

51. Former FATF reviewer, Washington, D.C., February 9, 2015.

52. "Demystifying Chinese Investment in Australia," KPMG, May 25, 2015, 4–5.

53. "They're Going to Buy the Whole Lot: Chinese Property Investment Tipped to Boom," news.com.au, July 22, 2015, http://www.news.com.au/finance/real-estate/theyre-going-to-buy-the-whole-lot-chinese-property-investment-tipped-to-boom/story-fndban6l-1227452851915.

54. "New Fees, Fines for Foreign Property Investors," *Brisbane Times*, February 25, 2015.

55. "Chinese Governor Charged over Opium Fuelled Lifestyle," *Telegraph*, December 14, 2012; Yang Chi-yu, "Report Outlines Lavish Life of Yunnan 'Drug Using Governor,'" September 27, 2011, http://www.wantchinatimes.com/news-subclass-cnt.aspx?id=20110927000065&cid=1303.

56. Author's interview, Australian Federal Police, Brisbane, Australia, February 27, 2015.

57. "How Chinese Fortunes Are Hidden in Australia," *Australian Financial Review*, October 24, 2014.

58. "Inside China's 'Fox Hunt' Anti-Corruption Crackdown," *Australian Financial Review*, October 25, 2014.

59. John Garnault, "A Family Affair," *Foreign Policy*, May 30, 2012, http://foreignpolicy.com/2012/05/30/a-family-affair/.

60. "In Thrall of the Empire of the Sons," *Sydney Morning Herald*, May 26, 2012.

61. "Point Piper's Altona Mansion Sale Dodged Foreign Investment Laws," June 3, 2015, http://news.domain.com.au/domain/real-estate-news/point-pipers-altona-mansion-sale-dodged-foreign-investment-laws-20150603-ghfheb.html.

62. Author's interview, Australian bank, Brisbane, Australia, August 5, 2013.

63. "How Chinese Fortunes Are Hidden."

64. Author's interview, Australian Attorney-General's Department, March 5, 2013; "China Takes Anti-Corruption Drive Overseas," *Financial Times*, September 16, 2014.

65. "Australia Set to Seize Assets of Corrupt Chinese Officials," *Sydney Morning Herald*, October 20, 2014.

66. Author's interview, former World Bank official, Washington, D.C, February 10, 2015.

67. Author's interview, private lawyer, Washington, D.C., February 10, 2015.

68. Jamie Fullerton, "Operation Skynet: China's Anti-Corruption Campaign Goes International as Beijing Reaches Out to Uncover Officials Fled Abroad," *Independent*, March 29, 2015.

69. Author's interviews: Department for International Development, London, June 17, 2013; Department of Justice, Washington, D.C., December 9, 2014; former FBI agent, Washington, D.C., February 9, 2015; former World Bank official, Washington, D.C., February 10, 2015; private

lawyer, Washington, D.C., February 10, 2015; Australian Attorney-General's Department, Brisbane, Australia, February 27, 2015; and National Crime Agency, London, December 14, 2015.

70. "Hunt for Corrupt Officials Fleeing Overseas."

71. "China Casts 'Sky Net' in New Hunt for Corrupt Fugitive Officials," *Bloomberg*, March 27, 2015.

72. "Chinese Police Pursued a Man to Australia on a 'Fox Hunt' without Permission," *Sydney Morning Herald*, April 15, 2015; "Obama Administration Warns Beijing against Covert Agents Operating in the US," *New York Times*, August 16, 2015; "Chinese Police Run Secret Operations in B.C. to Hunt Allegedly Corrupt Officials and Money," *National Post*, March 5, 2015.

73. Australian Institute of Criminology, "Transnational Crime Brief: Charges and Offences of Money Laundering," No. 4, March 2009, 1.

74. Global Witness, *Undue Diligence: How Banks Do Business with Corrupt Regimes* (London, 2009); StAR, *Politically Exposed Persons: A Policy Paper on Strengthening Preventive Measures* (Washington, D.C., 2009); US Senate Permanent Subcommittee on Investigations, *Keeping Foreign Corruption Out of the United States: Four Case Histories* (Washington, D.C., 2010); Financial Services Authority, *Banks' Management of High Money-Laundering Risk Situations* (London, 2011).

75. See also Financial Action Task Force, *Mutual Evaluation Report: Australia*, 57.

76. Author's interviews: Australian Federal Police, Brisbane, Australia, July 7, 2013, and AUSTRAC, Sydney, Australia, July 21, 2011; Financial Action Task Force, *Mutual Evaluation Report: Australia*, 57; "Chinese Investors Flooding Billions into the Australian Real Estate Market Prompt Money Laundering Fears," ABC News, October 12, 2015, http://www.abc.net.au/news/2015-10-12/chinese-investors-flooding-billions-into-australian-real-estate/6841816.

77. Author's interview, international auditor, New York City, May 4, 2015.

78. "Dirty Money: How Corrupt PNG Cash Is Reaching Australia," SBS Dateline, June 23, 2015, http://www.sbs.com.au/news/dateline/story/dirty-money-how-corrupt-png-cash-reaching-australia.

79. Financial Action Task Force, *Money Laundering and Terrorist Financing through the Real Estate Sector* (Paris, 2007); Louise I. Shelley, "Money Laundering into Real Estate," in *Convergence: Illicit Networks and National Security in the Age of Globalization*, edited by Michael Miklaucic and Jacqueline Brewer (Washington, D.C.: National Defense University Press, 2013), 131–146; Brigitte Unger and Joras Ferwada (eds.), *Money Laundering in the Real Estate Sector: Suspicious Properties* (Cheltenham, UK: Edward Elgar, 2011).

80. Financial Action Task Force, *Mutual Evaluation Report: Australia*, 57.

81. Australian House of Representatives, *Report on Foreign Investment in Residential Real Estate* (Canberra, Australia, 2014), 68.

82. Australian House of Representatives, *Foreign Investment in Residential Real Estate*, v; "Foreign Buyer Enforcement Needs Strengthening: Committee," ABC News, November 27, 2014, http://www.abc.net.au/news/2014-11-27/foreign-buyer-rule-enforcement-needs-to-be-strengthened/5921518.

83. Australian House of Representatives, *Foreign Investment in Residential Real Estate*, iv.

84. "Chinese Investors Flooding Billions."

85. "Chinese Investors Flooding Billions."

86. Author's interview, Australian Federal Police, Brisbane, Australia, June 18, 2014.

87. "Dirty Money: How Corrupt PNG Cash Is Reaching Australia."

88. Author's interviews: Australian Federal Police, Brisbane, Australia, June 18, 2014, and Global Witness, Brisbane, Australia, August 10, 2014.

89. Author's interviews: Australian Federal Police, Brisbane, Australia, July 7, 2013; June 18, 2014; and February 27, 2015; Financial Action Task Force, *Mutual Evaluation Report: Australia*, 57; "Chinese Investors Flooding Billions."

90. District Court Criminal Jurisdiction, Adelaide, February 20, 2015, No. DCCRM-14-2307, Regina vs. Pantaleo Capoccia.

91. Financial Action Task Force, *Mutual Evaluation Report: Australia*, 57.

92. Lorana Bartels, "Unexplained Wealth Laws in Australia," Trends and Issues in Crime and Criminal Justice No. 395 (Canberra: Australian Institute of Criminology, July 2010).

93. Transparency International UK, *Empowering the UK to Recover Corrupt Assets*, 26.

94. Financial Action Task Force, *Mutual Evaluation Report: Australia*, 8, 15, 56, 57, 60, 67.

95. OECD, *Phase 3 Report on Implementing the OECD Anti-Bribery Convention in Australia* (Paris, 2012), 5; see also Transparency International, *Progress Report: Enforcement of the OECD Anti-Bribery Convention* (Berlin, 2011).

96. Author's interview, Australian Attorney-General's Department, Canberra, Australia, March 5, 2013.

97. Jo-Anne Gilbert and J. C. Sharman, "Turning a Blind Eye to Bribery: Explaining Failures to Comply with the International Anti-Corruption Regime," *Political Studies* 64 (2016): 76–89.

98. Allan McConnell, Anika Gauja, and Linda Courtney Botterill, "Policy Fiascos, Blame Management and AWB Limited: The Howard Government's Escape from the Iraq Wheat Scandal," *Australian Journal of Political Science* 43 (2008): 599–616.

99. "Dirty Money," Four Corners, May 24, 2010, http://www.abc.net.au/4corners/content/2010/s2905618.htm; "RBA Firm 'Bribed Banker,'" *The Age*, January 24, 2011; "RBA Must Investigate the Securency Board," *National Times*, January 24, 2011.

100. "Australia 'Gags' a Massive Banknote Scandal," *Asia Sentinel*, July 30, 2014, http://www.asiasentinel.com/econ-business/australia-gags-massive-banknote-scandal/.

101. For the original, see https://wikileaks.org/aus-suppression-order/WikiLeaks-Australian-suppression-order.pdf.

102. OECD, *Australia: Follow-Up to the Phase 3 Report and Recommendations* (Paris, 2015), 4.

Conclusion

1. Daniel W. Drezner, *All Politics Is Global: Explaining International Regulatory Regimes* (Princeton: Princeton University Press, 2007); Deborah D. Avant, Martha Finnemore, and Susan K. Sell (eds.), *Who Governs the Globe?* (Cambridge: Cambridge University Press, 2010); Tim Büthe and Walter Mattli, *The New Global Rulers: The Privatization of Regulation in the World Economy* (Princeton: Princeton University Press, 2011).

2. Alexander Wendt, *Social Theory of International Politics* (Cambridge: Cambridge University Press, 1999); Frank Schimmelfennig, "The Community Trap: Liberal Norms, Rhetorical Action, and the Eastern Enlargement of the European Union," *International Organization* 55 (2001): 47–80; Jeffrey T. Checkel, "International Institutions and Socialization in Europe: Introduction and Framework," *International Organization* 59 (2005): 801–826; Alastair Iain Johnston, "Conclusions and Extensions: Toward Mid-Range Theorizing and Beyond Europe," *International Organization* 59 (2005): 1013–1044.

3. See http://www.justice.gov/criminal-fraud/chronological-list.

4. OECD, *Foreign Bribery Report: An Analysis of the Crime of Bribery of Foreign Officials* (Paris, 2014), 31.

5. See http://www.justice.gov/criminal-fraud/case/related-enforcement-actions/2014.

6. See the brilliant journalism of Rob Evans and David Leigh on this case for the *Guardian* at http://www.theguardian.com/world/bae.

7. OECD, *Foreign Bribery Report*, 13–14.

8. "The Anti-Bribery Business," *Economist*, May 9, 2015, http://www.economist.com/news/business/21650557-enforcement-laws-against-corporate-bribery-increases-there-are-risks-it-may-go.

9. Transparency International UK, *Empowering the UK to Recover Corrupt Assets: Unexplained Wealth Orders and Other New Approaches to Illicit Enrichment and Asset Recovery* (London, 2015), 29.

10. "Half of Councils Use Anti-Terror Law to Spy on 'Bin Crimes,'" *Telegraph*, November 1, 2008, http://www.telegraph.co.uk/news/uknews/3333366/Half-of-councils-use-anti-terror-laws-to-spy-on-bin-crimes.html.

11. US Senate Select Committee on Intelligence, *Committee Study of the Central Intelligence Agency's Detention and Interrogation Program* (Washington, D.C., 2014); Jane Mayer, *The Dark Side: The Inside Story of How the War on Terror Turned into a War on American Ideals* (New York: Anchor, 2008).

12. Alexander Cooley and John Heathershaw, *Dictators beyond Borders* (New Haven: Yale University Press, 2016).

13. Rahda Ivory, *Corruption, Asset Recovery, and the Protection of Property in Public International Law: The Human Rights of Bad Guys* (Cambridge: Cambridge University Press, 2014).

14. Author's interviews: international bank, Hong Kong, October 18, 2011; Liechtenstein Bankers' Association, Vaduz, Liechtenstein, June 24, 2013; international bank, New York City, November 21, 2014; US Senate Permanent Subcommittee on Investigations, Washington, D.C., December, 14 2014; international bank, London, June 23, 2015; and International Centre for Asset Recovery, Basel, Switzerland, October, 14 2015.

15. Michael Levi, "Serious Tax Fraud and Non-Compliance: A Review of Evidence on the Differential Impact of Criminal and Non-Criminal Proceedings," *Criminology and Public Policy* 9 (2010): 493–513; Sally S. Simpson, "White-Collar Crime: A Review of Recent Developments and Promising Directions for Future Research," *Annual Review of Sociology* 39 (2013): 309–331.

16. Author's interviews: international bank, Sydney, Australia, November 19, 2011; former Australian Federal Police officer, Brisbane, Australia, August 27, 2014; international bank, New York City, November 21, 2014; former US Treasury official, Washington, D.C., December 10, 2014; International Monetary Fund, Washington, D.C., February 9, 2015; Stolen Asset Recovery Initiative, Washington, D.C., February 12, 2015; international accountancy firm, New York City, May 4, 2015; international bank, London, June 23, 2015; and former US Financial Crimes and Enforcement official, London, November 10, 2015; author's observations, Brown University Financial Integrity conference, various public and private sector attendees, Providence, Rhode Island, May 5–6, 2015.

17. Transparency International, *Global Corruption Report* (Berlin, 2004); Asian Development Bank/OECD Anti-Corruption Initiative for the Asia-Pacific, *Mutual Legal Assistance, Extradition, and Recovery of Proceeds of Corruption in Asia and the Pacific* (Manila, 2007); StAR, *Stolen Asset Recovery (StAR) Initiative: Challenges, Opportunity, and Action Plan* (Washington, D.C., 2007).

18. StAR, *Few and Far: The Hard Facts on Stolen Asset Recovery* (Washington, D.C., 2014).

19. Kodjo Attiso and Gretta Fenner Zinkernagel, "Past Experience with Agreements for the Disposal of Confiscated Assets," in *Emerging Trends in Asset Recovery*, edited by Gretta Fenner Zinkernagel, Charles Monteith, and Pedro Gomez Pereira (Bern: Peter Lang, 2013), 336, 338.

20. Max Mader, "Civil Society Facilitators of Asset Recovery: The Two Swiss Cases Mobutu and Abacha," in *Non-State Actors and Asset Recovery*, edited by Daniel Thelesklaf and Pedro Gomes Pereira. Bern: Peter Lang, 2011, 109–130.

21. Attiso and Zinkernagel, "Agreements for the Disposal of Confiscated Assets," 340.

22. Alessandra Fontana, "Making Development Assistance Work at Home: DfID's Approach to Clamping Down on International Bribery and Money Laundering in the UK," U4 Practice Insight (Bergen, Norway: CMI, 2011), 1.

23. Thomas Rixen, *The Political Economy of International Tax Governance* (Houndmills, UK: Palgrave, 2008); William Vlcek, *Offshore Finance and Small States: Sovereignty, Size and Money* (Houndmills, UK: Palgrave, 2006); Richard Eccleston, *The Dynamics of Global Economic*

Governance: The Financial Crisis, the OECD and the Politics of International Tax Cooperation (Cheltenham, UK: Edward Elgar, 2014); Gabriel Zucman, *The Hidden Wealth of Nations: The Scourge of Tax Havens* (Chicago: University of Chicago Press, 2015).

24. Author's interviews: US Senate Permanent Subcommittee on Investigations, Washington, D.C., December, 14, 2014; Papua New Guinea Task Force Sweep, Brisbane, Australia, April 9, 2015; UK Department for International Development, London, September 17, 2015; and Swiss Department of Foreign Affairs, Bern, Switzerland, October 12, 2015.

25. Daniel W. Drezner, *The Sanctions Paradox: Economic Statecraft and International Relations* (Cambridge: Cambridge University Press, 1999).

26. David Cortright and George A. Lopez (eds.), *Smart Sanctions: Targeting Economic Statecraft* (Lanham, MD: Rowman and Littlefield, 2002).

27. Bill Browder, *Red Notice: How I Became Putin's No. 1 Enemy* (New York: Simon and Schuster, 2014).

28. Juan C. Zarate, *Treasury's War: The Unleashing of a New Era of Financial Warfare* (New York: Public Affairs, 2013), 25.

29. For the current list, see http://www.treasury.gov/resource-center/sanctions/Programs/Documents/narco_designations_kingpin.pdf.

30. Zarate, *Treasury's War*; author's interview, US Treasury, Washington, D.C., February 12, 2015.

31. Author's interviews: private lawyer, Washington, D.C., December 8, 2014, and February 10, 2015.

32. Author's interviews: private lawyer, Washington, D.C., December 8, 2014, and February 10, 2015.

33. J. C. Sharman, "The Bark *Is* the Bite: International Organizations and Blacklisting," *Review of International Political Economy* 16 (2009): 573–596.

34. Zarate, *Treasury's War*, 8.

35. Author's interviews: Transparency International, Berlin, September 13–14, 2015, and Transparency International UK, London, December 10, 2015.

36. Andrew Hudson, "Not a Great Asset: The UN Security Council's Counter-Terrorism Regime: Violating Human Rights," *Berkeley Journal of International Law* 32 (2007): 203–227; Elspeth Guild, "The Uses and Abuses of Counter-Terrorism Policies in Europe: The Case of the Terrorist Lists," *Journal of Common Market Studies* 46 (2008): 173–193.

37. Cooley and Heathershaw, *Dictators beyond Borders*.

38. Washington Office on Latin America, "Report on the International Commission against Impunity in Guatemala (CICIG)," July 1, 2015, http://www.wola.org/publications/WOLA_report_international_commission_against_impunity_guatemala.

39. "International Commission against Impunity in Guatemala Identifies Guatemalan Political Leaders Responsible for Customs Corruption," *International Enforcement Law Reporter* 31 (2015): 376–377.

40. Michael Lohmuller, "Honduras' OAS-Backed Anti-Corruption Body Takes Flight," InSight Crime, January 16, 2016, http://www.insightcrime.org/news-briefs/honduras-oas-backed-anti-corruption-body-takes-flight.

41. Bruce Yandle, "Boot-Leggers and Baptists: The Education of a Regulatory Economist," *Regulation* 7 (1983): 12–16.

42. StAR, *Public Wrongs, Private Actions: Civil Lawsuits to Recover Stolen Assets* (Washington, D.C., 2014).

43. Margaret Keck and Kathryn Sikkink, *Activists beyond Borders: Advocacy Networks in International Politics* (Ithaca: Cornell University Press, 1998).

44. Maud Perdriel-Vaissiere, "How to Turn Article 51 into Reality," in *Non-State Actors in Asset Recovery*, edited by Daniel Thelesklaf and Pedro Gomes Pereira (Bern: Peter Lang, 2011), 26.

45. Muria Garcia Sanz and Manuel Sese, "Political Corruption and Human Rights in Equatorial Guinea," in *Emerging Trends in Asset Recovery*, edited by Gretta Fenner Zinkernagel, Charles Monteith, and Pedro Gomez Pereira (Bern: Peter Lang, 2013), 295–302; author's interview, Open Society Foundations, New York City, February 13, 2015.

46. "Justices Side with 'Hopeless Challenge,'" *Financial Times*, April 11, 2008, http://www.ft.com/cms/s/0/d510dffa-075e-11dd-b41e-0000779fd2ac.html#axzz3jfZ3twBV.

47. Jed S. Rakoff and Howard W. Goldstein, *RICO: Civil and Criminal Law and Strategy* (New York: Law Journal Press, 2013).

48. "Taking the Gangster Rap," *Economist*, August 8, 2015.

49. For a detailed coverage of constructive trust related to corruption and money laundering, see Arthur Lenhoff, "The Constructive Trust as a Remedy for Corruption in Public Office," *Columbia Law Review* 54 (1954): 214–217; Zoe Lester, "Anti–Money Laundering: A Risk Perspective" (Ph.D. dissertation, University of Sydney, 2009), 123–131.

50. Anne Lugon-Moulin, "The Role of Donors in Supporting NSAs," in *Non-State Actors in Asset Recovery*, edited by Daniel Thelesklaf and Pedro Gomes Pereira (Bern: Peter Lang, 2011), 154.

51. "Siemens to Pay $100 million as Part of World Bank Group Settlement," World Bank, press release 2009/001EXT, http://star.worldbank.org/corruption-cases/sites/corruption-cases/files/settlements/Siemens_World_Bank_Settlement_Press_Release_2009.pdf.

52. Transparency International UK, *Combating Money Laundering and Recovering Looted Gains: Raising the UK's Game* (London, 2009), 56; author's interview, Transparency International UK, London, December 10, 2015.

53. Transparency International UK, *Raising the UK's Game*, 56.

54. Kensington International Limited v Republic of the Congo [2005] EWHC 2684 Queen's Bench Division (Commercial Court), (Cooke J); Global Witness, *Undue Diligence: How Banks Do Business with Corrupt Regimes* (London, 2009), 50–59.

55. Devi Sookun, *Stop Vulture Fund Lawsuits: A Handbook* (London: Commonwealth Secretariat, 2010), 44.

56. Global Witness, *Undue Diligence*, 59.

57. See http://en.mercopress.com/2015/02/23/us-justice-will-release-confidential-information-on-a-kirchner-s-family-business-associate.

58. "Cracking Shells," *Economist*, April 11, 2015.

59. Richard Sakwa, *Putin and the Oligarch: The Khodorkovsky-Yukos Affair* (London: I. B. Tauris, 2014).

60. Christopher S. Gibson, "Yukos Universal Limited (Isle of Man) vs. The Russian Federation: A Classic Case of Indirect Expropriation," *ICSID Review: Foreign Investment Law Journal* 30 (2015): 303–314.

61. Transparency International UK, *Empowering the UK*, 23–24.

BIBLIOGRAPHY

Author's interviews

Liechtenstein Bankers' Association, Vaduz, Liechtenstein, January 29, 2004
World Bank, Washington, D.C., September 7, 2004
US Department of Justice, Perth, Australia, July 1, 2007
International bank, Singapore, October 20, 2009
International Monetary Fund, Washington, D.C., February 24, 2010
FBI, Washington, D.C., May 18, 2010
Zambian Corruption Task Force, Washington, D.C., May 18, 2010
International bankers, Zurich, Switzerland, September 16–17, 2010
Prosecutor, Sofia, Bulgaria, September 29, 2010
Stolen Asset Recovery Initiative, Washington, D.C., March 21, 2011
US Senate Permanent Subcommittee on Investigations, Washington, D.C., March 21, 2011
Australian Federal Police, Brisbane, Australia, April 20, 2011
Asia-Pacific Group on Money Laundering, Sydney, Australia, May 26, 2011
Australian Attorney-General's Department, Canberra, Australia, May 27, 2011
Australian G20 Anti-Corruption Working Group delegate, Canberra, Australia, May 27, 2011
AUSTRAC, Sydney, Australia, July 21, 2011

Transparency International, Berlin, Germany, September 5–6, 2011
Metropolitan Police, London, UK, September 8, 2011
UK G20 Anti-Corruption Working Group delegate, London, UK, September 8, 2011
International bank, Sydney, Australia, November 19, 2011
Asian Development Bank Institute, Tokyo, Japan, October 13, 2011
International bank, Hong Kong, October 18, 2011
Stolen Asset Recovery Initiative, Washington, D.C., April 25, 2012
US Department of Justice, Washington, D.C., April 27, 2012
UK Department for International Development, London, UK, May 17, 2012
Former bank compliance officer, London, UK, May 18, 2012
Global Witness, London, UK, May 18, 2012
Papua New Guinea Financial Intelligence Unit, Brisbane, Australia, October 2, 2012
Papua New Guinea Ombudsman's Commission, Brisbane, Australia, October 2, 2012
Australian Attorney-General's Department, Canberra, Australia, March 5, 2013
Private lawyer, Washington, D.C., April 10, 2013
Stolen Asset Recovery Initiative, Washington, D.C., April 10–11, 2013
US State Department, Washington, D.C., April 12, 2013
United Nations Office on Drugs and Crime, Washington, D.C., April 13, 2013
Private lawyer, London, UK, June 17, 2013
UK Department for International Development, London, UK, June 17, 2013
UK G20 Anti-Corruption Working Group delegate, London, UK, June 17, 2013
International bank, Geneva, Switzerland, June 20, 2013
Liechtenstein Bankers' Association, Vaduz, Liechtenstein, June 24, 2013
Liechtenstein Financial Markets Authority, Vaduz, Liechtenstein, June 24, 2013
Australian Federal Police, Brisbane, Australia, July 7, 2013
Papua New Guinea Task Force Sweep, Brisbane, Australia, August 2, 2013
Australian bank, Brisbane, Australia, August 5, 2013
Former FBI agent, Washington, D.C., September 22, 2013
Papua New Guinea Task Force Sweep, Brisbane, Australia, October 26, 2013
Papua New Guinea Task Force Sweep, Brisbane, Australia, January 2, 2014
US Senate Permanent Subcommittee on Investigations, Washington, D.C., April 24, 2014
International bank, Nassau, The Bahamas, May 13, 2014
International auditor, by phone, June 4, 2014
Australian Federal Police, Brisbane, Australia, June 18, 2014
Papua New Guinea Task Force Sweep, Brisbane, Australia, June 25, 2014
Papua New Guinea Task Force Sweep, Brisbane, Australia, August 2, 2014
Global Witness, Brisbane, Australia, August 10, 2014
Former Australian Federal Police officer, Brisbane, Australia, August 27, 2014
Global Witness, New York City, September 24, 2014
Former head of Philippine Center for Investigative Journalism, New York City, October 29, 2014
International bank, New York City, October 30, 2014
International bank, New York City, November 21, 2014
Journalist, New York City, December 5, 2014

Private lawyer, Washington, D.C., December 8, 2014

Stolen Asset Recovery Initiative, Washington, D.C., December 9, 2014

US Department of Justice, Washington, D.C., December 9, 2014

Former US Treasury official, Washington, D.C., December 10, 2014

Jack Blum, Washington, D.C., December 10, 2014

US Senate Permanent Subcommittee on Investigations, Washington, D.C., December 14, 2014

Former FATF reviewer, Washington, D.C., February 9, 2015

Former FBI agent, Washington, D.C., February 9, 2015

International Monetary Fund, Washington, D.C., February 9, 2015

Former World Bank official, Washington, D.C, February 10, 2015

Private lawyer, Washington, D.C., February 10, 2015

Stolen Asset Recovery Initiative, Washington, D.C., February 12, 2015

US Treasury, Washington, D.C., February 12, 2015

Open Society Foundations, New York City, February 13, 2015

Australian Attorney-General's Department, Brisbane, Australia, February 27, 2015

Australian Federal Police, Brisbane, Australia, February 27, 2015

Papua New Guinea Task Force Sweep, Brisbane, Australia, April 9, 2015

International accountancy firm, New York City, May 4, 2015

International auditor, New York City, May 4, 2015

Former Swiss prosecutor, Providence, Rhode Island, May 6, 2015

Swiss banker, Providence, Rhode Island, May 6, 2015

C4ADS, by phone, May 28, 2015

International bankers and lawyers, Geneva, Switzerland, June 16–18, 2015

International bank, London, UK, June 23, 2015

Transparency International, Berlin, Germany, September 13–14, 2015

UK Department for International Development, London, UK, September 17, 2015

Swiss Department of Foreign Affairs, Bern, Switzerland, October 12, 2015

Former Swiss Financial Intelligence Unit official, Zurich, Switzerland, October 13, 2015

International Centre for Asset Recovery, Basel, Switzerland, October 13, 2015

Swiss Financial Intelligence Unit, Bern, Switzerland, October 13, 2015

Former Swiss prosecutor, Basel, Switzerland, October 14, 2015

International Centre for Asset Recovery, Basel, Switzerland, October 14, 2015

Berne Declaration, Lausanne, Switzerland, October 16, 2015

National Crime Agency, London, UK, October 28, 2015

Former US Financial Crimes and Enforcement Network official, London, UK, November 10, 2015

Kenyan Ethics and Anti-Corruption Commission, London, UK, November 16–17, 2015

Private lawyer, London, UK, December 9, 2015

Transparency International UK, London, UK, December 10, 2015

National Crime Agency, London, UK, December 14, 2015

Global Witness, London, UK, December 15, 2015

Author's observation

Asian Development Bank/OECD Anti-Corruption Initiative for the Asia-Pacific, Regional Anti-Corruption Summit, Hanoi, Vietnam, October 23–24, 2010
Wealth planning conference, Hong Kong, November 9–10, 2010
Wealth planning conference, Geneva, Switzerland, June 18–20, 2013
G20 Anti-Corruption Working Group meeting, Sydney, Australia, February 28, 2014
Wealth planning conference, Nassau, The Bahamas, May 12–14, 2014
Wealth planning conference, New York City, October 30, 2014
Jai Ramaswamy, Department of Justice, Center for the Advancement of Public Integrity conference, Columbia University, New York City, November 14, 2014
Wealth planning conference, Geneva, Switzerland, June 16–18, 2015
Wealth planning conference, London, UK, December 2, 2015

Written sources

Abbott, Elizabeth. *Haiti: The Duvaliers and Their Legacy*. New York: McGraw-Hill, 1988.
Abbott, Kenneth W., and Duncan Snidal. "Values and Interests: International Legalization in the Fight against Corruption." *Journal of Legal Studies* 31 (2002): 141–178.
Adam, Rita, and Valentin Zellweger. "The Proposed Swiss Comprehensive Act on Asset Recovery." In *Emerging Trends in Asset Recovery*, edited by Gretta Fenner Zinkernagel, Charles Monteith, and Pedro Gomez Pereira. Bern: Peter Lang, 2013, 173–181.
African Development Bank. "African Economic Outlook: Equatorial Guinea." Tunis, 2012.
Andreas, Peter, and Kelly M. Greenhill (eds.). *Sex, Drugs, and Body Counts: The Politics of Numbers in Global Crime and Conflict*. Ithaca: Cornell University Press, 2010.
Asian Development Bank/OECD Anti-Corruption Initiative for the Asia-Pacific. *Mutual Legal Assistance, Extradition, and Recovery of Proceeds of Corruption in Asia and the Pacific*. Manila, 2007.
———. *Asset Recovery and Mutual Legal Assistance in Asia and the Pacific*. Manila, 2008.
Askin, Steve, and Carole Collins. "External Collusion with Kleptocracy: Can Zaire Recapture Its Stolen Wealth?" *Review of African Political Economy* 57 (1993): 72–85.
Associação Mãos Livres/Corruption Watch UK. *Deception in High Places: The Corrupt Angola-Russia Debt Deal*. London, 2013.
Attiso, Kodjo, and Gretta Fenner Zinkernagel. "Past Experience with Agreements for the Disposal of Confiscated Assets." In *Emerging Trends in Asset Recovery*, edited by Gretta Fenner Zinkernagel, Charles Monteith, and Pedro Gomez Pereira. Bern: Peter Lang, 2013, 329–345.
Australian House of Representatives. *Report on Foreign Investment in Residential Real Estate*. Canberra, Australia, 2014.
Australian Institute of Criminology. "Transnational Crime Brief: Charges and Offences of Money Laundering." No. 4, 2009, 1–2.
Avant, Deborah D., Martha Finnemore, and Susan K. Sell (eds.). *Who Governs the Globe?* Cambridge: Cambridge University Press, 2010.
Bacarese, Alan. "Asset Recovery in a Common Law System: The United Kingdom." In *Recovering Stolen Assets*, edited by Mark Pieth. Bern: Peter Lang, 2008, 147–163.
Baker, Raymond. *Capitalism's Achilles Heel: Dirty Money and How to Renew the Free-Market System*. Hoboken, NJ: Wiley, 2005.

Balmaceda, Margarita M. *Energy Dependency, Politics and Corruption in the Former Soviet Union: Russia's Power, Oligarchs' Corruption and Ukraine's Missing Energy Policy, 1995–2006*. London: Routledge, 2008.

Barma, Naazneen H. "The Rentier State at Work: Comparative Experiences of the Resource Curse in East Asia and the Pacific." *Asia and the Pacific Policy Studies* 2 (2014): 257–272.

Bartels, Lorana. "Unexplained Wealth Laws in Australia." Trends and Issues in Crime and Criminal Justice No. 395. Canberra: Australian Institute of Criminology, July 2010.

Bassiouni, M. Cherif. "Corruption Cases against Officials of the Mubarak Regime." Paper published by the Egyptian-American Rule of Law Association, March 23, 2012.

Beattie, David. *Liechtenstein: A Modern History*. London: I. B. Tauris, 2004.

Bertossa, Bernard. "What Makes Asset Recovery So Difficult in Practice? A Practitioner's Perspective." In *Recovering Stolen Assets*, edited by Mark Pieth. Bern: Peter Lang, 2008, 19–37.

Boycko, Maxim, Andrei Shleifer, and Robert Vishny. *Privatizing Russia*. Cambridge, MA: MIT Press, 1995.

Borlini, Leonardo S., and Giulio Nessi. "International Asset Recovery: Origins, Evolution and Current Challenges." Baffi Center Research Paper, February 6, 2014.

Bowen, Sally, and Jane Holligan. *The Imperfect Spy: The Many Lives of Vladimiro Montesinos*. Lima: Peisa, 2003.

Brademas, John, and Fritz Heimann. "Tackling International Corruption: No Longer Taboo." *Foreign Affairs* 77 (1998): 17–22.

Braillard, Philippe. *Switzerland as a Financial Centre: Structures and Policies*. Berlin: Springer, 1988.

Browder, Bill. *Red Notice: How I Became Putin's No. 1 Enemy*. New York: Simon and Schuster, 2014.

Buchan, Bruce, and Lisa Hill. *An Intellectual History of Political Corruption*. London: Palgrave, 2014.

Bukovansky, Mlada. "The Hollowness of Anti-Corruption Discourse." *Review of International Political Economy* 13 (2006): 181–209.

Burgis, Tom. *The Looting Machine: Warlords, Oligarchs, Corporations, Smugglers, and the Theft of Africa's Wealth*. New York: Public Affairs, 2015.

Büthe, Tim, and Walter Mattli. *The New Global Rulers: The Privatization of Regulation in the World Economy*. Princeton: Princeton University Press, 2011.

Camdessus, Michael. "The IMF and Good Governance." Address by the Managing Director of the IMF at Transparency International, Paris, January 21, 1998. Available at www.imf.org/external/np/speeches/1998/012198.HTM.

Campos, Nauro F., Ralitza Dimova, and Ahmad Saleh. "Whither Corruption? A Quantitative Survey of the Literature on Corruption and Growth." IZA Discussion Paper No. 5334. 2010.

Carpenter, Charli. *Lost Causes: Agenda-Vetting in Global Issue Networks and the Shaping of Human Security*. Ithaca: Cornell University Press, 2014.

Carver, Jeremy. "The Hunt for Looted State Assets: The Case of Benazir Bhutto." In Transparency International, *Global Corruption Report*. Berlin, 2004, 102–104.

Chaikin, David. "Policy and Legal Obstacles in Recovering Dictators' Plunder." *Bond Law Review* 17 (2005): 27–46.

Chaikin, David, and J. C. Sharman. *Corruption and Money Laundering: A Symbiotic Relationship*. New York: Palgrave, 2009.

Chayes, Sarah. *Thieves of State: Why Corruption Threatens Global Security*. New York: W. W. Norton, 2015.

Checkel, Jeffrey T. "International Institutions and Socialization in Europe: Introduction and Framework." *International Organization* 59 (2005): 801–826.

Christie's International Real Estate. "Luxury Defined: An Insight into the Luxury Residential Property Market." No city, 2015.

Commission for Africa. *Our Common Interest*. London, 2005.

Cooley, Alexander, and John Heathershaw. *Dictators beyond Borders*. New Haven: Yale University Press, 2016.

Cortright, David, and George A. Lopez (eds.). *Smart Sanctions: Targeting Economic Statecraft*. Lanham, MD: Rowman and Littlefield, 2002.

Daniel, Tim. "Repatriation of Looted State Assets: Selected Case Studies and the UN Convention Against Corruption." In Transparency International, *Global Corruption Report*. Berlin, 2004, 100–107.

Daniel, Tim, and James Maton. "Recovering the Proceeds of Corruption: General Sani Abacha—A Nation's Thief." In *Recovering Stolen Assets*, edited by Mark Pieth. Bern: Peter Lang, 2008, 63–78.

——. "Civil Proceedings to Recover Corruptly Acquired Assets of Public Officials." In *Recovering Stolen Assets*, edited by Mark Pieth. Bern: Peter Lang, 2008, 243–266.

Davis, Kevin E. "Why Does the U.S. Regulate Foreign Bribery: Moralism, Self-Interest or Altruism?" *New York University Annual Survey of American Law* 67 (2012): 497–512.

Dawisha, Karen. *Putin's Kleptocracy: Who Owns Russia?* New York: Simon and Schuster, 2014.

Dornbierer, Andrew, and Gretta Fenner Zinkernagel. "Introduction." In *Emerging Trends in Asset Recovery*, edited by Gretta Fenner Zinkernagel, Charles Monteith, and Pedro Gomez Pereira. Bern: Peter Lang, 2013, xv–xxiv.

Downs, George M., David M. Rocke, and Peter N. Barsoom. "Is the Good News about Compliance Good News about Cooperation?" *International Organization* 50 (1996): 379–406.

Drezner, Daniel W. *All Politics Is Global: Explaining International Regulatory Regimes*. Princeton: Princeton University Press, 2007.

——. *The Sanctions Paradox: Economic Statecraft and International Relations*. Cambridge: Cambridge University Press, 1999.

Easterly, William. "What Did Structural Adjustment Adjust? The Association of Policies and Growth with Repeated IMF and World Bank Adjustment Loans." *Journal of Development Economics* 76 (2006): 1–22.

Eccleston, Richard. *The Dynamics of Global Economic Governance: The Financial Crisis, the OECD and the Politics of International Tax Cooperation*. Cheltenham, UK: Edward Elgar, 2014.

Eigen, Peter. "Combatting Corruption around the World." *Journal of Democracy* 7 (1996): 158–168.

——. "International Corruption: Organized Civil Society for Better Global Gover-nance." *Social Research* 80 (2013): 1287–1308.

Elster, Jon. *Nuts and Bolts for the Social Sciences*. Cambridge: Cambridge University Press, 1989.

Financial Action Task Force. *Anti–Money Laundering and Counter-Terrorist Financing Measures Mutual Evaluation Report: Australia*. Paris, 2015.

——. *Laundering the Proceeds of Corruption*. Paris, 2011.

——. *Money Laundering and Terrorist Financing through the Real Estate Sector*. Paris, 2007.

——. *Third Mutual Evaluation Report: Anti–Money Laundering and Combating the Financing of Terrorism; United Kingdom*. Paris, 2007.

Financial Services Authority. *Banks' Management of High Money-Laundering Risk Situations*. London, 2011.

Findley, Michael G., Daniel L. Nielson, and J. C. Sharman. *Global Shell Games: Experiments in Transnational Relations, Crime and Terrorism*. Cambridge: Cambridge University Press, 2014.

FINMA Annual Report, 2012. Bern: Swiss Financial Market Supervisory Authority, 2012.

Finnemore, Martha, and Kathryn Sikkink. "International Norm Dynamics and Political Change." *International Organization* 52 (1998): 887–917.

Fontana, Alessandra. "Making Development Assistance Work at Home: DfID's Approach to Clamping Down on International Bribery and Money Laundering in the UK." U4 Practice Insight. Bergen, Norway: CMI, 2011.

Garcia Sanz, Muria, and Manuel Sese. "Political Corruption and Human Rights in Equatorial Guinea." In *Emerging Trends in Asset Recovery*, edited by Gretta Fenner Zinkernagel, Charles Monteith, and Pedro Gomez Pereira. Bern: Peter Lang, 2013, 295–302.

Gibson, Christopher S. "Yukos Universal Limited (Isle of Man) vs. The Russian Federation: A Classic Case of Indirect Expropriation." *ICSID Review: Foreign Investment Law Journal* 30 (2015): 303–314.

Gilbert, Jo-Anne, and J. C. Sharman. "Turning a Blind Eye to Bribery: Explaining Failures to Comply with the International Anti-Corruption Regime." *Political Studies* 64 (2016): 74–89.

Githongo, John. Letter to President Mwai Kibaki. Nairobi, Kenya, November 22, 2005.

Global Witness. *Forests, Famine and War—The Key to Cambodia's Future*. London, 1996.

——. *International Thief Thief: How British Banks Are Complicit in Nigerian Corruption*. London, 2010.

——. *Lowering the Bar: How American Lawyers Told Us How to Funnel Suspect Funds into the United States*. Washington, D.C., 2016.

——. *The Secret Life of a Shopaholic: How an African Dictator's Playboy Son Went on a Spending Spree in the United States*. London, 2009.

——. *Undue Diligence: How Banks Do Business with Corrupt Regimes*. London, 2009.

Golden, Miriam A., and Eric C. C. Chang. "Competitive Corruption: Factional Conflict and Political Malfeasance in Postwar Italian Christian Democracy." *World Politics* 53 (2001): 588–622.

Guanieri, Carlo. "Courts Enforcing Political Accountability: The Role of Criminal Justice in Italy." In *Consequential Courts: Judicial Roles in Global Perspective*, edited by Diana Kapiszewski, Gordon Silverstein, and Robert A. Kagan. Cambridge: Cambridge University Press, 2013, 163–180.

Guild, Elspeth. "The Uses and Abuses of Counter-Terrorism Policies in Europe: The Case of the Terrorist Lists." *Journal of Common Market Studies* 46 (2008): 173–193.

Gully-Hart, Paul. "International Asset Recovery of Corruption-Related Assets: Switzerland." In *Recovering Stolen Assets*, edited by Mark Pieth. Bern: Peter Lang, 2008, 165–185.

Gutterman, Ellen. "The Legitimacy of Transnational NGOs: Lessons from the Experience of Transparency International in Germany and France." *Review of International Studies* 40 (2014): 391–418.

Hartman, Jennifer M. "Government by Thieves: Revealing the Monsters behind the Kleptocratic Masks." *Syracuse Journal of International Law and Commerce* 24 (1997): 157–175.

Heilbrunn, John R. "Oil and Water? Elite Politicians and Corruption in France." *Comparative Politics* 37 (2005): 277–296.

Helgesson, Karin Svedberg, and Ulrika Mörth. "Involuntary Public Policy-Making by For-Profit Professionals: European Lawyers on Anti–Money Laundering and Terrorism Financing." *Journal of Common Market Studies* 54 (2016): 1216–1232.

Heywood, Paul. "Political Corruption: Problems and Perspectives." *Political Studies* 45 (1997): 417–435.

Hollingsworth, Mark, and Stewart Lansley. *Londongrad: From Russia with Cash: The Inside Story of the Oligarchs*. London: Fourth Estate, 2010.

Holmes, Leslie. *The End of Communist Power: Anti-Corruption Campaigns and Legitimation Crisis*. Oxford: Oxford University Press, 1993.

———. "Postcommunist Transitions and Corruption: Mapping Patterns." *Social Research* 80 (2013): 1163–1186.

———. *Rotten States? Communism, Post-Communism, and Neo-Liberalism*. Raleigh, NC: Duke University Press, 2006.

Hotchkiss, Carolyn. "The Sleeping Dog Stirs: New Signs of Life in Efforts to End Corruption in International Business." *Journal of Public Policy and Marketing* 17 (1998): 108–115.

Huang, Yasheng. *Capitalism with Chinese Characteristics: Entrepreneurship and the State*. Cambridge: Cambridge University Press, 2008.

Hudson, Andrew. "Not a Great Asset: The UN Security Council's Counter-Terrorism Regime: Violating Human Rights." *Berkeley Journal of International Law* 32 (2007): 203–227.

Huntington, Samuel. *Political Order in Changing Societies*. New Haven: Yale University Press, 1968.

Ige, Bola. "Abacha and the Bankers: Cracking the Conspiracy." *Forum on Crime and Society* 2 (2002): 111–117.

International Monetary Fund. "The OECD Convention on Combating the Bribery of Foreign Officials in International Business Transactions." Washington, D.C., 2001.

Ivory, Radha. *Corruption, Asset Recovery, and the Protection of Property in Public International Law: The Human Rights of Bad Guys*. Cambridge: Cambridge University Press, 2014.

Jakobi, Anja P. *Common Goods and Evils? The Formation of Global Crime Governance*. Oxford: Oxford University Press, 2013.

Johannessen, Niels. "Tax Evasion and Swiss Bank Deposits." *Journal of Public Economics* 111 (2014): 46–62.

Johannessen, Niels, and Gabriel Zucman. "The End of Bank Secrecy? An Evaluation of the G20 Tax Crack-Down." *American Economic Journal: Economic Policy* 6 (2014): 65–91.

Johnston, Alastair Iain. "Conclusions and Extensions: Toward Mid-Range Theorizing and Beyond Europe." *International Organization* 59 (2005): 1013–1044.

Johnston, Michael C. *Syndromes of Corruption: Wealth, Power, and Democracy*. Cambridge: Cambridge University Press, 2005.

Joly, Eva. *Justice under Siege: One Woman's Battle against a European Oil Company*. London: Arcadia Books, 2007.

Jorge, Guillermo. "The Peruvian Efforts to Recover Proceeds from Montesinos's Criminal Network of Corruption." In Asian Development Bank/OECD Anti-Corruption Initiative for the Asia-Pacific, *Asset Recovery and Mutual Legal Assistance in Asia and the Pacific*. Manila, 2008, 189–223.

Kang, David C. "Bad Loans to Good Friends: Money Politics and the Developmental State in South Korea." *International Organization* 56 (2002): 177–207.

Kaplan, William. *A Secret Trial: Brian Mulroney, Stevie Cameron, and the Public Trust*. Montreal: McGill-Queens University Press, 2004.

Katzenstein, Peter (ed.). *The Culture of National Security: Norms and Identity in World Politics*. New York: Columbia University Press, 1996.

Kaufmann, Daniel. "Corruption: The Facts." *Foreign Policy* 107 (1997): 114–131.

Keck, Margaret, and Kathryn Sikkink. *Activists beyond Borders: Advocacy Networks in International Politics*. Ithaca: Cornell University Press, 1998.

Keene, Edward. "A Case Study in the Construction of International Hierarchy: British Treaty-Making and the Slave Trade in the Early Nineteenth Century." *International Organization* 61 (2007): 311–339.

Kelly, Sean. *America's Tyrant: The CIA and Mobutu of Zaire*. Lanham, MD: University Press of America, 1993.

Kerry, John. *The New War: The Web of Crime That Threatens America's Security*. New York: Simon and Schuster, 1997.

Kenya National Audit Office. "Special Audit Report of the Controller and Auditor General on Financing, Procurement and Implementation of Security Related Projects." Nairobi, Kenya, April 2006.

Kim, Hun Joon, and Kathryn Sikkink. "Explaining the Deterrence Effect of Human Rights Prosecutions for Transitional Countries." *International Studies Quarterly* 54 (2010): 939–963.

Klitgaard, Robert. *Tropical Gangsters: One Man's Experience with Development and Decadence in Deepest Africa*. New York: Basic Books, 1990.

Kofele-Kale, Ndiva. "Patrimonicide: The International Economic Crime of Indigenous Spoliation." *Vanderbilt Journal of Transnational Law* 28 (1995): 45–117.

Krasner, Stephen D. (ed.). *International Regimes*. Ithaca: Cornell University Press, 1982.

Krueger, Anne O. "The Political Economy of the Rent-Seeking Society." *American Economic Review* 64 (1974): 291–303.

Kumlin, Staffan, and Peter Esaiasson. "Scandal Fatigue? Scandal, Elections and Satisfaction with Democracy in Western Europe, 1977–2007." *British Journal of Political Science* 42 (2012): 263–282.

Kuran, Timur. "Sparks and Prairie Fires: A Theory of Unanticipated Political Revolution." *Public Choice* 61 (1989): 41–74.

Lambsdorff, Johann Graf. "Consequences and Causes of Corruption: What Do We Know from a Cross-Section of Countries?" Working Paper. University of Passau, 2005.

———. *The New Institutional Economics of Corruption and Reform: Theory, Policy and Evidence*. Cambridge: Cambridge University Press, 2007.

Larmour, Peter. "Administrative Theory, Interpersonal Relations and Anti-Corruption Practice in Papua New Guinea." Policy and Governance Discussion Paper 07–02. Canberra: Crawford School of Economics and Government, 2007.

Leff, Nathaniel. "Economic Development through Bureaucratic Corruption." *American Behavioral Scientist* 8 (1964): 8–14.

Lenhoff, Arthur. "The Constructive Trust as a Remedy for Corruption in Public Office." *Columbia Law Review* 54 (1954): 214–217.

Lester, Zoe. "Anti–Money Laundering: A Risk Perspective." Ph.D. dissertation, University of Sydney, 2009.

Levi, Michael. "Serious Tax Fraud and Non-Compliance: A Review of Evidence on the Differential Impact of Criminal and Non-Criminal Proceedings." *Criminology and Public Policy* 9 (2010): 493–513.

Levi, Michael, and Peter Reuter. "Money Laundering." In *Crime and Justice: A Review of Research*, edited by M. Tony. Chicago: University of Chicago Press, 2006, 289–375.

Longchamp, Olivier, and Mark Herkenrath. "Money Laundering, Liability and Sanctions for Financial Intermediaries—The Issue of Having the Assets of Politically Exposed Persons in Switzerland." In *Emerging Trends in Asset Recovery*, edited by Gretta Fenner Zinkernagel, Charles Monteith, and Pedro Gomez Pereira. Bern: Peter Lang, 2013, 127–136.

Lü, Xiaobo. *Cadres and Corruption: The Organizational Involution of the Chinese Communist Party*. Palo Alto, CA: Stanford University Press, 2000.

Lugon-Moulin, Anne. "The Role of Donors in Supporting NSAs." In *Non-State Actors in Asset Recovery*, edited by Daniel Thelesklaf and Pedro Gomes Pereira. Bern: Peter Lang, 2011, 147–160.

Maass, Peter. *Crude World: The Violent Twilight of Oil*. New York: Vintage Books, 2009.

Mader, Max. "Civil Society Facilitators of Asset Recovery: Two Swiss Cases; Mobutu and Abacha." In *Non-State Actors and Asset Recovery*, edited by Daniel Thelesklaf and Pedro Gomes Pereira. Bern: Peter Lang, 2011, 109–130.

Madruga, Antenor. "Expectations of Developing Economies: A View from the Americas." In *Recovering Stolen Assets*, edited by Mark Pieth. Bern: Peter Lang, 2008, 369–386.

Marcelo, Simeon V. "The Long Road from Zurich to Manila: The Recovery of the Marcos Swiss Dollar Deposits." In *Recovering Stolen Assets*, edited by Mark Pieth. Bern: Peter Lang, 2008, 89–110.

Mason, Phil. "Being Janus: A Donor Agency's Approach to Asset Recovery." In *Emerging Trends in Asset Recovery*, edited by Gretta Fenner Zinkernagel, Charles Monteith, and Pedro Gomez Pereira. Bern: Peter Lang, 2013, 197–204.

Mauro, Paolo. "Corruption and Growth." *Quarterly Journal of Economics* 110 (1995): 681–712.

———. "The Persistence of Corruption and Slow Economic Growth." *IMF Staff Papers* 51 (2004): 1–18.

Mayer, Jane. *The Dark Side: The Inside Story of How the War on Terror Turned into a War on American Ideals*. New York: Anchor, 2008.

McConnell, Allan, Anika Gauja, and Linda Courtney Botterill. "Policy Fiascos, Blame Management and AWB Limited: The Howard Government's Escape from the Iraq Wheat Scandal." *Australian Journal of Political Science* 43 (2008): 599–616.

McCoy, Jennifer, and Heather Heckel. "The Emergence of a Global Anti-Corruption Norm." *International Politics* 38 (2001): 65–90.

McMillan, John, and Pablo Zoido. "How to Subvert Democracy: Montesinos in Peru." *Journal of Economic Perspectives* 18 (2004): 69–92.

Meier, Henri B., John E. Marthinsen, and Pascal A. Gantebein. *Swiss Finance: Capital Markets, Banking, and the Swiss Value Chain*. Hoboken, NJ: Wiley, 2012.

Monfrini, Enrico. "The Abacha Case." In *Recovering Stolen Assets*, edited by Mark Pieth. Bern: Peter Lang, 2008, 41–63.

Morier, Pierre-Yves. "Is Autonomous Confiscation the Acme of Asset Recovery?" In *Recovering Stolen Assets*, edited by Mark Pieth. Bern: Peter Lang, 2008, 267–278.

Morrissey, Oliver. "British Aid Policy in the 'Short-Blair' Years." In *Perspectives on European Development Co-operation: Policy and Performance of Individual Donor Countries and the EU*, edited by Paul Hoebink and Olav Stokke. London: Routledge, 2005, 161–183.

Mueller, John. *Retreat from Doomsday: The Obsolescence of Major War*. New York: Basic Books, 1989.

Murphy, Kevin M., Andrei Vishny, and Robert W. Shleifer. "The Allocation of Talent." *Quarterly Journal of Economics* 106 (1991): 503–530.

Nadelmann, Ethan A. "Global Prohibition Regimes: The Evolution of Norms in International Society." *International Organization* 44 (1990): 479–526.

Naím, Moisés. "The Corruption Eruption." *Brown Journal of World Affairs* 2 (1995): 245–261.

Ndikumana, Leonce, and James Boyce. "Congo's Odious Debt: External Borrowing and Capital Flight in Zaire." *Development and Change* 29 (1998): 195–217.

Nicholls, Colin, Tim Daniel, Alan Bacarese, and John Hatchard. *Corruption and the Misuse of Public Office*. 2nd ed. Oxford: Oxford University Press, 2011.

North, Douglass C. *Institutions, Institutional Change, and Economic Performance*. Cambridge: Cambridge University Press, 1990.

Nyblade, Benjamin, and Steven R. Reed. "Who Cheats? Who Loots? Political Competition and Corruption in Japan, 1947–1993." *American Journal of Political Science* 52 (2008): 926–941.

Nye, Joseph S. "Corruption and Political Development." *American Political Science Review* 61 (1967): 417–427.

OECD. *Foreign Bribery Report: An Analysis of the Crime of Bribery of Foreign Officials.* Paris, 2014.

——. *Australia: Follow-Up to the Phase 3 Report and Recommendations.* Paris, 2015.

——. *Measuring Responses to Illicit Financial Flows from Developing Countries.* Paris, 2013.

——. *Phase 3 Report on Implementing the OECD Anti-Bribery Convention in Australia.* Paris, 2012.

Oliver, Kenneth. "'Excellent!' I Cried. 'Elementary!' said He. Mutual Legal Assistance and the Present Challenges Faced by the Legal Community in the Never-Ending Quest for the Recovery of Stolen Assets." In *Non-State Actors and Asset Recovery*, edited by Daniel Thelesklaf and Pedro Gomes Pereira. Bern: Peter Lang, 2011, 160–182.

Palan, Ronen. *The Offshore World: Sovereign Markets, Virtual Places, and Nomad Millionaires.* Ithaca: Cornell University Press, 2003.

Palan, Ronen, Richard Murphy, and Christian Chavagneux. *Tax Havens: How Globalization Really Works.* Ithaca: Cornell University Press, 2010.

Papua New Guinea Financial Intelligence Unit. "Due Diligence in Relation to Government Cheques and Payments." Port Moresby, Papua New Guinea, 2010.

Papua New Guinea Government. *Commission of Inquiry Generally into the Department of Finance: Final Report.* Port Moresby, Papua New Guinea, 2009.

Park, Susan. *World Bank Group Interactions with Environmentalists: Changing International Organisation Identities.* Manchester, UK: Manchester University Press, 2010.

People's Bank of China. "A Study on Methods of Transferring Assets outside China by Chinese Corruptors and Monitoring Methods for This Problem." Beijing, 2008.

Perdriel-Vaissiere, Maud. "How to Turn Article 51 into Reality." In *Non-State Actors in Asset Recovery*, edited by Daniel Thelesklaf and Pedro Gomes Pereira. Bern: Peter Lang, 2011, 17–37.

Persson, Anna, Bo Rothstein, and Jan Teorell. "Why Anti-Corruption Reforms Fail: Systemic Corruption as a Collective Action Problem." *Governance* 26 (2013): 449–471.

Peters, Rebecca G. "Money Laundering in Switzerland." *Northwestern Journal of International Law and Business* 11 (1990): 105–139.

Pierson, Paul. "Big, Slow-Moving, and . . . Invisible: Macrosocial Processes in the Study of Comparative Politics." In *Comparative Historical Analysis in the Social Sciences*, edited by James Mahoney and Dietrich Rueschemeyer. Cambridge: Cambridge University Press, 2003, 177–207.

Pleines, Heiko. "Manipulating Politics: Domestic Investors in Ukrainian Privatisation Auctions, 2000–2004." *Europe Asia Studies* 60 (2008): 1177–1197.

Porta, Donatella della, Salvatore Sberna, and Alberto Vannucci. "Centripetal and Centrifugal Corruption in Post-Democratic Italy." *Italian Politics* 30 (2015): 198–217.

Porta, Donatella della, and Alberto Vannucci. "Corruption and Anti-Corruption: The Political Defeat of 'Clean Hands' in Italy." *West European Politics* 30 (2007): 830–853.

Price, Richard. "Reversing the Gun Sights: Transnational Civil Society Targets Landmines." *International Organization* 52 (1998): 613–644.

———. "Transnational Civil Society and Advocacy in World Politics." *World Politics* 55 (2003): 579–606.

Rakoff, Jed S., and Howard W. Goldstein. *RICO: Civil and Criminal Law and Strategy*. New York: Law Journal Press, 2013.

Reisman, W. Michael. "Harnessing International Law to Restrain and Recapture Indigenous Spoliations." *American Journal of International Law* 83 (1989): 56–59.

Reno, William. "Congo: From State Collapse to 'Absolutism,' to State Failure." *Third World Quarterly* 27 (2006): 43–56.

———. "Ironies of Post–Cold War Structural Adjustment in Africa." *Review of African Political Economy* 23 (1996): 7–18.

———. *Warlord Politics and African States*. Boulder, CO: Lynne Rienner, 1998.

Reyntjens, Filip. *The Great African War: Congo and Regional Geopolitics, 1996–2002*. Cambridge: Cambridge University Press, 2009.

Ribadu, Nuhu. *Show Me the Money: Leveraging Anti–Money Laundering Tools to Fight Corruption in Nigeria*. Washington, D.C.: Center for Global Development, 2010.

Rixen, Thomas. *The Political Economy of International Tax Governance*. Houndmills, UK: Palgrave, 2008.

Rixen, Thomas, and Peter Schwarz. "The Effectiveness of the EU Savings Tax Directive—Evidence from Four Countries." *Journal of Common Market Studies* 50 (2012): 151–168.

Rose-Ackerman, Susan. *Corruption and Government: Causes, Consequences, and Reform*. Cambridge: Cambridge University Press, 1999.

———. *Corruption: A Study in Political Economy*. New York: Academic Press, 1978.

———. "Democracy and 'Grand' Corruption." *International Social Science Journal* 48 (1996): 365–380.

Ross, Michael L. "The Political Economy of the Resource Curse." *World Politics* 51 (1999): 297–322.

Saad, Ahmed, Urs Feller, Marcel Frey, Kamal Shah, and Charlotte Welsh. "Recovering Stolen Assets: The Egyptian Experience." In *Emerging Trends in Asset Recovery*, edited by Gretta Fenner Zinkernagel, Charles Monteith, and Pedro Gomez Pereira. Bern: Peter Lang 2013, 17–26.

Sachs, Jeffrey, and Katharina Pistor. *The Rule of Law and Economic Reform in Russia*. Boulder, CO: Westview Press, 1997.

Sakwa, Richard. *Putin and the Oligarch: The Khodorkovsky-Yukos Affair*. London: I. B. Tauris, 2014.

Salvioni, Sergio. "Recovering the Proceeds of Corruption: Ferdinand Marcos of the Philippines." In *Recovering Stolen Assets*, edited by Mark Pieth. Bern: Peter Lang, 2008, 79–88.

Sandholtz, Wayne. *Prohibiting Plunder: How Norms Change*. Oxford: Oxford University Press, 2007.

Sandholtz, Wayne, and Mark M. Gray. "International Integration and National Corruption." *International Organization* 57 (2003): 761–800.

Schatzburg, Michael G. *Mobutu or Chaos? The United States in Zaire, 1960–1990*. Lanham, MD: University Press of America, 1991.

Scher, Daniel. "Asset Recovery: Repatriating Africa's Looted Billions." *African Security Review* 14 (2005): 17–26.

Schimmelfennig, Frank. "The Community Trap: Liberal Norms, Rhetorical Action, and the Eastern Enlargement of the European Union." *International Organization* 55 (2001): 47–80.

Sharman, J. C. "The Bark *Is* the Bite: International Organizations and Blacklisting." *Review of International Political Economy* 16 (2009): 573–596.

———. *Havens in a Storm: The Struggle for Global Tax Regulation*. Ithaca: Cornell University Press, 2006.

———. *The Money Laundry: Regulating Criminal Finance in the Global Economy*. Ithaca: Cornell University Press, 2011.

———. "Regional Deals and the Global Imperative: The External Dimension of the European Union Savings Tax Directive." *Journal of Common Market Studies* 46 (2008): 1049–1069.

Shelley, Louise I. "Money Laundering into Real Estate." In *Convergence: Illicit Networks and National Security in the Age of Globalization*, edited by Michael Miklaucic and Jacqueline Brewer. Washington, D.C.: National Defense University Press, 2013, 131–146.

Shleifer, Andrei, and Robert W. Vishny. "Corruption." *Quarterly Journal of Economics* 109 (1993): 599–617.

Sikkink, Kathryn. *The Justice Cascade: How Human Rights Prosecutions Are Changing World Politics*. New York: W. W. Norton, 2013.

Silverstein, Ken. *The Secret World of Oil*. New York: Verso, 2014.

Simmons, Beth. "International Law and State Behavior: Commitment and Compliance in International Monetary Affairs." *American Political Science Review* 94 (2000): 819–835.

Simpson, Sally S. "White-Collar Crime: A Review of Recent Developments and Promising Directions for Future Research." *Annual Review of Sociology* 39 (2013): 309–331.

Sookun, Devi. *Stop Vulture Fund Lawsuits: A Handbook*. London: Commonwealth Secretariat, 2010.

StAR. *Barriers to Asset Recovery: An Analysis of Key Barriers and Recommendations for Action*. Washington, D.C., 2011.

———. *Few and Far: The Hard Facts on Stolen Asset Recovery*. Washington, D.C., 2014.

———. *Good Practices Guide for Non-Conviction Based Forfeiture*. Washington, D.C., 2009.

———. *Politically Exposed Persons: A Policy Paper on Strengthening Preventive Measures*. Washington, D.C., 2009.

———. *Public Wrongs, Private Actions: Civil Lawsuits to Recover Stolen Assets*. Washington, D.C., 2014.

———. *The Puppet Masters: How the Corrupt Use Legal Structures to Hide Their Stolen Assets and What to Do about It*. Washington, D.C., 2011.

———. *Stolen Asset Recovery (StAR) Initiative: Challenges, Opportunity, and Action Plan*. Washington, D.C., 2007.

———. "World Bank and United Nations Office on Drugs and Crime: Work Plan." Washington, D.C., November 24, 2008.

Swiss Federal Banking Commission. "Abacha Funds at Swiss Banks." Bern, August 30, 2000.

Tanzi, Vito. "Corruption, Governmental Activities, and Markets." IMF Working Paper 94/99. Washington, D.C., 1994.

Tanzi, Vito, and Hamid Davoodi. "Roads to Nowhere: How Corruption in Public Investment Hurts Growth." Economic Issues Series No. 12. Washington, D.C.: IMF, 1998.

Tänzler, Dirk, Konstandinos Maras, and Angelos Giannakopoulos. "The German Myth of a Corruption-Free Modern Country." In *The Social Construction of Corruption in Europe*, edited by Dirk Tänzler, Konstandinos Maras, and Angelos Giannakopoulos. Farnham, UK: Ashgate, 2012, 87–106.

Transparency International. *Global Corruption Report*. Berlin, 2004.

——. *Progress Report: Enforcement of the OECD Anti-Bribery Convention*. Berlin, 2011.

Transparency International UK. *Combating Money Laundering and Recovering Looted Gains: Raising the UK's Game*. London, 2009.

——. *Corruption on Your Doorstep: How Corrupt Capital Is Used to Buy Property in the UK*. London, 2015.

——. *Empowering the UK to Recover Corrupt Assets: Unexplained Wealth Orders and Other New Approaches to Illicit Enrichment and Asset Recovery*. London, 2015.

Treisman, Daniel. "What Have We Learned about Corruption from Ten Years of Cross-National Research?" *Annual Review of Political Science* 10 (2007): 211–244.

U4. "Making Hay while the Sun Shines: Experiences with the Zambian Task Force on Corruption." Practice Insight. Bergen, Norway: CMI, 2011.

UK National Risk Assessment of Money Laundering and Terrorist Financing. London: Home Office and Her Majesty's Treasury, 2015.

Unger, Brigitte, and Joras Ferwada (eds.). *Money Laundering in the Real Estate Sector: Suspicious Properties*. Cheltenham, UK: Edward Elgar, 2011.

United Nations Ad Hoc Committee for Negotiation of a Convention Against Corruption. Fourth Session, Vienna, January 13–24, 2003.

United Nations Office for Drug Control and Crime Prevention. *Financial Havens, Secrecy and Money Laundering*. Vienna, 1998.

United Nations Office on Drugs and Crime. "Estimating Illicit Financial Flows Resulting from Drug Trafficking and Other Transnational Organized Crimes." Vienna, 2011.

——. "Global Study on the Transfer of Funds of Illicit Origin, Especially Funds Derived from Acts of Corruption." 2002. Available at https://www.unodc.org/pdf/crime/convention_corruption/session_4/12e.pdf.

US Department of Commerce. *U.S. and Allied Efforts to Recover and Restore Gold and Other Assets Stolen or Hidden by Germany during World War II*. Washington, D.C., 1997.

US Senate Permanent Subcommittee on Investigations. *Keeping Foreign Corruption Out of the United States: Four Case Histories*. Washington, D.C., 2010.

——. *Money Laundering and Foreign Corruption: Enforcement and Effectiveness of the Patriot Act*. Washington, D.C., 2004.

——. *Offshore Tax Evasion: Efforts to Collect Unpaid Taxes on Billions in Offshore Accounts*. Washington, D.C., 2014.

——. *Private Banking and Money Laundering: A Case Study of Opportunities and Vulnerabilities*. Washington, D.C., 1999.

———. *U.S. Vulnerability to Money Laundering, Drugs, and Terrorist Financing: HSBC Case History*. Washington, D.C., 2012.

US Senate Select Committee on Intelligence. *Committee Study of the Central Intelligence Agency's Detention and Interrogation Program*. Washington, D.C., 2014.

Valdivia, Luis Largas. "Corruption and Criminal Organization: Peru's Experience." In Asian Development Bank/OECD Anti-Corruption Initiative for the Asia-Pacific, *Asset Recovery and Mutual Legal Assistance in Asia and the Pacific*. Manila, 2008, 224–231.

van Oranje, Mabel, and Henry Parham. "Publishing What We Learned: An Assessment of the Publish What You Pay Coalition." 2009. Available at https://eiti.org/files/Publishing%20What%20We%20Learned.pdf.

Vlasic, Mark V., and Gregory Cooper. "Beyond the Duvalier Legacy: What the New 'Arab Spring' Governments Can Learn from Haiti and the Benefits of Stolen Asset Recovery." *Northwestern Journal of International Human Rights* 10 (2011): 19–26.

Vlassis, Dmitri, and Dorothee Gottwald. "Implementing the Asset Recovery Provisions of UNCAC." In *Recovering Stolen Assets*, edited by Mark Pieth. Bern: Peter Lang, 2008, 353–368.

Vlcek, William. *Offshore Finance and Small States: Sovereignty, Size and Money*. Houndmills, UK: Palgrave, 2006.

Vogl, Frank. *Waging War on Corruption: Inside the Movement Fighting the Abuse of Power*. Lanham, MD: Rowman and Littlefield, 2012.

von Stein, Jana. "Do Treaties Constrain or Screen? Selection Bias and Treaty Compliance." *American Political Science Review* 99 (2005): 611–622.

Wachanga, Jesse Mwangi. "Hurdles in Asset Recovery and Fighting Corruption by Developing Countries: The Kenya Experience." In *Emerging Trends in Asset Recovery*, edited by Gretta Fenner Zinkernagel, Charles Monteith, and Pedro Gomez Pereira. Bern: Peter Lang, 2013, 147–158.

Walton, Grant. "Defining Corruption Where the State Is Weak: The Case of Papua New Guinea." *Journal of Development Studies* 51 (2015): 15–31.

Wang, Hongying, and James N. Rosenau. "Transparency International and Corruption as an Issue of Global Governance." *Global Governance* 7 (2001): 25–49.

Weaver, Catherine. *Hypocrisy Trap: The World Bank and the Poverty of Reform*. Princeton: Princeton University Press, 2008.

Wechsler, William. "Follow the Money." *Foreign Affairs* 80 (2001): 40–57.

Wedel, Janine R. "Rethinking Corruption in an Age of Ambiguity." *Annual Review of Law and Social Science* 8 (2012): 453–498.

Wedeman, Andrew. *Double Paradox: Rapid Growth and Rising Corruption in China*. Ithaca: Cornell University Press, 2012.

———. "Looters, Rent-Scrapers, and Dividend Collectors: Corruption and Growth in Zaire, South Korea, and the Philippines." *Journal of Developing Areas* 31 (1997): 457–478.

Wendt, Alexander. *Social Theory of International Politics*. Cambridge: Cambridge University Press, 1999.

Williams, Robert E. "From Malabo to Malibu: Addressing Corruption and Human Rights Abuse in an African Petrostate." *Human Rights Quarterly* 33 (2011): 620–648.

Wilson, Andrew. *Ukraine's Orange Revolution*. New Haven: Yale University Press, 2006.

Wolfensohn, James D. *A Global Life: My Journey among Rich and Poor, from Sydney to Wall Street to the World Bank*. New York: Public Affairs, 2010.

World Bank. "Helping Countries Combat Corruption: The Role of the World Bank." Washington, D.C., 1997.

———. "Sub-Saharan Africa: From Crisis to Sustainable Growth; A Long-Term Perspective Study." Washington, D.C., 1989.

Wrong, Michela. *In the Footsteps of Mr Kurtz*. London: Fourth Estate, 2000.

———. *It's Our Turn to Eat: The Story of a Kenyan Whistle-Blower*. London: Fourth Estate, 2009.

Wyss, Rudolf. "Proactive Co-operation within the Mutual Legal Assistance Procedure." In *Emerging Trends in Asset Recovery*, edited by Gretta Fenner Zinkernagel, Charles Monteith, and Pedro Gomez Pereira. Bern: Peter Lang, 2013, 105–113.

Yandle, Bruce. "Boot-Leggers and Baptists: The Education of a Regulatory Economist." *Regulation* 7 (1983): 12–16.

Zarate, Juan C. *Treasury's War: The Unleashing of a New Era of Financial Warfare*. New York: Public Affairs, 2013.

Zucman, Gabriel. *The Hidden Wealth of Nations: The Scourge of Tax Havens*. Chicago: University of Chicago Press, 2015.

INDEX

CPSIA information can be obtained
at www.ICGtesting.com
Printed in the USA
LVOW12*2109270217

525564LV00005B/166/P

9 781501 705519